NON SANZ DROICT.

THE
Famous Historie of
Troylus *and* Cresseid.

Excellently expressing the beginning
of their loues, with the conceited wooing
of *Pandarus* Prince of *Licia.*

Written by William Shakespeare.

LONDON
Imprinted by *G. Eld* for *R. Bonian* and *H. Walley,* and
are to be sold at the spred Eagle in Paules
Church-yeard, ouer against the
great North doore.
1609.

Title page of the first printed version of *Troilus and Cressida*, 1609.

William Shakespeare

TROILUS AND CRESSIDA

With New and Updated Critical Essays and a Revised Bibliography

Edited by Daniel Seltzer

THE SIGNET CLASSIC SHAKESPEARE
General Editor: Sylvan Barnet

𝒞

A SIGNET CLASSIC

SIGNET CLASSIC
Published by New American Library, a division of
Penguin Putnam Inc., 375 Hudson Street, New York, New York 10014, U.S.A.
Penguin Books Ltd, 80 Strand, London WC2R 0RL, England
Penguin Books Australia Ltd, Ringwood, Victoria, Australia
Penguin Books Canada Ltd, 10 Alcorn Avenue, Toronto, Ontario, Canada M4V 3B2
Penguin Books (N.Z.) Ltd, 182–190 Wairau Road, Auckland 10, New Zealand

Penguin Books Ltd, Registered Offices:
Harmondsworth, Middlesex, England

Published by Signet Classic, an imprint of New American Library,
a division of Penguin Putnam Inc.

First Signet Classic Printing (Second Revised Edition), August 2002
10 9 8 7 6 5 4 3 2 1

Library of Congress Catalog Card Number: 2002019115

Printed in the United States of America

Contents

Shakespeare: An Overview

Biographical Sketch

Between the record of his baptism in Stratford on 26 April 1564 and the record of his burial in Stratford on 25 April 1616, some forty official documents name Shakespeare, and many others name his parents, his children, and his grandchildren. Further, there are at least fifty literary references to him in the works of his contemporaries. More facts are known about William Shakespeare than about any other playwright of the period except Ben Jonson. The facts should, however, be distinguished from the legends. The latter, inevitably more engaging and better known, tell us that the Stratford boy killed a calf in high style, poached deer and rabbits, and was forced to flee to London, where he held horses outside a playhouse. These traditions are only traditions; they may be true, but no evidence supports them, and it is well to stick to the facts.

Mary Arden, the dramatist's mother, was the daughter of a substantial landowner; about 1557 she married John Shakespeare, a tanner, glove-maker, and trader in wool, grain, and other farm commodities. In 1557 John Shakespeare was a member of the council (the governing body of Stratford), in 1558 a constable of the borough, in 1561 one of the two town chamberlains, in 1565 an alderman (entitling him to the appellation of "Mr."), in 1568 high bailiff—the town's highest political office, equivalent to mayor. After 1577, for an unknown reason he drops out of local politics. What *is* known is that he had to mortgage his wife's property, and that he was involved in serious litigation.

The birthday of William Shakespeare, the third child and the eldest son of this locally prominent man, is unrecorded, but the Stratford parish register records that the infant was baptized on 26 April 1564. (It is quite possible that he was born on 23 April, but this date has probably been assigned by tradition because it is the date on which, fifty-two years later, he died, and perhaps because it is the feast day of St. George, patron saint of England.) The attendance records of the Stratford grammar school of the period are not extant, but it is reasonable to assume that the son of a prominent local official attended the free school—it had been established for the purpose of educating males precisely of his class—and received substantial training in Latin. The masters of the school from Shakespeare's seventh to fifteenth years held Oxford degrees; the Elizabethan curriculum excluded mathematics and the natural sciences but taught a good deal of Latin rhetoric, logic, and literature, including plays by Plautus, Terence, and Seneca.

On 27 November 1582 a marriage license was issued for the marriage of Shakespeare and Anne Hathaway, eight years his senior. The couple had a daughter, Susanna, in May 1583. Perhaps the marriage was necessary, but perhaps the couple had earlier engaged, in the presence of witnesses, in a formal "troth plight" which would render their children legitimate even if no further ceremony were performed. In February 1585, Anne Hathaway bore Shakespeare twins, Hamnet and Judith.

That Shakespeare was born is excellent; that he married and had children is pleasant; but that we know nothing about his departure from Stratford to London or about the beginning of his theatrical career is lamentable and must be admitted. We would gladly sacrifice details about his children's baptism for details about his earliest days in the theater. Perhaps the poaching episode is true (but it is first reported almost a century after Shakespeare's death), or perhaps he left Stratford to be a schoolmaster, as another tradition holds; perhaps he was moved (like Petruchio in *The Taming of the Shrew*) by

> Such wind as scatters young men through the world,
> To seek their fortunes farther than at home
> Where small experience grows.   (1.2.49–51)

In 1592, thanks to the cantankerousness of Robert Greene, we have our first reference, a snarling one, to Shakespeare as an actor and playwright. Greene, a graduate of St. John's College, Cambridge, had become a playwright and a pamphleteer in London, and in one of his pamphlets he warns three university-educated playwrights against an actor who has presumed to turn playwright:

> There is an upstart crow, beautified with our feathers, that with his *tiger's heart wrapped in a player's hide* supposes he is as well able to bombast out a blank verse as the best of you, and being an absolute Johannes-factotum [i.e., jack-of-all-trades] is in his own conceit the only Shake-scene in a country.

The reference to the player, as well as the allusion to Aesop's crow (who strutted in borrowed plumage, as an actor struts in fine words not his own), makes it clear that by this date Shakespeare had both acted and written. That Shakespeare is meant is indicated not only by *Shake-scene* but also by the parody of a line from one of Shakespeare's plays, *3 Henry VI*: "O, tiger's heart wrapped in a woman's hide" (1.4.137). If in 1592 Shakespeare was prominent enough to be attacked by an envious dramatist, he probably had served an apprenticeship in the theater for at least a few years.

In any case, although there are no extant references to Shakespeare between the record of the baptism of his twins in 1585 and Greene's hostile comment about "Shake-scene" in 1592, it is evident that during some of these "dark years" or "lost years" Shakespeare had acted and written. There are a number of subsequent references to him as an actor. Documents indicate that in 1598 he is a "principal comedian," in 1603 a "principal tragedian," in 1608 he is one of the "men players." (We do not have, however, any solid information about which roles he may have played; later traditions say he played Adam in *As You Like It* and the ghost in *Hamlet*, but nothing supports the assertions. Probably his role as dramatist came to supersede his role as actor.) The profession of actor was not for a gentleman, and it occasionally drew the scorn of university men like Greene who resented writing speeches for persons less educated than themselves, but it

was respectable enough; players, if prosperous, were in
effect members of the bourgeoisie, and there is nothing to
suggest that Stratford considered William Shakespeare less
than a solid citizen. When, in 1596, the Shakespeares were
granted a coat of arms—i.e., the right to be considered
gentlemen—the grant was made to Shakespeare's father,
but probably William Shakespeare had arranged the matter
on his own behalf. In subsequent transactions he is occasionally styled a gentleman.

Although in 1593 and 1594 Shakespeare published two
narrative poems dedicated to the Earl of Southampton,
Venus and Adonis and *The Rape of Lucrece*, and may well
have written most or all of his sonnets in the middle nineties,
Shakespeare's literary activity seems to have been almost
entirely devoted to the theater. (It may be significant that
the two narrative poems were written in years when the
plague closed the theaters for several months.) In 1594
he was a charter member of a theatrical company called
the Chamberlain's Men, which in 1603 became the royal
company, the King's Men, making Shakespeare the king's
playwright. Until he retired to Stratford (about 1611, apparently), he was with this remarkably stable company. From
1599 the company acted primarily at the Globe theater, in
which Shakespeare held a one-tenth interest. Other Elizabethan dramatists are known to have acted, but no other is
known also to have been entitled to a share of the profits.

Shakespeare's first eight published plays did not have his
name on them, but this is not remarkable; the most popular
play of the period, Thomas Kyd's *The Spanish Tragedy*,
went through many editions without naming Kyd, and
Kyd's authorship is known only because a book on the profession of acting happens to quote (and attribute to Kyd)
some lines on the interest of Roman emperors in the drama.
What is remarkable is that after 1598 Shakespeare's name
commonly appears on printed plays—some of which are not
his. Presumably his name was a drawing card, and pub-
lishers used it to attract potential buyers. Another indication
of his popularity comes from Francis Meres, author of *Pal-
ladis Tamia: Wit's Treasury* (1598). In this anthology of
snippets accompanied by an essay on literature, many playwrights are mentioned, but Shakespeare's name occurs

more often than any other, and Shakespeare is the only play-wright whose plays are listed.

From his acting, his play writing, and his share in a playhouse, Shakespeare seems to have made considerable money. He put it to work, making substantial investments in Stratford real estate. As early as 1597 he bought New Place, the second-largest house in Stratford. His family moved in soon afterward, and the house remained in the family until a granddaughter died in 1670. When Shakespeare made his will in 1616, less than a month before he died, he sought to leave his property intact to his descendants. Of small bequests to relatives and to friends (including three actors, Richard Burbage, John Heminges, and Henry Condell), that to his wife of the second-best bed has provoked the most comment. It has sometimes been taken as a sign of an unhappy marriage (other supposed signs are the apparently hasty marriage, his wife's seniority of eight years, and his residence in London without his family). Perhaps the second-best bed was the bed the couple had slept in, the best bed being reserved for visitors. In any case, had Shakespeare not excepted it, the bed would have gone (with the rest of his household possessions) to his daughter and her husband.

On 25 April 1616 Shakespeare was buried within the chancel of the church at Stratford. An unattractive monument to his memory, placed on a wall near the grave, says that he died on 23 April. Over the grave itself are the lines, perhaps by Shakespeare, that (more than his literary fame) have kept his bones undisturbed in the crowded burial ground where old bones were often dislodged to make way for new:

> Good friend, for Jesus' sake forbear
> To dig the dust enclosed here.
> Blessed be the man that spares these stones
> And cursed be he that moves my bones.

A Note on the Anti-Stratfordians, Especially Baconians and Oxfordians

Not until 1769—more than a hundred and fifty years after Shakespeare's death—is there any record of anyone expressing doubt about Shakespeare's authorship of the plays and poems. In 1769, however, Herbert Lawrence nominated Francis Bacon (1561–1626) in *The Life and Adventures of Common Sense*. Since then, at least two dozen other nominees have been offered, including Christopher Marlowe, Sir Walter Raleigh, Queen Elizabeth I, and Edward de Vere, 17th earl of Oxford. The impulse behind all anti-Stratfordian movements is the scarcely concealed snobbish opinion that "the man from Stratford" simply could not have written the plays because he was a country fellow without a university education and without access to high society. Anyone, the argument goes, who used so many legal terms, medical terms, nautical terms, and so forth, and who showed some familiarity with classical writing, must have attended a university, and anyone who knew so much about courtly elegance and courtly deceit must himself have moved among courtiers. The plays do indeed reveal an author whose interests were exceptionally broad, but specialists in any given field—law, medicine, arms and armor, and so on—soon find that the plays do not reveal deep knowledge in specialized matters; indeed, the playwright often gets technical details wrong.

The claim on behalf of Bacon, forgotten almost as soon as it was put forth in 1769, was independently reasserted by Joseph C. Hart in 1848. In 1856 it was reaffirmed by W. H. Smith in a book, and also by Delia Bacon in an article; in 1857 Delia Bacon published a book, arguing that Francis Bacon had directed a group of intellectuals who wrote the plays.

Francis Bacon's claim has largely faded, perhaps because it was advanced with such evident craziness by Ignatius Donnelly, who in *The Great Cryptogram* (1888) claimed to break a code in the plays that proved Bacon had written not only the plays attributed to Shakespeare but also other Renaissance works, for instance the plays of Christopher Marlowe and the essays of Montaigne.

Consider the last two lines of the Epilogue in *The Tempest*:

> As you from crimes would pardoned be,
> Let your indulgence set me free.

What was Shakespeare—sorry, Francis Bacon, Baron Verulam—*really* saying in these two lines? According to Baconians, the lines are an anagram reading, "Tempest of Francis Bacon, Lord Verulam; do ye ne'er divulge me, ye words." Ingenious, and it is a pity that in the quotation the letter *a* appears only twice in the cryptogram, whereas in the deciphered message it appears three times. Oh, no problem; just alter "Verulam" to "Verul'm" and it works out very nicely.

Most people understand that with sufficient ingenuity one can torture any text and find in it what one wishes. For instance: Did Shakespeare have a hand in the King James Version of the Bible? It was nearing completion in 1610, when Shakespeare was forty-six years old. If you look at the 46th Psalm and count forward for forty-six words, you will find the word *shake*. Now if you go to the end of the psalm and count backward forty-six words, you will find the word *spear*. Clear evidence, according to some, that Shakespeare slyly left his mark in the book.

Bacon's candidacy has largely been replaced in the twentieth century by the candidacy of Edward de Vere (1550–1604), 17th earl of Oxford. The basic ideas behind the Oxford theory, advanced at greatest length by Dorothy and Charlton Ogburn in *This Star of England* (1952, rev. 1955), a book of 1297 pages, and by Charlton Ogburn in *The Mysterious William Shakespeare* (1984), a book of 892 pages, are these: (1) The man from Stratford could not possibly have had the mental equipment and the experience to have written the plays—only a courtier could have written them; (2) Oxford had the requisite background (social position, education, years at Queen Elizabeth's court); (3) Oxford did not wish his authorship to be known for two basic reasons: writing for the public theater was a vulgar pursuit, and the plays show so much courtly and royal disreputable behavior that they would have compromised Oxford's position at court. Oxfordians offer countless details to support the claim. For example, Hamlet's phrase "that ever I was born to set it right" (1.5.89) barely conceals "E. Ver, I was born to set it right," an unambiguous announcement of de Vere's authorship, according to *This Star of England* (p. 654). A second example: Consider Ben

Jonson's poem entitled "To the Memory of My Beloved Master William Shakespeare," prefixed to the first collected edition of Shakespeare's plays in 1623. According to Oxfordians, when Jonson in this poem speaks of the author of the plays as the "swan of Avon," he is alluding not to William Shakespeare, who was born and died in Stratford-on-Avon and who throughout his adult life owned property there; rather, he is alluding to Oxford, who, the Ogburns say, used "William Shakespeare" as his pen name, and whose manor at Bilton was on the Avon River. Oxfordians do not offer any evidence that Oxford took a pen name, and they seem unconcerned that Oxford had sold the manor in 1581, forty-two years before Jonson wrote his poem. Surely a reference to the Shakespeare who was born in Stratford, who had returned to Stratford, and who had died there only seven years before Jonson wrote the poem is more plausible. And exactly why Jonson, who elsewhere also spoke of Shakespeare as a playwright, and why Heminges and Condell, who had acted with Shakespeare for about twenty years, should speak of Shakespeare as the author in their dedication in the 1623 volume of collected plays is never adequately explained by Oxfordians. Either Jonson, Heminges and Condell, and numerous others were in on the conspiracy, or they were all duped—equally unlikely alternatives. Another difficulty in the Oxford theory is that Oxford died in 1604, and some of the plays are clearly indebted to works and events later than 1604. Among the Oxfordian responses are: At his death Oxford left some plays, and in later years these were touched up by hacks, who added the material that points to later dates. *The Tempest*, almost universally regarded as one of Shakespeare's greatest plays and pretty clearly dated to 1611, does indeed date from a period after the death of Oxford, but it is a crude piece of work that should not be included in the canon of works by Oxford.

The anti-Stratfordians, in addition to assuming that the author must have been a man of rank and a university man, usually assume two conspiracies: (1) a conspiracy in Elizabethan and Jacobean times, in which a surprisingly large number of persons connected with the theater knew that the actor Shakespeare did not write the plays attributed to him but for some reason or other pretended that he did; (2) a conspiracy of today's Stratfordians, the professors who teach Shakespeare in the colleges and universities, who are said to have a vested interest in preserving Shakespeare as the author of the plays they teach. In fact, (1) it is inconceivable that the secret of Shakespeare's non-authorship could have been preserved by all of the people who supposedly were in on the conspiracy, and (2) academic fame awaits any scholar today who can disprove Shakespeare's authorship.

The Stratfordian case is convincing not only because hundreds or even thousands of anti-Stratford arguments—of the sort that say "ever I was born" has the secret double meaning "E. Ver, I was born"—add up to nothing at all but also because irrefutable evidence connects the man from Stratford with the London theater and with the authorship of particular plays. The anti-Stratfordians do not seem to understand that it is not enough to dismiss the Stratford case by saying that a fellow from the provinces simply couldn't have written the plays. Nor do they understand that it is not enough to dismiss all of the evidence connecting Shakespeare with the plays by asserting that it is perjured.

The Shakespeare Canon

We return to William Shakespeare. Thirty-seven plays as well as some nondramatic poems are generally held to constitute the Shakespeare canon, the body of authentic works. The exact dates of composition of most of the works are highly uncertain, but evidence of a starting point and/or of a final limiting point often provides a framework for informed guessing. For example, *Richard II* cannot be earlier than 1595, the publication date of some material to which it is indebted; *The Merchant of Venice* cannot be later than 1598, the year Francis Meres mentioned it. Sometimes arguments for a date hang on an alleged topical allusion, such as the lines about the unseasonable weather in *A Midsummer Night's Dream*, 2.1.81–117, but such an allusion, if indeed it is an allusion to an event in the real world, can be variously interpreted, and in any case there is always the possibility that a topical allusion was inserted years later, to bring the play up to date. (The issue of alterations in a text between the time that Shakespeare drafted it and the time that it was printed—alterations due to censorship or playhouse practice or Shakespeare's own second thoughts—will be discussed in "The Play Text as a Collaboration" later in this overview.) Dates are often attributed on the basis of style, and although conjectures about style usually rest on other conjectures (such as Shakespeare's development as a playwright, or the appropriateness of lines to character), sooner or later one must rely on one's literary sense. There is no documentary proof, for example, that *Othello* is not as early as *Romeo and Juliet*, but one feels that *Othello* is a later, more mature work, and because the first record of its performance is 1604, one is glad enough to set its composition at that date and not push it back into Shakespeare's early years. (*Romeo and Juliet* was first published in 1597, but evidence suggests that it was written a little earlier.) The following chronology, then, is indebted not only to facts but also to informed guesswork and sensitivity. The dates, necessarily imprecise for some works, indicate something like a scholarly consensus concerning the time of original composition. Some plays show evidence of later revision.

Plays. The first collected edition of Shakespeare, published in 1623, included thirty-six plays. These are all accepted as Shakespeare's, though for one of them, *Henry VIII*, he is thought to have had a collaborator. A thirty-seventh play, *Pericles*, published in 1609 and attributed to Shakespeare on the title page, is also widely accepted as being partly by Shakespeare even though it is not included in the 1623 volume. Still another play not in the 1623 volume, *The Two Noble Kinsmen*, was first published in 1634, with a title page attributing it to John Fletcher and Shakespeare. Probably most students of the subject now believe that Shakespeare did indeed have a hand in it. Of the remaining plays attributed at one time or another to Shakespeare, only one, *Edward III*, anonymously published in 1596, is now regarded by some scholars as a serious candidate. The prevailing opinion, however, is that this rather simple-minded play is not Shakespeare's; at most he may have revised some passages, chiefly scenes with the Countess of

Salisbury. We include *The Two Noble Kinsmen* but do not include *Edward III* in the following list.

1588–94	*The Comedy of Errors*
1588–94	*Love's Labor's Lost*
1589–91	*2 Henry VI*
1590–91	*3 Henry VI*
1589–92	*1 Henry VI*
1592–93	*Richard III*
1589–94	*Titus Andronicus*
1593–94	*The Taming of the Shrew*
1592–94	*The Two Gentlemen of Verona*
1594–96	*Romeo and Juliet*
1595	*Richard II*
1595–96	*A Midsummer Night's Dream*
1596–97	*King John*
1594–96	*The Merchant of Venice*
1596–97	*1 Henry IV*
1597	*The Merry Wives of Windsor*
1597–98	*2 Henry IV*
1598–99	*Much Ado About Nothing*
1598–99	*Henry V*
1599	*Julius Caesar*
1599–1600	*As You Like It*
1599–1600	*Twelfth Night*
1600–1601	*Hamlet*
1601–1602	*Troilus and Cressida*
1602–1604	*All's Well That Ends Well*
1603–1604	*Othello*
1604	*Measure for Measure*
1605–1606	*King Lear*
1605–1606	*Macbeth*
1606–1607	*Antony and Cleopatra*
1605–1608	*Timon of Athens*
1607–1608	*Coriolanus*
1607–1608	*Pericles*
1609–10	*Cymbeline*
1610–11	*The Winter's Tale*
1611	*The Tempest*

| 1612–13 | *Henry VIII* |
| 1613 | *The Two Noble Kinsmen* |

Poems. In 1989 Donald W. Foster published a book in which he argued that "A Funeral Elegy for Master William Peter," published in 1612, ascribed only to the initials W.S., *may* be by Shakespeare. Foster later published an article in a scholarly journal, *PMLA* 111 (1996), in which he asserted the claim more positively. The evidence begins with the initials, and includes the fact that the publisher and the printer of the elegy had published Shakespeare's *Sonnets* in 1609. But such facts add up to rather little, especially because no one has found any connection between Shakespeare and William Peter (an Oxford graduate about whom little is known, who was murdered at the age of twenty-nine). The argument is based chiefly on statistical examinations of word patterns, which are said to correlate with Shakespeare's known work. Despite such correlations, however, many readers feel that the poem does not sound like Shakespeare. True, Shakespeare has a great range of styles, but his work is consistently imaginative and interesting. Many readers find neither of these qualities in "A Funeral Elegy."

1592–93	*Venus and Adonis*
1593–94	*The Rape of Lucrece*
1593–1600	*Sonnets*
1600–1601	*The Phoenix and the Turtle*

Shakespeare's English

1. Spelling and Pronunciation. From the philologist's point of view, Shakespeare's English is modern English. It requires footnotes, but the inexperienced reader can comprehend substantial passages with very little help, whereas for the same reader Chaucer's Middle English is a foreign language. By the beginning of the fifteenth century the chief grammatical changes in English had taken place, and the final unaccented -*e* of Middle English had been lost (though

it survives even today in spelling, as in *name*); during the fifteenth century the dialect of London, the commercial and
political center, gradually displaced the provincial dialects,
at least in writing; by the end of the century, printing had
helped to regularize and stabilize the language, especially
spelling. Elizabethan spelling may seem erratic to us (there
were dozens of spellings of *Shakespeare*, and a simple word
like *been* was also spelled *beene* and *bin*), but it had much in
common with our spelling. Elizabethan spelling was conser-
vative in that for the most part it reflected an older pronunciation (Middle English) rather than the sound of the
language as it was then spoken, just as our spelling continues
to reflect medieval pronunciation—most obviously in the
now silent but formerly pronounced letters in a word such as
knight. Elizabethan pronunciation, though not identical with
ours, was much closer to ours than to that of the Middle
Ages. Incidentally, though no one can be certain about what
Elizabethan English sounded like, specialists tend to believe
it was rather like the speech of a modern stage Irishman
(*time* apparently was pronounced *toime*, *old* pronounced
awld, *day* pronounced *die*, and *join* pronounced *jine*) and not
at all like the Oxford speech that most of us think it was.

An awareness of the difference between our pronunciation and Shakespeare's is crucial in three areas—in accent,
or number of syllables (many metrically regular lines may
look irregular to us); in rhymes (which may not look like
rhymes); and in puns (which may not look like puns).
Examples will be useful. Some words that were at least on
occasion stressed differently from today are *aspèct*, *còm-
plete*, *fòrlorn*, *revènue*, and *sepùlcher*. Words that sometimes had an additional syllable are *emp[e]ress*, *Hen[e]ry*,
mon[e]th, and *villain* (three syllables, *vil-lay-in*). An additional syllable is often found in possessives, like *moon*'s
(pronounced *moones*) and in words ending in *-tion* or *-sion*.
Words that had one less syllable than they now have are
needle (pronounced *neel*) and *violet* (pronounced *vilet*).
Among rhymes now lost are *one* with *loan*, *love* with *prove*,
beast with *jest*, *eat* with *great*. (In reading, trust your sense
of metrics and your ear, more than your eye.) An example of
a pun that has become obliterated by a change in pronunciation is Falstaff's reply to Prince Hal's "Come, tell us your

reason" in *1 Henry IV*: "Give you a reason on compulsion?
If reasons were as plentiful as blackberries, I would give no
man a reason upon compulsion, I" (2.4.237–40). The *ea* in
reason was pronounced rather like a long *a,* like the *ai* in
raisin, hence the comparison with blackberries.

Puns are not merely attempts to be funny; like metaphors
they often involve bringing into a meaningful relationship
areas of experience normally seen as remote. In *2 Henry IV,*
when Feeble is conscripted, he stoically says, "I care not. A
man can die but once. We owe God a death" (3.2.242–43),
punning on *debt,* which was the way *death* was pronounced.
Here an enormously significant fact of life is put into simple
commercial imagery, suggesting its commonplace quality.
Shakespeare used the same pun earlier in *1 Henry IV,* when
Prince Hal says to Falstaff, "Why, thou owest God a death,"
and Falstaff replies, " 'Tis not due yet: I would be loath
to pay him before his day. What need I be so forward with
him that calls not on me?" (5.1.126–29).

Sometimes the puns reveal a delightful playfulness;
sometimes they reveal aggressiveness, as when, replying to
Claudius's "But now, my cousin Hamlet, and my son,"
Hamlet says, "A little more than kin, and less than kind!"
(1.2.64–65). These are Hamlet's first words in the play, and
we already hear him warring verbally against Claudius.
Hamlet's "less than kind" probably means (1) Hamlet is not
of Claudius's family or nature, *kind* having the sense it still
has in our word *mankind*; (2) Hamlet is not kindly (affectionately) disposed toward Claudius; (3) Claudius is not
naturally (but rather unnaturally, in a legal sense incestu-
ously) Hamlet's father. The puns evidently were not put in
as sops to the groundlings; they are an important way of
communicating a complex meaning.

2. *Vocabulary.* A conspicuous difficulty in reading Shakespeare is rooted in the fact that some of his words are no
longer in common use—for example, words concerned with
armor, astrology, clothing, coinage, hawking, horsemanship, law, medicine, sailing, and war. Shakespeare had a
large vocabulary—something near thirty thousand words—
but it was not so much a vocabulary of big words as a
vocabulary drawn from a wide range of life, and it is partly

his ability to call upon a great body of concrete language that gives his plays the sense of being in close contact with life. When the right word did not already exist, he made it up. Among words thought to be his coinages are *accommodation, all-knowing, amazement, bare-faced, countless, dexterously, dislocate, dwindle, fancy-free, frugal, indistinguishable, lackluster, laughable, overawe, premeditated, sea change, star-crossed*. Among those that have not survived are the verb *convive*, meaning to feast together, and *smilet*, a little smile.

Less overtly troublesome than the technical words but more treacherous are the words that seem readily intelligible to us but whose Elizabethan meanings differ from their modern ones. When Horatio describes the Ghost as an "erring spirit," he is saying not that the ghost has sinned or made an error but that it is wandering. Here is a short list of some of the most common words in Shakespeare's plays that often (but not always) have a meaning other than their most usual modern meaning:

'a	he
abuse	deceive
accident	occurrence
advertise	inform
an, and	if
annoy	harm
appeal	accuse
artificial	skillful
brave	fine, splendid
censure	opinion
cheer	(1) face (2) frame of mind
chorus	a single person who comments on the events
closet	small private room
competitor	partner
conceit	idea, imagination
cousin	kinsman
cunning	skillful
disaster	evil astrological influence
doom	judgment
entertain	receive into service

envy	malice
event	outcome
excrement	outgrowth (of hair)
fact	evil deed
fancy	(1) love (2) imagination
fell	cruel
fellow	(1) companion (2) low person (often an insulting term if addressed to someone of approximately equal rank)
fond	foolish
free	(1) innocent (2) generous
glass	mirror
hap, haply	chance, by chance
head	army
humor	(1) mood (2) bodily fluid thought to control one's psychology
imp	child
intelligence	news
kind	natural, acting according to nature
let	hinder
lewd	base
mere(ly)	utter(ly)
modern	commonplace
natural	a fool, an idiot
naughty	(1) wicked (2) worthless
next	nearest
nice	(1) trivial (2) fussy
noise	music
policy	(1) prudence (2) stratagem
presently	immediately
prevent	anticipate
proper	handsome
prove	test
quick	alive
sad	serious
saw	proverb
secure	without care, incautious
silly	innocent

sensible	capable of being perceived by the senses
shrewd	sharp
so	provided that
starve	die
still	always
success	that which follows
tall	brave
tell	count
tonight	last night
wanton	playful, careless
watch	keep awake
will	lust
wink	close both eyes
wit	mind, intelligence

All glosses, of course, are mere approximations; sometimes one of Shakespeare's words may hover between an older meaning and a modern one, and as we have seen, his words often have multiple meanings.

3. Grammar. A few matters of grammar may be surveyed, though it should be noted at the outset that Shakespeare sometimes made up his own grammar. As E.A. Abbott says in *A Shakespearian Grammar,* "Almost any part of speech can be used as any other part of speech": a noun as a verb ("he childed as I fathered"); a verb as a noun ("She hath made compare"); or an adverb as an adjective ("a seldom pleasure"). There are hundreds, perhaps thousands, of such instances in the plays, many of which at first glance would not seem at all irregular and would trouble only a pedant. Here are a few broad matters.

Nouns: The Elizabethans thought the *-s* genitive ending for nouns (as in *man's*) derived from *his*; thus the line " 'gainst the count his galleys I did some service," for "the count's galleys."

Adjectives: By Shakespeare's time adjectives had lost the endings that once indicated gender, number, and case. About the only difference between Shakespeare's adjectives and ours is the use of the now redundant *more* or *most* with the comparative ("some more fitter place") or superlative

("This was the most unkindest cut of all"). Like double comparatives and double superlatives, double negatives were acceptable; Mercutio "will not budge for no man's pleasure."

Pronouns: The greatest change was in pronouns. In Middle English *thou, thy,* and *thee* were used among familiars and in speaking to children and inferiors; *ye, your,* and *you* were used in speaking to superiors (servants to masters, nobles to the king) or to equals with whom the speaker was not familiar. Increasingly the "polite" forms were used in all direct address, regardless of rank, and the accusative *you* displaced the nominative *ye.* Shakespeare sometimes uses *ye* instead of *you,* but even in Shakespeare's day *ye* was archaic, and it occurs mostly in rhetorical appeals.

Thou, thy, and *thee* were not completely displaced, however, and Shakespeare occasionally makes significant use of them, sometimes to connote familiarity or intimacy and sometimes to connote contempt. In *Twelfth Night* Sir Toby advises Sir Andrew to insult Cesario by addressing him as *thou:* "If thou thou'st him some thrice, it shall not be amiss" (3.2.46–47). In *Othello* when Brabantio is addressing an unidentified voice in the dark he says, "What are you?" (1.1.91), but when the voice identifies itself as the foolish suitor Roderigo, Brabantio uses the contemptuous form, saying, "I have charged thee not to haunt about my doors" (93). He uses this form for a while, but later in the scene, when he comes to regard Roderigo as an ally, he shifts back to the polite *you,* beginning in line 163, "What said she to you?" and on to the end of the scene. For reasons not yet satisfactorily explained, Elizabethans used *thou* in addresses to God—"O God, thy arm was here," the king says in *Henry V* (4.8.108)—and to supernatural characters such as ghosts and witches. A subtle variation occurs in *Hamlet.* When Hamlet first talks with the Ghost in 1.5, he uses *thou,* but when he sees the Ghost in his mother's room, in 3.4, he uses *you,* presumably because he is now convinced that the Ghost is not a counterfeit but is his father.

Perhaps the most unusual use of pronouns, from our point of view, is the neuter singular. In place of our *its, his* was often used, as in "How far that little candle throws *his* beams." But the use of a masculine pronoun for a neuter noun came to seem unnatural, and so *it* was used for the possessive as well as the nominative: "The hedge-sparrow fed the cuckoo so long / That it had it head bit off by it young." In the late sixteenth century the possessive form *its* developed, apparently by analogy with the *-s* ending used to indicate a genitive noun, as in *book*'s, but *its* was not yet common usage in Shakespeare's day. He seems to have used *its* only ten times, mostly in his later plays. Other usages, such as "you have seen Cassio and she together" or the substitution of *who* for *whom,* cause little problem even when noticed.

Verbs, Adverbs, and Prepositions: Verbs cause almost no difficulty: The third person singular present form commonly ends in *-s,* as in modern English (e.g., "He blesses"), but sometimes in *-eth* (Portia explains to Shylock that mercy "blesseth him that gives and him that takes"). Broadly speaking, the *-eth* ending was old-fashioned or dignified or "literary" rather than colloquial, except for the words *doth, hath,* and *saith.* The *-eth* ending (regularly used in the King James Bible, 1611) is very rare in Shakespeare's dramatic prose, though not surprisingly it occurs twice in the rather formal prose summary of the narrative poem *Lucrece.* Sometimes a plural subject, especially if it has collective force, takes a verb ending in *-s,* as in "My old bones aches." Some of our strong or irregular preterites (such as *broke*) have a different form in Shakespeare (*brake*); some verbs that now have a weak or regular preterite (such as *helped*) in Shakespeare have a strong or irregular preterite (*holp*). Some adverbs that today end in *-ly* were not inflected: "grievous sick," "wondrous strange." Finally, prepositions often are not the ones we expect: "We are such stuff as dreams are made on," "I have a king here to my flatterer."

Again, none of the differences (except meanings that have substantially changed or been lost) will cause much difficulty. But it must be confessed that for some elliptical passages there is no widespread agreement on meaning. Wise editors resist saying more than they know, and when they are uncertain they add a question mark to their gloss.

Shakespeare's Theater

In Shakespeare's infancy, Elizabethan actors performed wherever they could—in great halls, at court, in the courtyards of inns. These venues implied not only different audiences but also different playing conditions. The innyards must have made rather unsatisfactory theaters: on some days they were unavailable because carters bringing goods to London used them as depots; when available, they had to be rented from the innkeeper. In 1567, presumably to avoid such difficulties, and also to avoid regulation by the Common Council of London, which was not well disposed toward theatricals, one John Brayne, brother-in-law of the carpenter turned actor James Burbage, built the Red Lion in an eastern suburb of London. We know nothing about its shape or its capacity; we can say only that it may have been the first building in Europe constructed for the purpose of giving plays since the end of antiquity, a thousand years earlier. Even after the building of the Red Lion theatrical activity continued in London in makeshift circumstances, in marketplaces and inns, and always uneasily. In 1574 the Common Council required that plays and playing places in London be licensed because

> sundry great disorders and inconveniences have been found to ensue to this city by the inordinate haunting of great multitudes of people, specially youth, to plays, interludes, and shows, namely occasion of frays and quarrels, evil practices of incontinency in great inns having chambers and secret places adjoining to their open stages and galleries.

The Common Council ordered that innkeepers who wished licenses to hold performance put up a bond and make contributions to the poor.

The requirement that plays and innyard theaters be licensed, along with the other drawbacks of playing at inns and presumably along with the success of the Red Lion, led James Burbage to rent a plot of land northeast of the city walls, on property outside the jurisdiction of the city. Here he built England's second playhouse, called simply the Theatre. About all that is known of its construction is that it was wood. It soon had imitators, the most famous being the Globe (1599), essentially an amphitheater built across the Thames (again outside the city's jurisdiction), constructed with timbers of the Theatre, which had been dismantled when Burbage's lease ran out.

Admission to the theater was one penny, which allowed spectators to stand at the sides and front of the stage that jutted into the yard. An additional penny bought a seat in a covered part of the theater, and a third penny bought a more comfortable seat and a better location. It is notoriously difficult to translate prices into today's money, since some things that are inexpensive today would have been expensive in the past and vice versa—a pipeful of tobacco (imported, of course) cost a lot of money, about three pennies, and an orange (also imported) cost two or three times what a chicken cost—but perhaps we can get some idea of the low cost of the penny admission when we realize that a penny could also buy a pot of ale. An unskilled laborer made about five or sixpence a day, an artisan about twelve pence a day, and the hired actors (as opposed to the sharers in the company, such as Shakespeare) made about ten pence a performance. A printed play cost five or sixpence. Of course a visit to the theater (like a visit to a baseball game today) usually cost more than the admission since the spectator probably would also buy food and drink. Still, the low entrance fee meant that the theater was available to all except the very poorest people, rather as movies and most athletic events are today. Evidence indicates that the audience ranged from apprentices who somehow managed to scrape together the minimum entrance fee and to escape from their masters for a few hours, to prosperous members of the middle class and aristocrats who paid the additional fee for admission to the galleries. The exact proportion of men to women cannot be determined, but women of all classes certainly were present. Theaters were open every afternoon but Sundays for much of the year, except in times of plague, when they were closed because of fear of infection. By the way, no evidence suggests the presence of toilet facilities. Presumably the patrons relieved themselves by making a quick trip to the fields surrounding the playhouses.

There are four important sources of information about the

structure of Elizabethan public playhouses—drawings, a contract, recent excavations, and stage directions in the plays. Of drawings, only the so-called de Witt drawing (c. 1596) of the Swan—really his friend Aernout van Buchell's copy of Johannes de Witt's drawing—is of much significance. The drawing, the only extant representation of the interior of an Elizabethan theater, shows an amphitheater of three tiers, with a stage jutting from a wall into the yard or

Johannes de Witt, a Continental visitor to London, made a drawing of the Swan theater in about the year 1596. The original drawing is lost; this is Aernout van Buchell's copy of it.

center of the building. The tiers are roofed, and part of the stage is covered by a roof that projects from the rear and is supported at its front on two posts, but the groundlings, who paid a penny to stand in front of the stage or at its sides, were exposed to the sky. (Performances in such a playhouse were held only in the daytime; artificial illumination was not used.) At the rear of the stage are two massive doors; above the stage is a gallery.

The second major source of information, the contract for the Fortune (built in 1600), specifies that although the Globe (built in 1599) is to be the model, the Fortune is to be square, eighty feet outside and fifty-five inside. The stage is to be forty-three feet broad, and is to extend into the middle of the yard, i.e., it is twenty-seven and a half feet deep.

The third source of information, the 1989 excavations of the Rose (built in 1587), indicate that the Rose was fourteen-sided, about seventy-two feet in diameter with an inner yard almost fifty feet in diameter. The stage at the Rose was about sixteen feet deep, thirty-seven feet wide at the rear, and twenty-seven feet wide downstage. The relatively small dimensions and the tapering stage, in contrast to the rectangular stage in the Swan drawing, surprised theater historians and have made them more cautious in generalizing about the Elizabethan theater. Excavations at the Globe have not yielded much information, though some historians believe that the fragmentary evidence suggests a larger theater, perhaps one hundred feet in diameter.

From the fourth chief source, stage directions in the plays, one learns that entrance to the stage was by the doors at the rear (*"Enter one citizen at one door, and another at the other"*). A curtain hanging across the doorway—or a curtain hanging between the two doorways—could provide a place where a character could conceal himself, as Polonius does, when he wishes to overhear the conversation between Hamlet and Gertrude. Similarly, withdrawing a curtain from the doorway could "discover" (reveal) a character or two. Such discovery scenes are very rare in Elizabethan drama, but a good example occurs in *The Tempest* (5.1.171), where a stage direction tells us, *"Here Prospero discovers Ferdinand and Miranda playing at chess."* There was also some sort of playing space "aloft" or "above" to represent, for instance, the top of a city's walls or a room above the street. Doubtless each theater had its own peculiarities, but perhaps we can talk about a "typical" Elizabethan theater if we realize that no theater need exactly fit the description, just as no mother is the average mother with 2.7 children.

This hypothetical theater is wooden, round, or polygonal (in *Henry V* Shakespeare calls it a "wooden *O*") capable of holding some eight hundred spectators who stood in the yard around the projecting elevated stage—these spectators were the "groundlings"—and some fifteen hundred additional spectators who sat in the three roofed galleries. The stage, protected by a "shadow" or "heavens" or roof, is entered from two doors; behind the doors is the "tiring house" (attiring house, i.e., dressing room), and above the stage is some sort of gallery that may sometimes hold spectators but can be used (for example) as the bedroom from which Romeo—according to a stage direction in one text—"goeth down." Some evidence suggests that a throne can be lowered onto the platform stage, perhaps from the "shadow"; certainly characters can descend from the stage through a trap or traps into the cellar or "hell." Sometimes this space beneath the stage accommodates a sound-effects man or musician (in *Antony and Cleopatra "music of the hautboys* [oboes] *is under the stage"*) or an actor (in *Hamlet* the *"Ghost cries under the stage"*). Most characters simply walk on and off through the doors, but because there is no curtain in front of the platform, corpses will have to be carried off (Hamlet obligingly clears the stage of Polonius's corpse, when he says, "I'll lug the guts into the neighbor room"). Other characters may have fallen at the rear, where a curtain on a doorway could be drawn to conceal them.

Such may have been the "public theater," so called because its inexpensive admission made it available to a wide range of the populace. Another kind of theater has been called the "private theater" because its much greater admission charge (sixpence versus the penny for general admission at the public theater) limited its audience to the wealthy or the prodigal. The private theater was basically a large room, entirely roofed and therefore artificially illuminated, with a stage at one end. The theaters thus were distinct in two ways: One was essentially an amphitheater that catered to the general public; the other was a hall that catered to the wealthy. In 1576 a hall theater was established in Blackfriars, a Dominican priory in London that had been suppressed in 1538 and confiscated by the Crown and thus was not under the city's jurisdiction. All the actors in this Blackfriars theater were boys about eight to thirteen years old (in the public theaters similar boys played female parts; a boy Lady Macbeth played to a man Macbeth). Near the end of this section on Shakespeare's theater we will talk at some length about possible implications in this convention of using boys to play female roles, but for the moment we should say that it doubtless accounts for the relative lack of female roles in Elizabethan drama. Thus, in *A Midsummer Night's Dream*, out of twenty-one named roles, only four are female; in *Hamlet*, out of twenty-four, only two (Gertrude and Ophelia) are female. Many of Shakespeare's characters have fathers but no mothers—for instance, King Lear's daughters. We need not bring in Freud to explain the disparity; a dramatic company had only a few boys in it.

To return to the private theaters, in some of which all of the performers were children—the "eyrie of . . . little eyases" (nest of unfledged hawks—2.2.347–48) which Rosencrantz mentions when he and Guildenstern talk with Hamlet. The theater in Blackfriars had a precarious existence, and ceased operations in 1584. In 1596 James Burbage, who had already made theatrical history by building the Theatre, began to construct a second Blackfriars theater. He died in 1597, and for several years this second Blackfriars theater was used by a troupe of boys, but in 1608 two of Burbage's sons and five other actors (including Shakespeare) became joint operators of the theater, using it in the winter when the open-air Globe was unsuitable. Perhaps such a smaller theater, roofed, artificially illuminated, and with a tradition of a wealthy audience, exerted an influence in Shakespeare's late plays.

Performances in the private theaters may well have had intermissions during which music was played, but in the public theaters the action was probably uninterrupted, flowing from scene to scene almost without a break. Actors would enter, speak, exit, and others would immediately enter and establish (if necessary) the new locale by a few properties and by words and gestures. To indicate that the scene took place at night, a player or two would carry a torch. Here are some samples of Shakespeare establishing the scene:

This is Illyria, lady.　　　　　　　　　(*Twelfth Night*, 1.2.2)

Well, this is the Forest of Arden.　　　(*As You Like It*, 2.4.14)

This castle has a pleasant seat; the air
Nimbly and sweetly recommends itself
Unto our gentle senses.　　　　　　　(*Macbeth*, 1.6.1–3)

The west yet glimmers with some streaks of day.
　　　　　　　　　　　　　　　　　(*Macbeth*, 3.3.5)

Sometimes a speech will go far beyond evoking the minimal setting of place and time, and will, so to speak, evoke the social world in which the characters move. For instance, early in the first scene of *The Merchant of Venice* Salerio suggests an explanation for Antonio's melancholy. (In the following passage, *pageants* are decorated wagons, floats, and *cursy* is the verb "to curtsy," or "to bow.")

Your mind is tossing on the ocean,
There where your argosies with portly sail—
Like signiors and rich burghers on the flood,
Or as it were the pageants of the sea—
Do overpeer the petty traffickers
That cursy to them, do them reverence,
As they fly by them with their woven wings.　　(1.1.8–14)

Late in the nineteenth century, when Henry Irving produced the play with elaborate illusionistic sets, the first scene showed a ship moored in the harbor, with fruit vendors and dock laborers, in an effort to evoke the bustling and exotic life of Venice. But Shakespeare's words give us this exotic, rich world of commerce in his highly descriptive language when Salerio speaks of "argosies with portly sail" that fly with "woven wings"; equally important, through Salerio Shakespeare conveys a sense of the orderly, hierarchical society in which the lesser ships, "the petty traffickers," curtsy and thereby "do . . . reverence" to their superiors, the merchant prince's ships, which are "Like signiors and rich burghers."

On the other hand, it is a mistake to think that except for verbal pictures the Elizabethan stage was bare. Although Shakespeare's Chorus in *Henry V* calls the stage an "unworthy scaffold" (Prologue 1.10) and urges the spectators to "eke out our performance with your mind" (Prologue 3.35), there was considerable spectacle. The last act of *Macbeth,* for instance, has five stage directions calling for *"drum and colors,"* and another sort of appeal to the eye is indicated by the stage direction *"Enter Macduff, with Macbeth's head."* Some scenery and properties may have been substantial; doubtless a throne was used, but the pillars supporting the roof would have served for the trees on which Orlando pins his poems in *As You Like It*.

Having talked about the public theater—"this wooden *O*"—at some length, we should mention again that Shakespeare's plays were performed also in other locales. Alvin Kernan, in *Shakespeare, the King's Playwright: Theater in the Stuart Court 1603–1613* (1995) points out that "several of [Shakespeare's] plays contain brief theatrical performances, set always in a court or some noble house. When Shakespeare portrayed a theater, he did not, except for the choruses in *Henry V*, imagine a public theater" (p. 195). (Examples include episodes in *The Taming of the Shrew*, *A Midsummer Night's Dream*, *Hamlet*, and *The Tempest*.)

A Note on the Use of Boy Actors in Female Roles

Until fairly recently, scholars were content to mention that the convention existed; they sometimes also mentioned that it continued the medieval practice of using males in female roles, and that other theaters, notably in ancient Greece and in China and Japan, also used males in female roles. (In classical Noh drama in Japan, males still play the female roles.) Prudery may have been at the root of the academic failure to talk much about the use of boy actors, or maybe there really is not much more to say than that it was a convention of a male-centered culture (Stephen Greenblatt's view, in *Shakespearean Negotiations* [1988]). Further, the very nature of a convention is that it is not thought about: Hamlet is a Dane and Julius Caesar is a Roman, but in Shakespeare's plays they speak English, and we in the audience never give this odd fact a thought. Similarly, a character may speak in the presence of others and we understand, again without thinking about it, that he or she is not heard by the figures on the stage (the aside); a character alone on the stage may speak (the soliloquy), and we do not take the character to be unhinged; in a realistic (box) set, the fourth wall, which allows us to see what is going on, is miraculously missing. The no-nonsense view, then, is that the boy actor was an accepted convention, accepted unthinkingly—just as today we know that Kenneth Branagh is not Hamlet, Al Pacino is not Richard III, and Denzel Washington is not the Prince of Aragon. In this view, the audience takes the performer for the role, and that is that; such is the argument we now make for race-free casting, in which African-Americans and Asians can play roles of persons who lived in medieval Denmark and ancient Rome. But gender perhaps is different, at least today. It is a matter of abundant academic study: The Elizabethan theater is now sometimes called a transvestite theater, and we hear much about cross-dressing.

Shakespeare himself in a very few passages calls attention to the use of boys in female roles. At the end of *As You Like It* the boy who played Rosalind addresses the audience, and says, "O men, . . . if I were a woman, I would kiss as many of you as had beards that pleased me." But this is in the Epilogue; the plot is over, and the actor is stepping out of the play and into the audience's everyday world. A second reference to the practice of boys playing female roles occurs in *Antony and Cleopatra*, when Cleopatra imagines that she and Antony will be the subject of crude plays, her role being performed by a boy:

> The quick comedians
> Extemporally will stage us, and present
> Our Alexandrian revels: Antony
> Shall be brought drunken forth, and I shall see
> Some squeaking Cleopatra boy my greatness.   (5.2.216–20)

In a few other passages, Shakespeare is more indirect. For instance, in *Twelfth Night* Viola, played of course by a boy, disguises herself as a young man and seeks service in the house of a lord. She enlists the help of a Captain, and (by way of explaining away her voice and her beardlessness) says,

> I'll serve this duke
> Thou shalt present me as an eunuch to him.   (1.2.55–56)

In *Hamlet*, when the players arrive in 2.2, Hamlet jokes with the boy who plays a female role. The boy has grown since Hamlet last saw him: "By'r Lady, your ladyship is nearer to heaven than when I saw you last by the altitude of a chopine" (a lady's thick-soled shoe). He goes on: "Pray God your voice . . . be not cracked" (434–38).

Exactly how sexual, how erotic, this material was and is, is now much disputed. Again, the use of boys may have been unnoticed, or rather not thought about—an unexamined convention—by most or all spectators most of the time, perhaps *all* of the time, except when Shakespeare calls the convention to the attention of the audience, as in the passages just quoted. Still, an occasional bit seems to invite erotic thoughts. The clearest example is the name that Rosalind takes in *As You Like It*, Ganymede—the beautiful youth whom Zeus abducted. Did boys dressed to play female roles carry homoerotic appeal for straight men (Lisa Jardine's view, in *Still Harping on Daughters* [1983]), or for gay men, or for some or all women in the audience? Further, when the boy actor played a woman who (for the purposes of the plot) disguised herself as a male, as Rosalind, Viola, and Portia do—so we get a boy playing a woman playing a man—what sort of appeal was generated, and for what sort of spectator?

Some scholars have argued that the convention empowered women by letting female characters display a freedom unavailable in Renaissance patriarchal society; the convention, it is said, undermined rigid gender distinctions. In this view, the convention (along with plots in which female characters for a while disguised themselves as young men) allowed Shakespeare to say what some modern gender critics say: Gender is a constructed role rather than a biological given, something we make, rather than a fixed binary opposition of male and female (see Juliet Dusinberre, in *Shakespeare and the Nature of Women* [1975]). On the other hand, some scholars have maintained that the male disguise assumed by some female characters serves only to reaffirm traditional social distinctions since female characters who don male garb (notably Portia in *The Merchant of Venice* and Rosalind in *As You Like It*) return to their female garb and at least implicitly (these critics say) reaffirm the status quo. (For this last view, see Clara Claiborne Park, in an essay in *The Woman's Part*, ed. Carolyn Ruth Swift Lenz et al. [1980].) Perhaps no one answer is right for all plays; in *As You Like It* cross-dressing empowers Rosalind, but in *Twelfth Night* cross-dressing comically traps Viola.

Shakespeare's Dramatic Language: Costumes, Gestures and Silences; Prose and Poetry

Because Shakespeare was a dramatist, not merely a poet, he worked not only with language but also with costume, sound effects, gestures, and even silences. We have already discussed some kinds of spectacle in the preceding section, and now we will begin with other aspects of visual language; a theater, after all, is literally a "place for seeing." Consider the opening stage direction in *The Tempest*, the first play in the first published collection of Shakespeare's plays: *"A tempestuous noise of thunder and Lightning heard: Enter a Ship-master, and a Boteswain."*

Costumes: What did that shipmaster and that boatswain wear? Doubtless they wore something that identified them as men of the sea. Not much is known about the costumes that Elizabethan actors wore, but at least three points are clear: (1) many of the costumes were splendid versions of contemporary Elizabethan dress; (2) some attempts were made to approximate the dress of certain occupations and of antique or exotic characters such as Romans, Turks, and Jews; (3) some costumes indicated that the wearer was supernatural. Evidence for elaborate Elizabethan clothing can be found in the plays themselves and in contemporary comments about the "sumptuous" players who wore the discarded clothing of noblemen, as well as in account books that itemize such things as "a scarlet cloak with two broad gold laces, with gold buttons down the sides."

The attempts at approximation of the dress of certain occupations and nationalities also can be documented from the plays themselves, and it derives additional confirmation from a drawing of the first scene of Shakespeare's *Titus Andronicus*—the only extant Elizabethan picture of an identifiable episode in a play. (See pp. xxxviii–xxxix.) The drawing, probably done in 1594 or 1595, shows Queen Tamora pleading for mercy. She wears a somewhat medieval-looking robe and a crown; Titus wears a toga and a wreath, but two soldiers behind him wear costumes fairly close to Elizabethan dress. We do not know, however, if the drawing represents an actual stage production in the public theater, or perhaps a private production, or maybe only a reader's visualization of an episode. Further, there is some conflicting evidence: In *Julius Caesar* a reference is made to Caesar's doublet (a close-fitting jacket), which, if taken literally, suggests that even the protagonist did not wear Roman clothing; and certainly the lesser characters, who are said to wear hats, did not wear Roman garb.

It should be mentioned, too, that even ordinary clothing can be symbolic: Hamlet's "inky cloak," for example, sets him apart from the brightly dressed members of Claudius's court and symbolizes his mourning; the fresh clothes that are put on King Lear partly symbolize his return to sanity. Consider, too, the removal of disguises near the end of some plays. For instance, Rosalind in *As You Like It* and Portia and Nerissa in *The Merchant of Venice* remove their male attire, thus again becoming fully themselves.

Gestures and Silences: Gestures are an important part of a dramatist's language. King Lear kneels before his daughter Cordelia for a benediction (4.7.57–59), an act of humility that contrasts with his earlier speeches banishing her and that contrasts also with a comparable gesture, his ironic

kneeling before Regan (2.4.153–55). Northumberland's failure to kneel before King Richard II (3.3.71–72) speaks volumes. As for silences, consider a moment in *Coriolanus*: Before the protagonist yields to his mother's entreaties (5.3.182), there is this stage direction: *"Holds her by the hand, silent."* Another example of "speech in dumbness" occurs in *Macbeth*, when Macduff learns that his wife and children have been murdered. He is silent at first, as Malcolm's speech indicates: "What, man! Ne'er pull your hat upon your brows. Give sorrow words" (4.3.208–09). (For a discussion of such moments, see Philip C. McGuire's *Speechless Dialect: Shakespeare's Open Silences* [1985].)

Of course when we think of Shakespeare's work, we think primarily of his language, both the poetry and the prose.

Prose: Although two of his plays (*Richard II* and *King John*) have no prose at all, about half the others have at least one quarter of the dialogue in prose, and some have notably more: *1 Henry IV* and *2 Henry IV*, about half; *As You Like It*

and *Twelfth Night*, a little more than half; *Much Ado About Nothing*, more than three quarters; and *The Merry Wives of Windsor*, a little more than five sixths. We should remember that despite Molière's joke about M. Jourdain, who was amazed to learn that he spoke prose, most of us do not speak prose. Rather, we normally utter repetitive, shapeless, and often ungrammatical torrents; prose is something very different—a sort of literary imitation of speech at its most coherent.

Today we may think of prose as "natural" for drama; or even if we think that poetry is appropriate for high tragedy we may still think that prose is the right medium for comedy. Greek, Roman, and early English comedies, however, were written in verse. In fact, prose was not generally considered a literary medium in England until the late fifteenth century; Chaucer tells even his bawdy stories in verse. By the end of the 1580s, however, prose had established itself on the English comic stage. In tragedy, Marlowe made some use of prose, not simply in the speeches of clownish servants but even in the speech of a tragic hero, Doctor Faustus. Still, before Shakespeare, prose normally was used in the theater only for special circumstances: (1) letters and proclamations, to set them off from the poetic dialogue; (2) mad characters, to indicate that normal thinking has become disordered; and (3) low comedy, or speeches uttered by clowns even when they are not being comic. Shakespeare made use of these conventions, but he also went far beyond them. Sometimes he begins a scene in prose and then shifts into verse as the emotion is heightened; or conversely, he may shift from verse to prose when a speaker is lowering the emotional level, as when Brutus speaks in the Forum.

Shakespeare's prose usually is not prosaic. Hamlet's prose includes not only small talk with Rosencrantz and Guildenstern but also princely reflections on "What a piece of work is a man" (2.2.312). In conversation with Ophelia, he shifts from light talk in verse to a passionate prose denunciation of women (3.1.103), though the shift to prose here is perhaps also intended to suggest the possibility of madness. (Consult Brian Vickers, *The Artistry of Shakespeare's Prose* [1968].)

Poetry: Drama in rhyme in England goes back to the Middle Ages, but by Shakespeare's day rhyme no longer dominated poetic drama; a finer medium, blank verse (strictly speaking, unrhymed lines of ten syllables, with the stress on every second syllable) had been adopted. But before looking at unrhymed poetry, a few things should be said about the chief uses of rhyme in Shakespeare's plays. (1) A couplet (a pair of rhyming lines) is sometimes used to convey emotional heightening at the end of a blank verse speech; (2) characters sometimes speak a couplet as they leave the stage, suggesting closure; (3) except in the latest plays, scenes fairly often conclude with a couplet, and sometimes, as in *Richard II*, 2.1.145–46, the entrance of a new character within a scene is preceded by a couplet, which wraps up the earlier portion of that scene; (4) speeches of two characters occasionally are linked by rhyme, most notably in *Romeo and Juliet*, 1.5.95–108, where the lovers speak a sonnet between them; elsewhere a taunting reply occasionally rhymes with the previous speaker's last line; (5) speeches with sententious or gnomic remarks are sometimes in rhyme, as in the duke's speech in *Othello* (1.3.199–206); (6) speeches of sardonic mockery are sometimes in rhyme—for example, Iago's speech on women in *Othello* (2.1.146–58)—and they sometimes conclude with an emphatic couplet, as in Bolingbroke's speech on comforting words in *Richard II* (1.3.301–2); (7) some characters are associated with rhyme, such as the fairies in *A Midsummer Night's Dream*; (8) in the early plays, especially *The Comedy of Errors* and *The Taming of the Shrew*, comic scenes that in later plays would be in prose are in jingling rhymes; (9) prologues, choruses, plays-within-the-play, inscriptions, vows, epilogues, and so on are often in rhyme, and the songs in the plays are rhymed.

Neither prose nor rhyme immediately comes to mind when we first think of Shakespeare's medium: It is blank verse, unrhymed iambic pentameter. (In a mechanically exact line there are five iambic feet. An iambic foot consists of two syllables, the second accented, as in *away*; five feet make a pentameter line. Thus, a strict line of iambic pentameter contains ten syllables, the even syllables being stressed more heavily than the odd syllables. Fortunately, Shakespeare usually varies the line somewhat.) The first speech in *A Midsummer Night's Dream*, spoken by Duke Theseus to his betrothed, is an example of blank verse:

> Now, fair Hippolyta, our nuptial hour
> Draws on apace. Four happy days bring in
> Another moon; but, O, methinks, how slow
> This old moon wanes! She lingers my desires,
> Like to a stepdame, or a dowager,
> Long withering out a young man's revenue.   (1.1.1–6)

As this passage shows, Shakespeare's blank verse is not mechanically unvarying. Though the predominant foot is the iamb (as in *apace* or *desires*), there are numerous variations. In the first line the stress can be placed on "fair," as the regular metrical pattern suggests, but it is likely that "Now" gets almost as much emphasis; probably in the second line "Draws" is more heavily emphasized than "on," giving us a trochee (a stressed syllable followed by an unstressed one); and in the fourth line each word in the phrase "This old moon wanes" is probably stressed fairly heavily, conveying by two spondees (two feet, each of two stresses) the oppressive tedium that Theseus feels.

In Shakespeare's early plays much of the blank verse is end-stopped (that is, it has a heavy pause at the end of each line), but he later developed the ability to write iambic pentameter verse paragraphs (rather than lines) that give the illusion of speech. His chief techniques are (1) enjambing, i.e., running the thought beyond the single line, as in the first three lines of the speech just quoted; (2) occasionally replacing an iamb with another foot; (3) varying the position of the chief pause (the caesura) within a line; (4) adding an occasional unstressed syllable at the end of a line, traditionally called a feminine ending; (5) and beginning or ending a speech with a half line.

Shakespeare's mature blank verse has much of the rhythmic flexibility of his prose; both the language, though richly figurative and sometimes dense, and the syntax seem natural. It is also often highly appropriate to a particular character. Consider, for instance, this speech from *Hamlet*, in which Claudius, King of Denmark ("the Dane"), speaks to Laertes:

> And now, Laertes, what's the news with you?
> You told us of some suit. What is't, Laertes?
> You cannot speak of reason to the Dane
> And lose your voice. What wouldst thou beg, Laertes,
> That shall not be my offer, not thy asking?   (1.2.42–46)

Notice the short sentences and the repetition of the name "Laertes," to whom the speech is addressed. Notice, too, the shift from the royal "us" in the second line to the more intimate "my" in the last line, and from "you" in the first three lines to the more intimate "thou" and "thy" in the last two lines. Claudius knows how to ingratiate himself with Laertes.

For a second example of the flexibility of Shakespeare's blank verse, consider a passage from *Macbeth*. Distressed by the doctor's inability to cure Lady Macbeth and by the imminent battle, Macbeth addresses some of his remarks to the doctor and others to the servant who is arming him. The entire speech, with its pauses, interruptions, and irresolution (in "Pull't off, I say," Macbeth orders the servant to remove the armor that the servant has been putting on him), catches Macbeth's disintegration. (In the first line, *physic* means "medicine," and in the fourth and fifth lines, *cast the water* means "analyze the urine.")

> Throw physic to the dogs, I'll none of it.
> Come, put mine armor on. Give me my staff.
> Seyton, send out.—Doctor, the thanes fly from me.—
> Come, sir, dispatch. If thou couldst, doctor, cast
> The water of my land, find her disease
> And purge it to a sound and pristine health,
> I would applaud thee to the very echo,
> That should applaud again.—Pull't off, I say.—
> What rhubarb, senna, or what purgative drug,
> Would scour these English hence? Hear'st thou of them?
>
> (5.3.47–56)

Blank verse, then, can be much more than unrhymed iambic pentameter, and even within a single play Shakespeare's blank verse often consists of several styles, depending on the speaker and on the speaker's emotion at the moment.

The Play Text as a Collaboration

Shakespeare's fellow dramatist Ben Jonson reported that the actors said of Shakespeare, "In his writing, whatsoever he penned, he never blotted out line," i.e., never crossed out material and revised his work while composing. None of Shakespeare's plays survives in manuscript (with the possible exception of a scene in *Sir Thomas More*), so we cannot fully evaluate the comment, but in a few instances the published work clearly shows that he revised his manuscript. Consider the following passage (shown here in facsimile) from the best early text of *Romeo and Juliet*, the Second Quarto (1599):

Ro. Would I were ſleepe and peace ſo ſweet to reſt
The grey eyde morne ſmiles on the ſrowning night,
Checkring the Eaſterne Clouds with ſtreaks of light,
And darkneſſe fleckted like a drunkard reeles,
From ſorth daies pathway, made by *Tytans* wheeles.
Hence will I to my ghoſtly Friers cloſe cell,
His helpe to craue, and my deare hap to tell.

                        Exit.

Enter Frier alone with a basket.   (night,
Fri. The grey-eyed morne ſmiles on the ſrowning
Checking the Eaſterne clowdes with ſtreaks of light:
And fleckeld darkneſſe like a drunkard reeles,
From ſorth daies path, and *Titans* burning wheeles:
Now ere the ſun aduance his burning eie,

Romeo rather elaborately tells us that the sun at dawn is
dispelling the night (morning is smiling, the eastern clouds
are checked with light, and the sun's chariot—Titan's
wheels—advances), and he will seek out his spiritual father,
the Friar. He exits and, oddly, the Friar enters and says pretty
much the same thing about the sun. Both speakers say that
"the gray-eyed morn smiles on the frowning night," but there
are small differences, perhaps having more to do with the
business of printing the book than with the author's
composition: For Romeo's "checkring," "fleckted," and
"pathway," we get the Friar's "checking," "fleckeld," and
"path." (Notice, by the way, the inconsistency in Elizabethan
spelling: Romeo's "clouds" become the Friar's "clowdes.")

Both versions must have been in the printer's copy, and it
seems safe to assume that both were in Shakespeare's manuscript. He must have written one version—let's say he first
wrote Romeo's closing lines for this scene—and then he
decided, no, it's better to give this lyrical passage to the
Friar, as the opening of a new scene, but he neglected to
delete the first version. Editors must make a choice, and they
may feel that the reasonable thing to do is to print the text as
Shakespeare intended it. But how can we know what he
intended? Almost all modern editors delete the lines from

Romeo's speech, and retain the Friar's lines. They don't do this because they know Shakespeare's intention, however. They give the lines to the Friar because the first published version (1597) of *Romeo and Juliet* gives only the Friar's version, and this text (though in many ways inferior to the 1599 text) is thought to derive from the memory of some actors, that is, it is thought to represent a performance, not just a script. Maybe during the course of rehearsals Shakespeare—an actor as well as an author—unilaterally decided that the Friar should speak the lines; if so (remember that we don't know this to be a fact) his final intention was to give the speech to the Friar. Maybe, however, the actors talked it over and settled on the Friar, with or without Shakespeare's approval. On the other hand, despite the 1597 version, one might argue (if only weakly) on behalf of giving the lines to Romeo rather than to the Friar, thus: (1) Romeo's comment on the coming of the daylight emphasizes his separation from Juliet, and (2) the figurative language seems more appropriate to Romeo than to the Friar. Having said this, in the Signet edition we have decided in this instance to draw on the evidence provided by earlier text and to give the lines to the Friar, on the grounds that since Q1 reflects a production, in the theater (at least on one occasion) the lines were spoken by the Friar.

A playwright sold a script to a theatrical company. The script thus belonged to the company, not the author, and author and company alike must have regarded this script not as a literary work but as the basis for a play that the actors would create on the stage. We speak of Shakespeare as the author of the plays, but readers should bear in mind that the texts they read, even when derived from a single text, such as the First Folio (1623), are inevitably the collaborative work not simply of Shakespeare with his company—doubtless during rehearsals the actors would suggest alterations—but also with other forces of the age. One force was governmental censorship. In 1606 parliament passed "an Act to restrain abuses of players," prohibiting the utterance of oaths and the name of God. So where the earliest text of *Othello* gives us "By heaven" (3.3.106), the first Folio gives "Alas," presumably reflecting the compliance of stage practice with the law. Similarly, the 1623 version of *King Lear* omits the oath "Fut" (probably from "By God's foot") at 1.2.142, again presumably reflecting the line as it was spoken on the stage. Editors who seek to give the reader the play that Shakespeare initially conceived—the "authentic" play conceived by the solitary Shakespeare—probably will restore the missing oaths and references to God. Other editors, who see the play as a collaborative work, a construction made not only by Shakespeare but also by actors and compositors and even government censors, may claim that what counts is the play as it was actually performed. Such editors regard the censored text as legitimate, since it is the play that was (presumably) finally put on. A performed text, they argue, has more historical reality than a text produced by an editor who has sought to get at what Shakespeare initially wrote. In this view, the text of a play is rather like the script of a film; the script is not the film, and the play text is not the performed play. Even if we want to talk about the play that Shakespeare "intended," we will find ourselves talking about a script that he handed over to a company with the intention that it be implemented by actors. The "intended" play is the one that the actors—we might almost say "society"—would help to construct.

Further, it is now widely held that a play is also the work of readers and spectators, who do not simply receive meaning, but who create it when they respond to the play. This idea is fully in accord with contemporary post-structuralist critical thinking, notably Roland Barthes's "The Death of the Author," in *Image-Music-Text* (1977) and Michel Foucault's "What Is an Author?," in *The Foucault Reader* (1984). The gist of the idea is that an author is not an isolated genius; rather, authors are subject to the politics and other social structures of their age. A dramatist especially is a worker in a collaborative project, working most obviously with actors—parts may be written for particular actors—but working also with the audience. Consider the words of Samuel Johnson, written to be spoken by the actor David Garrick at the opening of a theater in 1747:

> The stage but echoes back the public voice;
> The drama's laws, the drama's patrons give,
> For we that live to please, must please to live.

The audience—the public taste as understood by the playwright—helps to determine what the play is. Moreover, even members of the public who are not part of the playwright's immediate audience may exert an influence through censorship. We have already glanced at governmental censorship, but there are also other kinds. Take one of Shakespeare's most beloved characters, Falstaff, who appears in three of Shakespeare's plays, the two parts of *Henry IV* and *The Merry Wives of Windsor*. He appears with this name in the earliest printed version of the first of these plays, *1 Henry IV*, but we know that Shakespeare originally called him (after an historical figure) Sir John Oldcastle. Oldcastle appears in Shakespeare's source (partly reprinted in the Signet edition of *1 Henry IV*), and a trace of the name survives in Shakespeare's play, 1.2.43–44, where Prince Hal punningly addresses Falstaff as "my old lad of the castle." But for some reason—perhaps because the family of the historical Oldcastle complained—Shakespeare had to change the name. In short, the play as we have it was (at least in this detail) subject to some sort of censorship. If we think that a text should present what we take to be the author's intention, we probably will want to replace *Falstaff* with *Oldcastle*. But if we recognize that a play is a collaboration, we may welcome the change, even if it was forced on Shakespeare. Somehow *Falstaff*, with its hint of *false-staff*, i.e., inadequate prop, seems just right for this fat knight who, to our delight, entertains the young prince with untruths. We can go as far as saying that, at least so far as a play is concerned, an insistence on the author's original intention (even if we could know it) can sometimes impoverish the text.

The tiny example of Falstaff's name illustrates the point that the text we read is inevitably only a version—something in effect produced by the collaboration of the playwright with his actors, audiences, compositors, and editors—of a fluid text that Shakespeare once wrote, just as the *Hamlet* that we see on the screen starring Kenneth Branagh is not the *Hamlet* that Shakespeare saw in an open-air playhouse starring Richard Burbage. *Hamlet* itself, as we shall note in a moment, also exists in several versions. It is not surprising that there is now much talk about the *instability* of Shakespeare's texts.

Because he was not only a playwright but was also an actor and a shareholder in a theatrical company, Shakespeare probably was much involved with the translation of the play from a manuscript to a stage production. He may or may not have done some rewriting during rehearsals, and he may or may not have been happy with cuts that were made. Some plays, notably *Hamlet* and *King Lear*, are so long that it is most unlikely that the texts we read were acted in their entirety. Further, for both of these plays we have more than one early text that demands consideration. In *Hamlet*, the Second Quarto (1604) includes some two hundred lines not found in the Folio (1623). Among the passages missing from the Folio are two of Hamlet's reflective speeches, the "dram of evil" speech (1.4.13–38) and "How all occasions do inform against me" (4.4.32–66). Since the Folio has more numerous and often fuller stage directions, it certainly looks as though in the Folio we get a theatrical version of the play, a text whose cuts were probably made—this is only a hunch, of course—not because Shakespeare was changing his conception of Hamlet but because the playhouse demanded a modified play. (The problem is complicated, since the Folio not only cuts some of the Quarto but adds some material. Various explanations have been offered.)

Or take an example from *King Lear*. In the First and Second Quarto (1608, 1619), the final speech of the play is given to Albany, Lear's surviving son-in-law, but in the First Folio version (1623), the speech is given to Edgar. The Quarto version is in accord with tradition—usually the highest-ranking character in a tragedy speaks the final words. Why does the Folio give the speech to Edgar? One possible answer is this: The Folio version omits some of Albany's speeches in earlier scenes, so perhaps it was decided (by Shakespeare? by the players?) not to give the final lines to so pale a character. In fact, the discrepancies are so many between the two texts, that some scholars argue we do not simply have texts showing different theatrical productions. Rather, these scholars say, Shakespeare substantially revised the play, and we really have two versions of *King Lear* (and of *Othello* also, say some)—two different plays—not simply two texts, each of which is in some ways imperfect.

In this view, the 1608 version of *Lear* may derive from Shakespeare's manuscript, and the 1623 version may derive from his later revision. The Quartos have almost three hundred lines not in the Folio, and the Folio has about a hundred lines not in the Quartos. It used to be held that all the texts were imperfect in various ways and from various causes— some passages in the Quartos were thought to have been set from a manuscript that was not entirely legible, other passages were thought to have been set by a compositor who was new to setting plays, and still other passages were thought to have been provided by an actor who misremembered some of the lines. This traditional view held that an editor must draw on the Quartos and the Folio in order to get Shakespeare's "real" play. The new argument holds (although not without considerable strain) that we have two authentic plays, Shakespeare's early version (in the Quarto) and Shakespeare's—or his theatrical company's—revised version (in the Folio). Not only theatrical demands but also Shakespeare's own artistic sense, it is argued, called for extensive revisions. Even the titles vary: Q1 is called *True Chronicle Historie of the life and death of King Lear and his three Daughters*, whereas the Folio text is called *The Tragedie of King Lear*. To combine the two texts in order to produce what the editor thinks is the play that Shakespeare intended to write is, according to this view, to produce a text that is false to the history of the play. If the new view is correct, and we do have texts of two distinct versions of *Lear* rather than two imperfect versions of one play, it supports in a textual way the post-structuralist view that we cannot possibly have an unmediated vision of (in this case) a play by Shakespeare; we can only recognize a plurality of visions.

Editing Texts

Though eighteen of his plays were published during his lifetime, Shakespeare seems never to have supervised their publication. There is nothing unusual here; when a playwright sold a play to a theatrical company he surrendered his ownership to it. Normally a company would not publish the play, because to publish it meant to allow competitors to acquire the piece. Some plays did get published: Apparently hard-up actors sometimes pieced together a play for a publisher; sometimes a company in need of money sold a play; and sometimes a company allowed publication of a play that no longer drew audiences. That Shakespeare did not concern himself with publication is not remarkable; of his contemporaries, only Ben Jonson carefully supervised the publication of his own plays.

In 1623, seven years after Shakespeare's death, John Heminges and Henry Condell (two senior members of Shakespeare's company, who had worked with him for about twenty years) collected his plays—published and unpublished—into a large volume, of a kind called a folio. (A folio is a volume consisting of large sheets that have been folded once, each sheet thus making two leaves, or four pages. The size of the page of course depends on the size of the sheet—a folio can range in height from twelve to sixteen inches, and in width from eight to eleven; the pages in the 1623 edition of Shakespeare, commonly called the First Folio, are approximately thirteen inches tall and eight inches wide.) The eighteen plays published during Shakespeare's lifetime had been issued one play per volume in small formats called quartos. (Each sheet in a quarto has been folded twice, making four leaves, or eight pages, each page being about nine inches tall and seven inches wide, roughly the size of a large paperback.)

Heminges and Condell suggest in an address "To the great variety of readers" that the republished plays are presented in better form than in the quartos:

> Before you were abused with diverse stolen and surreptitious copies, maimed and deformed by the frauds and stealths of injurious impostors that exposed them; even those, are now offered to your view cured and perfect of their limbs, and all the rest absolute in their numbers, as he [i.e., Shakespeare] conceived them.

There is a good deal of truth to this statement, but some of the quarto versions are better than others; some are in fact preferable to the Folio text.

Whoever was assigned to prepare the texts for publication

in the first Folio seems to have taken the job seriously and yet not to have performed it with uniform care. The sources of the texts seem to have been, in general, good unpublished copies or the best published copies. The first play in the collection, *The Tempest*, is divided into acts and scenes, has unusually full stage directions and descriptions of spectacle, and concludes with a list of the characters, but the editor was not able (or willing) to present all of the succeeding texts so fully dressed. Later texts occasionally show signs of carelessness: in one scene of *Much Ado About Nothing* the names of actors, instead of characters, appear as speech prefixes, as they had in the Quarto, which the Folio reprints; proofreading throughout the Folio is spotty and apparently was done without reference to the printer's copy; the pagination of *Hamlet* jumps from 156 to 257. Further, the proofreading was done while the presses continued to print, so that each play in each volume contains a mix of corrected and uncorrected pages.

Modern editors of Shakespeare must first select their copy; no problem if the play exists only in the Folio, but a considerable problem if the relationship between a Quarto and the Folio—or an early Quarto and a later one—is unclear. In the case of *Romeo and Juliet*, the First Quarto (Q1), published in 1597, is vastly inferior to the Second (Q2), published in 1599. The basis of Q1 apparently is a version put together from memory by some actors. Not surprisingly, it garbles many passages and is much shorter than Q2. On the other hand, occasionally Q1 makes better sense than Q2. For instance, near the end of the play, when the parents have assembled and learned of the deaths of Romeo and Juliet, in Q2 the Prince says (5.3.208–9),

> Come, *Montague;* for thou art early vp
> To see thy sonne and heire, now earling downe.

The last three words of this speech surely do not make sense, and many editors turn to Q1, which instead of "now earling downe" has "more early downe." Some modern editors take only "early" from Q1, and print "now early down"; others take "more early," and print "more early down." Further, Q1 (though, again, quite clearly a garbled and abbreviated text) includes some stage directions that are not found in Q2, and today many editors who base their text on Q2 are glad to add these stage directions, because the directions help to give us a sense of what the play looked like on Shakespeare's stage. Thus, in 4.3.58, after Juliet drinks the potion, Q1 gives us this stage direction, not in Q2: *"She falls upon her bed within the curtains."*

In short, an editor's decisions do not end with the choice of a single copy text. First of all, editors must reckon with Elizabethan spelling. If they are not producing a facsimile, they probably modernize the spelling, but ought they to preserve the old forms of words that apparently were pronounced quite unlike their modern forms—*lanthorn, alablaster*? If they preserve these forms are they really preserving Shakespeare's forms or perhaps those of a compositor in the printing house? What is one to do when one finds *lanthorn* and *lantern* in adjacent lines? (The editors of this series in general, but not invariably, assume that words should be spelled in their modern form, unless, for instance, a rhyme is involved.) Elizabethan punctuation, too, presents problems. For example, in the First Folio, the only text for the play, Macbeth rejects his wife's idea that he can wash the blood from his hand (2.2.60–62):

> No: this my Hand will rather
> The multitudinous Seas incarnardine,
> Making the Greene one, Red.

Obviously an editor will remove the superfluous capitals, and will probably alter the spelling to "incarnadine," but what about the comma before "Red"? If we retain the comma, Macbeth is calling the sea "the green one." If we drop the comma, Macbeth is saying that his bloody hand will make the sea ("the Green") *uniformly* red.

An editor will sometimes have to change more than spelling and punctuation. Macbeth says to his wife (1.7.46–47):

> I dare do all that may become a man,
> Who dares no more, is none.

For two centuries editors have agreed that the second line is unsatisfactory, and have emended "no" to "do": "Who dares do more is none." But when in the same play (4.2.21–22) Ross says that fearful persons

> Floate vpon a wilde and violent Sea
> Each way, and moue,

need we emend the passage? On the assumption that the compositor misread the manuscript, some editors emend "each way, and move" to "and move each way"; others emend "move" to "none" (i.e., "Each way and none"). Other editors, however, let the passage stand as in the original. The editors of the Signet Classic Shakespeare have restrained themselves from making abundant emendations. In their minds they hear Samuel Johnson on the dangers of emendation: "I have adopted the Roman sentiment, that it is more honorable to save a citizen than to kill an enemy." Some departures (in addition to spelling, punctuation, and lineation) from the copy text have of course been made, but the original readings are listed in a note following the play, so that readers can evaluate the changes for themselves.

Following tradition, the editors of the Signet Classic Shakespeare have prefaced each play with a list of characters, and throughout the play have regularized the names of the speakers. Thus, in our text of *Romeo and Juliet*, all speeches by Juliet's mother are prefixed "Lady Capulet," although the 1599 Quarto of the play, which provides our copy text, uses at various points seven speech tags for this one character: *Capu. Wi.* (i.e., Capulet's wife), *Ca. Wi., Wi., Wife, Old La.* (i.e., Old Lady), *La.,* and *Mo.* (i.e., Mother). Similarly, in *All's Well That Ends Well*, the character whom we regularly call "Countess" is in the Folio (the copy text) variously identified as *Mother, Countess, Old Countess, Lady,* and *Old Lady.* Admittedly there is some loss in regularizing, since the various prefixes may give us a hint of the way Shakespeare (or a scribe who copied Shakespeare's manuscript) was thinking of the character in a particular scene—for instance, as a mother, or as an old lady. But too much can be made of these differing prefixes, since the social relationships implied are *not* always relevant to the given scene.

We have also added line numbers and in many cases act and scene divisions as well as indications of locale at the beginning of scenes. The Folio divided most of the plays into acts and some into scenes. Early eighteenth-century editors increased the divisions. These divisions, which provide a convenient way of referring to passages in the plays, have been retained, but when not in the text chosen as the basis for the Signet Classic text they are enclosed within square brackets, [ ], to indicate that they are editorial additions. Similarly, though no play of Shakespeare's was equipped with indications of the locale at the heads of scene divisions, locales have here been added in square brackets for the convenience of readers, who lack the information that costumes, properties, gestures, and scenery afford to spectators. Spectators can tell at a glance they are in the throne room, but without an editorial indication the reader may be puzzled for a while. It should be mentioned, incidentally, that there are a few authentic stage directions—perhaps Shakespeare's, perhaps a prompter's—that suggest locales, such as *"Enter Brutus in his orchard,"* and *"They go up into the Senate house."* It is hoped that the bracketed additions in the Signet text will provide readers with the sort of help provided by these two authentic directions, but it is equally hoped that the reader will remember that the stage was not loaded with scenery.

Shakespeare on the Stage

Each volume in the Signet Classic Shakespeare includes a brief stage (and sometimes film) history of the play. When we read about earlier productions, we are likely to find them eccentric, obviously wrongheaded—for instance, Nahum Tate's version of *King Lear*, with a happy ending, which held the stage for about a century and a half, from the late seventeenth century until the end of the first quarter of the nineteenth. We see engravings of David Garrick, the greatest actor of the eighteenth century, in eighteenth-century garb as King Lear, and we smile, thinking how absurd the production must have been. If we are more thoughtful, we say, with the English novelist L. P. Hartley, "The past is a foreign country: they do things differently there." But if the eighteenth-century staging is a foreign country, what of the plays of the late sixteenth and seventeenth centuries? A foreign language, a foreign theater, a foreign audience.

Probably all viewers of Shakespeare's plays, beginning with Shakespeare himself, at times have been unhappy with the plays on the stage. Consider three comments about production that we find in the plays themselves, which suggest Shakespeare's concerns. The Chorus in *Henry V* complains that the heroic story cannot possibly be adequately staged:

> But pardon, gentles all,
> The flat unraisèd spirits that hath dared
> On this unworthy scaffold to bring forth
> So great an object. Can this cockpit hold
> The vasty fields of France? Or may we cram
> Within this wooden *O* the very casques
> That did affright the air at Agincourt?
>
> . . . .
>
> Piece out our imperfections with your thoughts.
> (Prologue 1.8–14, 23)

Second, here are a few sentences (which may or may not represent Shakespeare's own views) from Hamlet's longish lecture to the players:

> Speak the speech, I pray you, as I pronounced it to you, trippingly on the tongue. But if you mouth it, as many of our players do, I had as lief the town crier spoke my lines. . . . O, it offends me to the soul to hear a robustious periwig-pated fellow tear a passion to tatters, to very rags, to split the ears of the groundlings. . . . And let those that play your clowns speak no more than is set down for them, for there be of them that will themselves laugh, to set on some quantity of barren spectators to laugh too, though in the meantime some necessary question of the play be then to be considered. That's villainous and shows a most pitiful ambition in the fool that uses it. (3.2.1–47)

Finally, we can quote again from the passage cited earlier in this introduction, concerning the boy actors who played the female roles. Cleopatra imagines with horror a theatrical version of her activities with Antony:

> The quick comedians
> Extemporally will stage us, and present
> Our Alexandrian revels: Antony
> Shall be brought drunken forth, and I shall see
> Some squeaking Cleopatra boy my greatness
> I' th' posture of a whore.   (5.2.216–21)

It is impossible to know how much weight to put on such passages—perhaps Shakespeare was just being modest about his theater's abilities—but it is easy enough to think that he was unhappy with some aspects of Elizabethan production. Probably no production can fully satisfy a playwright, and for that matter, few productions can fully satisfy *us;* we regret this or that cut, this or that way of costuming the play, this or that bit of business.

One's first thought may be this: Why don't they just do "authentic" Shakespeare, "straight" Shakespeare, the play as Shakespeare wrote it? But as we read the plays—words written to be performed—it sometimes becomes clear that we do not know *how* to perform them. For instance, in *Antony and Cleopatra* Antony, the Roman general who has succumbed to Cleopatra and to Egyptian ways, says, "The nobleness of life / Is to do thus" (1.1.36–37). But what is "thus"? Does Antony at this point embrace Cleopatra? Does he embrace and kiss her? (There are, by the way, very few scenes of kissing on Shakespeare's stage, possibly because boys played the female roles.) Or does he make a sweeping gesture, indicating the Egyptian way of life?

This is not an isolated example; the plays are filled with lines that call for gestures, but we are not sure what the gestures should be. *Interpretation* is inevitable. Consider a passage in *Hamlet*. In 3.1, Polonius persuades his daughter, Ophelia, to talk to Hamlet while Polonius and Claudius eavesdrop. The two men conceal themselves, and Hamlet encounters Ophelia. At 3.1.131 Hamlet suddenly says to her, "Where's your father?" Why does Hamlet, apparently out of nowhere—they have not been talking about Polonius—ask this question? Is this an example of the "antic disposition" (fantastic behavior) that Hamlet earlier (1.5.172) had told Horatio and others—including us—he would display? That is, is the question about the whereabouts of her father a seemingly irrational one, like his earlier question (3.1.103) to Ophelia, "Ha, ha! Are you honest?" Or, on the other hand, has Hamlet (as in many productions) suddenly glimpsed Polonius's foot protruding from beneath a drapery at the rear? That is, does Hamlet ask the question because he has suddenly seen something suspicious and now is testing Ophelia? (By the way, in productions that do give Hamlet a physical cue, it is almost always Polonius rather than Claudius who provides the clue. This itself is an act of interpretation on the part of the director.) Or (a third possibility) does Hamlet get a clue from Ophelia, who inadvertently betrays the spies by nervously glancing at their place of hiding? This is the interpretation used in the BBC television version, where Ophelia glances in fear toward the hiding place just after Hamlet says "Why wouldst thou be a breeder of sinners?" (121–22). Hamlet, realizing that he is being observed, glances here and there *before* he asks "Where's your father?" The question thus is a climax to what he has been doing while speaking the preceding lines. Or (a fourth interpretation) does Hamlet suddenly, without the aid of any clue whatsoever, intuitively (insightfully, mysteriously, wonderfully) sense that someone is spying? Directors must decide, of course—and so must readers.

Recall, too, the preceding discussion of the texts of the plays, which argued that the texts—though they seem to be before us in permanent black on white—are unstable. The Signet text of *Hamlet*, which draws on the Second Quarto (1604) and the First Folio (1623) is considerably longer than any version staged in Shakespeare's time. Our version, even if spoken very briskly and played without any intermission, would take close to four hours, far beyond "the two hours' traffic of our stage" mentioned in the Prologue to *Romeo and Juliet*. (There are a few contemporary references to the duration of a play, but none mentions more than three hours.) Of Shakespeare's plays, only *The Comedy of Errors*, *Macbeth*, and *The Tempest* can be done in less than three hours without cutting. And even if we take a play that exists only in a short text, *Macbeth*, we cannot claim that we are experiencing the very play that Shakespeare conceived, partly because some of the Witches' songs almost surely are non-Shakespearean additions, and partly because we are not willing to watch the play performed without an intermission and with boys in the female roles.

Further, as the earlier discussion of costumes mentioned, the plays apparently were given chiefly in contemporary, that is, in Elizabethan dress. If today we give them in the costumes that Shakespeare probably saw, the plays seem not contemporary but curiously dated. Yet if we use our own dress, we find lines of dialogue that are at odds with what we see; we may feel that the language, so clearly not our own, is inappropriate coming out of people in today's dress. A common solution, incidentally, has been to set the plays in the nineteenth century, on the grounds that this attractively distances the plays (gives them a degree of foreignness, allowing for interesting costumes) and yet doesn't put them into a museum world of Elizabethan England.

Inevitably our productions are adaptations, *our* adaptations, and inevitably they will look dated, not in a century but in twenty years, or perhaps even in a decade. Still, we cannot escape from our own conceptions. As the director Peter Brook has said, in *The Empty Space* (1968):

> It is not only the hair-styles, costumes and make-ups that look dated. All the different elements of staging—the shorthands of behavior that stand for emotions; gestures, gesticulations and tones of voice—are all fluctuating on an invisible stock exchange all the time. . . . A living theatre that thinks it can stand aloof from anything as trivial as fashion will wilt. (p. 16)

As Brook indicates, it is through today's hairstyles, costumes, makeup, gestures, gesticulations, tones of voice—this includes our *conception* of earlier hairstyles, costumes, and so forth if we stage the play in a period other than our own—that we inevitably stage the plays.

It is a truism that every age invents its own Shakespeare, just as, for instance, every age has invented its own classical world. Our view of ancient Greece, a slave-holding society in which even free Athenian women were severely circumscribed, does not much resemble the Victorians' view of ancient Greece as a glorious democracy, just as, perhaps, our view of Victorianism itself does not much resemble theirs. We cannot claim that the Shakespeare on our stage is the true Shakespeare, but in our stage productions we find a Shakespeare that speaks to us, a Shakespeare that our ancestors doubtless did not know but one that seems to us to be the true Shakespeare—at least for a while.

Our age is remarkable for the wide variety of kinds of staging that it uses for Shakespeare, but one development deserves special mention. This is the now common practice of race-blind or color-blind or nontraditional casting, which allows persons who are not white to play in Shakespeare. Previously blacks performing in Shakespeare were limited to a mere three roles, Othello, Aaron (in *Titus Andronicus*), and the Prince of Morocco (in *The Merchant of Venice*), and there were no roles at all for Asians. Indeed, African-Americans rarely could play even one of these three roles, since they were not welcome in white companies. Ira Aldridge (c.1806–1867), a black actor of undoubted talent, was forced to make his living by performing Shakespeare in England and in Europe, where he could play not only Othello but also—in whiteface—other tragic roles such as King Lear. Paul Robeson (1898–1976) made theatrical history when he played Othello in London in 1930, and there was some talk about bringing the production to the United States, but there was more talk about whether American audiences would tolerate the sight of a black man—a real black man, not a white man in blackface—kissing and then killing a white woman. The idea was tried out in summer stock in 1942, the reviews were enthusiastic, and in the following year Robeson opened on Broadway in a production that ran an astounding 296 performances. An occasional all-black company sometimes performed Shakespeare's plays, but otherwise blacks (and other minority members) were in effect shut out from performing Shakespeare. Only since about 1970 has it been common for nonwhites to play major roles along with whites. Thus, in a 1996–97 production of *Antony and Cleopatra*, a white Cleopatra, Vanessa Redgrave, played opposite a black Antony, David Harewood.

Multiracial casting is now especially common at the New York Shakespeare Festival, founded in 1954 by Joseph Papp, and in England, where even siblings such as Claudio and Isabella in *Measure for Measure* or Lear's three daughters may be of different races. Probably most viewers today soon stop worrying about the lack of realism, and move beyond the color of the performers' skin to the quality of the performance.

Nontraditional casting is not only a matter of color or race; it includes sex. In the past, occasionally a distinguished woman of the theater has taken on a male role—Sarah Bernhardt (1844–1923) as Hamlet is perhaps the most famous example—but such performances were widely regarded as eccentric. Although today there have been some performances involving cross-dressing (a drag *As You Like It* staged by the National Theatre in England in 1966 and in the United States in 1974 has achieved considerable fame in the annals of stage history), what is more interesting is the casting of women in roles that traditionally are male but that need not be. Thus, a 1993–94 English production of *Henry V* used a woman—*not* cross-dressed—in the role of the governor of Harfleur. According to Peter Holland, who reviewed the production in *Shakespeare Survey* 48 (1995), "having a female Governor of Harfleur feminized the city and provided a direct response to the horrendous threat of rape and murder that Henry had offered, his language and her body in direct connection and opposition" (p. 210). Ten years from now the device may not play so effectively, but today it speaks to us. Shakespeare, born in the Elizabethan Age, has been dead nearly four hundred years, yet he is, as Ben Jonson said, "not of an age but for all time." We must understand, however, that he is "for all time" precisely because each age finds in his abundance something for itself and something of itself.

And here we come back to two issues discussed earlier in this introduction—the instability of the text and, curiously, the Bacon/Oxford heresy concerning the authorship of the plays. *Of course* Shakespeare wrote the plays, and we should daily fall on our knees to thank him for them—and yet there is something to the idea that he is not their only author. Every editor, every director and actor, and every reader to some degree shapes them, too, for when we edit, direct, act, or read, we inevitably become Shakespeare's collaborator and re-create the plays. The plays, one might say, are so cunningly contrived that they guide our responses, tell us how we ought to feel, and make a mark on us, but (for better or for worse) we also make a mark on them.

—SYLVAN BARNET
Tufts University

Introduction

The modern student of *Troilus and Cressida*—reader, spectator, or actor—is faced with complex problems of staging, character, and moral ideas. The challenge of the play has been complicated (in many instances, unnecessarily) by a critical history full of dissension. Some of the insolubles connected with *Troilus* concern the auspices of its first performances, or, indeed, whether it was acted at all before it was printed. Others stem from a consideration of the nature of the play itself, because critics have always felt that it is strange and untypical, and somehow flawed, expounding an approach to life which Shakespeare found uncongenial even as he set it forth. It may be helpful, therefore, to review some basic facts, to indicate those questions that can never be settled with the documentation at our disposal, and then to move on to an appraisal of the work itself and its place in Shakespeare's career. Ultimately, we should try to see in the play the attempt Shakespeare was making to solve certain ethical questions in dramatic form.

The history of the play's first production is inextricably bound up in its early textual history. Literary critics as well as bibliographical historians have been interested in the latter for some years, perhaps because it seems unlikely that so strange a play should be accompanied only accidentally by a curious textual provenance. Believing that the tastes of its first audience might help explain the problematic nature of the play, critics have wanted to know where and for whom it was first performed. Certain aspects of the textual history of *Troilus and Cressida* seem to offer answers; this has led to great speculation, some of which has tended to obscure the facts.

The facts are these. In February of 1603, the permission of the Stationers' Company was granted to James Roberts to print, "when he hath gotten sufficient aucthority, the booke of Troilus and Cressida, as yt is acted by my Lord Chamberlens men." From whom Roberts had yet to secure "aucthority" is not immediately apparent; presumably it was from the actors themselves, who wanted to block publication for the time being. Nevertheless, the entry clearly documents the existence and performance of *Troilus and Cressida* by Shakespeare's company, probably during the winter of 1602–03. Roberts, for whatever reason, did not print the play. The first edition of *Troilus* did not appear until almost six years later, when two newcomers to the printing business, Richard Bonian and Henry Walley, published a quarto of the text in January, 1609. While the book was still in the press, Bonian and Walley altered its title page and added an extra leaf, which carried an epistle to the reader. The first title page announced the play: "As it was acted by the Kings Maiesties seruants at the Globe." The new title page of the quarto, the same as the first in other particulars, replaced this acknowledgment with the phrase: "Excellently expressing the beginning of their [Troilus and Cressida's] loues, with the conceited wooing of Pandarus Prince of Licia." Following the altered title page appeared the epistle to the reader, unsigned, claiming that the play was "neuer stal'd with the Stage, neuer clapper-clawd with the palmes of the vulger . . . not . . . sullied, with the smoaky breath of the multitude." Finally, in 1623, *Troilus* was printed by Heminges and Condell in their great folio collection of Shakespeare's plays, in a text occasionally fuller than that of the 1609 quarto, but also containing many errors (see note on the text of this edition). *Troilus* appears in the section of the Folio containing the tragedies, although its position in this section was altered after printing had begun. The alteration used to be grounds for an inference by some critics that even Shakespeare's editors and colleagues were not certain about the type of play with which they were dealing. More recently, however, textual critics have shown that the change was probably due only to the reluctance of Walley, the surviving publisher of the quarto, to give up his rights to the printer of the Folio—the delay meanwhile causing the latter to withdraw *Troilus* after three pages of it had been set up in type, and to reinsert it later when permission was granted. Thus, although Heminges and Condell apparently classified *Troilus and Cressida* as a "Tragedy," and although the writer of the 1609 epistle called it a "Comedy," its position in the Folio has nothing to do with the ambiguous nature of the play itself; after all, both title pages of the 1609 quarto call it a "History." Nothing is really proved by this contradictory nomenclature except how casual the Elizabethan and Jacobean vocabulary was when it came to naming genres.

Although unnecessary problems raised by the play's position in the Folio have been removed, the earlier printer's claim that *Troilus* had never been applauded "with the palmes of the vulger" has elicited various and conflicting interpretations: the play, indeed, was never acted; it entered rehearsals, proved too difficult, and was withdrawn; it was acted not for the "vulger" at the public theater, but for an audience of sophisticated and cynical wits at the Inns of Court; it was actually produced at the Globe but was a failure with the "multitude," therefore "neuer clapper-clawd." We should note that all these conjectures are possible only because of the altered title page and printer's epistle in the quarto; but neither of these bibliographical facts should obscure the evidence of the original entry in the Stationers' Register (that Shakespeare's company had acted the play by the beginning of 1603), nor that of the first 1609 title page (which tells us specifically that the play "was acted by the Kings Maiesties seruants at the Globe"). Any further suggestions about the theatrical provenance of the play are clearly conjectural. More important, interpretations of characters, mood, and general intention of *Troilus and Cressida* that are based on such conjecture should be considered with great caution.

One such interpretation that has attained considerable currency is that the play was acted by Shakespeare's company for the young lawyers at one of the Inns of Court, and that it was especially written and rehearsed for this occasion. Such circumstances, the theory maintains, would not only be in keeping with the cynical mood and legalistic rhetoric of the drama, but with the claims of the epistle, whose author is careful to state only that the play was never performed for the "vulger," and not that it had never been performed at all. If this is the case, however, it represents the only example during Shakespeare's career of any play actually subsidized for a special production in this manner. To purchase a single performance for a play already in the public repertory was something else entirely—Elizabeth's court did this frequently—but it was very costly to do so. Moreover, although much in the play would delight the ears of a cynic, and although some of the language in it is drawn (very generally) from legal vocabulary, the fact remains that the bitterness of this drama runs deeper than the self-conscious sneer which often accompanies sarcasm. There is metaphor drawn from the law in many other Shakespearean plays, and one should ask, in reading or seeing *Troilus,* whether some of its abstractions and overblown circumlocutions may not have a more general purpose than the pleasure of some law students attending a theatrical charade.

To suggest that Shakespeare wrote the play for the students to act themselves is even more unlikely. *Troilus and Cressida* is extremely difficult for amateurs to perform, even if they are very talented and very cynical. Pandarus' allusions to prostitutes and others employed in the "hold-door trade" would have been absurd in a performance for one of the Inns; illogical, indeed, before any audience except that of the public theater. This epilogue is as unsavory and ugly as anything in Thersites' "mastic" harangues, and although we may not like to think so, it, and the action preceding it, must have been spoken in a public theater by actors in Shakespeare's company.

Whether the public audience applauded it is another matter. *Troilus* may not have been performed more than once or twice, and it is very possible that Bonian and Walley, as they prepared the first title page for their 1609 quarto, knew only that the play was by an extremely successful dramatist and that it had once been acted at the Globe. Details of failures, even today, are not often remembered after seven or eight years. Whatever made them decide to alter the title page, deleting the acknowledgment to Shakespeare's company and inserting the epistle to the reader, we can never know. We must keep in mind, however, that possibly their correction was itself a mistake. In any case, the inserted phrase about the "conceited wooing of Pandarus Prince of Licia" was an easy line filler for the deleted acknowledgment, and no publisher has ever shrunk from a descriptive phrase which might promote sales of his book. The tone of the epistle indicates that Bonian and Walley knew a good thing when they saw it, and they were delighted to have in their possession a play by Shakespeare which six years earlier his own company apparently had tried to withhold from publication, and which had been in the repertory but was not generally known.

Our only positive evidence dates *Troilus* before February 1603, in performance at the Globe Theatre by the King's Men (then the Lord Chamberlain's Men). Although it is probably impossible to solve the riddle of this play's textual history, it is important to keep that mystery separate from the enigma of the play itself. There is no doubt that the peculiar strengths and failings of *Troilus and Cressida* are unique in the Shakespearean canon; even when compared to the other so-called "problem plays" *(Measure for Measure, All's Well That Ends Well)*, it stands by itself. *Troilus* contains speeches that illuminate difficult portions of other plays, but seem somehow incongruous in this one; most of its cast of characters were traditionally associated with ideals of romance and chivalry, but even as they describe heroic emotions and speak the old ringing epithets, these figures appear addicted to long-winded gossip, petty projects, morbid preoccupations, and selfishly narrow ambitions. Such incongruities remind us of the intentions and methods of satire, and it has been suggested that *Troilus and Cressida* was Shakespeare's specific attempt to write in the currently popular vein of "comical satire." But human depravity obviously saddened Shakespeare infinitely more than it angered

Marston, Jonson, or Chapman, and the satirical elements of the play have ultimately very little to do with the final impression it makes in reading, or with its overall effect in the theater. If the play has a satirical spokesman, it is Thersites, but Thersites' corrosive voice hardly speaks for balance or good sense, and, if the actor is brave enough to play him correctly, no audience smiles upon him except in embarrassment. At first, one may suspect satirical intention behind such incongruous components as Ulysses' eloquent perceptions and the insignificant use made of them, but much of the pathos of the play occurs in just those scenes that would be mercilessly satirical if Shakespeare were being consistent. It has been proposed, with good logic, that in *Troilus and Cressida* Shakespeare consciously imitated or unconsciously assimilated certain elements of cynicism and satire from the plays then being performed by child actors with great success at Blackfriars and Paul's. Perhaps less than a year before the composition of *Troilus,* Shakespeare allowed Hamlet himself to express surprise that these children should "carry it away," even in competition with "Hercules and his load too." Always alert to the economic problems of his profession as well as to the artistic ones, Shakespeare was inevitably influenced by the issues that the war of the theaters expressed, but although this influence surely affected some aspects of *Troilus and Cressida,* it can never be held accountable for the play as a whole.

In the problems that the drama presents for directors, actors, and stage designers, one may find, perhaps, a clue to its mystery, a way to understand why some parts of it are so emotionally and intellectually satisfying, others so flat and ill-conceived. Problems of modern production often reveal with lucidity the answers to many questions that a purely literary approach cannot solve. Although probably no modern production of this play can make it a satisfactory theatrical experience (as much may have been said of the script in 1602), one quality that does emerge in production tells us much about the development of Shakespeare's ideas around the time *Troilus* was written. That quality is one of energetic experimentation—experimentation not of the amateur, unsure of his materials, nor of the craftsman temporarily exhausted and therefore forgetting for the moment the almost automatic use of his tools. Rather, *Troilus* reminds one of a study by Michelangelo, boldly and completely rendered in some places, lightly blocked in elsewhere—the whole cartoon groping with line and space to build a conception that seems to develop before us, sometimes obscure but never tentative, and that will require ultimately another form, perhaps even a different medium, for its perfect expression.

In producing *Troilus and Cressida* for the stage, this quality of experimentation, of searching for form, comes to the director when he first tries to develop an overall conception of the action and the general style that should guide him when rehearsals begin, but he is likely to discover early in his efforts that this play defies such an attempt. This is why *Troilus and Cressida,* perhaps more frequently than any other play by Shakespeare, succumbs in preparation to that last effort of the desperate director, a striking form of modern dress. The modern theater has seen *Troilus* in Edwardian dress, modish evening clothes, Wild West costumes, and the uniforms of the American Civil War; and there is little doubt that such aberrations occur (invariably in the name of originality or "significance to the modern audience") because the director, in forgivable despair, has begun to mistrust the text itself.

A setting for this play usually presents problems. Perhaps the original plan of the director and his designer is to use a three-sided apron stage, approximating the projection of the platform in the Elizabethan public theaters; they have envisioned the dramatic potentials of certain speeches delivered from different parts of this remarkable acting area: the oaths of the two lovers, for example, just before Pandarus packs them off to bed; Ulysses' two great addresses, the first of which seems especially to require the magnificent plenitude of space provided by the apron stage; the great quintet near the end of the play, when Troilus, Ulysses, and Thersites watch and comment upon the surrender of Cressida to Diomedes; the last chaotic battle exchanges, which require maximum fluidity of movement. If, however, on the basis of such scenes, a setting is provided that utilizes the large, even epic proportions of the open platform, the director and actors will soon discover that in other portions of the play so much space becomes a burden instead of an advantage. Even scenes that begin with the promise of pomp and procession become, within twenty or thirty lines, scenes of intimate discussion. The Trojan princes marching over the stage (1.2.191–248) are much less important to the progress of the play than the innuendos and small talk of Cressida and Pandarus; nor is there suspense built in anticipation of the entrance of Troilus himself, for we have already seen him, and, having heard Cressida's replies to Pandarus' gossip, we are even prepared for her coy response when he appears. The combat between Hector and Ajax (4.5.113–16) is a red herring for the director, because this combat, when it finally happens, is dramatically uninteresting compared to other portions of the scene—Ulysses' enthusiastic praise of Troilus, for example, or Troilus and Ulysses' short exchange, which ends the episode; the combat is especiallly pale compared to the byplay between Achilles and Hector. If the director plans the moves of his actors to emphasize the apparent climax of the episode, he will find that the real interest of the scene has shifted elsewhere, that the point of the action is not what he thought it was, and that whatever this scene should be, it is not a scene of pageantry.

The actors themselves will face problems of characterization comparable to the vocal difficulties of an operatic baritone who, while studying his role, comes suddenly upon an aria written in the range of a tenor. If, for example, Hector is as sharply intelligent as he appears throughout the debate with Troilus and Paris (2.2), the actor playing him will have difficulty portraying the hero's flabby and illogical surrender at the end of the scene. It is true that men commit themselves every day to causes in which they do not believe, but this irony does not impregnate Hector's

> I am yours,
> You valiant offspring of great Priamus.
> I have a roisting challenge sent amongst
> The dull and factious nobles of the Greeks
> Will strike amazement to their drowsy spirits.
> I was advertised their great general slept
> Whilst emulation in the army crept;
> This, I presume, will wake him.   (2.2.206–13)

These lines neither satirize Hector nor (as has been suggested) reveal ironically the fate of reason in a situation of uncontrolled passion. Moreover, they do not contain the sort of formalized change of motivation that occurs frequently in Elizabethan plays, and which an actor must cope with as best he can. These lines are simply a manifestation of the history to which Shakespeare was bound and to which his previous development of Hector's intelligence and viewpoint was inimicable.

Experimentation with motive and personality that results in inconsistent characterization presents difficulties for actors in other roles. The actress playing Cressida appears on stage only twice after she has been exchanged by the Trojans for Antenor; earlier (3.2.63–197 and 4.2.101–03) she has managed somehow the character's unrealistic anticipation of her own treachery, but, after her tearful leave-taking of Troilus, in which her repeated cry, "Be true," has touched her own fears, Cressida must parade happily among the Grecian generals, who kiss her "in general," and receive Ulysses' coldly perceptive insult. Whatever the actress has made of Cressida earlier, she is now the brassy and degraded slut the Elizabethans had been taught to expect. She appears only once more, to fall to Diomedes, and the actress must decide how to effect this transition of character. Once again, the problem is not so much one of an unfamiliar convention, but of unreconciled strands of development.

Such difficulties of production, and others similar to them, suggest that one of Shakespeare's major problems in composing *Troilus* was not only consistency of character in the normal sense, but the nature of constancy itself, whether in politics or in love. Each of the troublesome matters noted above concerns the continuity of some factor pertinent to all parts of the text, whether that factor is stage setting or characterization. In 4.5. Hector's dialogue with Achilles assumes more importance than his short fight with Ajax, because it is Achilles and not Ajax who should have entered the lists against the Trojan champion. It would be in keeping with Elizabethan ideas of order and degree for Achilles to maintain the identity of an active hero, and Ulysses wishes to goad him on toward his proper role. But more important, we listen eagerly to the talk between Hector and Achilles because so much in the play concerns sentiments identical to those motivating these men: Hector's faith in the principles that define what is right and good, and Achilles' surrender to the "one touch of nature" that can make all human beings blind and selfish. The confrontation of these men demands full use of the open stage, with the other actors distributed so as to emphasize it, but the machinery of Ajax's exhibition bout still hangs fire, and Shakespeare, almost as though he were working out the problem before our eyes, develops his main line of interest without bothering to erase false starts and unnecessary detail.

There is no need to examine in every character the way in which inconstancy, as a thematic concern, vitiates dramatic consistency. One final example is provided importantly by the heroine of the play. In the first half of the action Cressida is full and varied, yet her later fall from constancy is so baldly unqualified that Shakespeare's interest seems to have been attracted more to the violence of the metamorphosis than to maintaining the credibility of the character. No simple reliance upon the Elizabethan rumor of Cressida's harlotry can explain her sudden and complete degeneration.

The nature of that constancy which can preserve felicity in love and stability in politics had concerned Shakespeare since he began writing plays, and it was to remain a fundamental concern throughout his career. *Troilus and Cressida* is a pivotal play in the canon because it looks forward and backward simultaneously, indicating the ways in which Shakespeare's view of constancy was developing, and the dramatic forms which eventually would have to be employed to render that development effectively. From the beginning, he had found great dramatic potential in the stability that can be maintained only by the king who mirrors in himself an ordered nation, and in the fidelity of love that can overcome laughable folly or dangerous misunderstanding. By far the greater part of his writing had been, consequently, in varying forms of romantic comedy and patriotic chronicle-histories (the latter a theatrical form that may actually have been Shakespeare's own conception). He had also dramatized, though with less frequency, that form of constancy within the individual which forces him to be so energetically true to himself in love or even in crime that he can no longer be tolerated in the world of living men. In the lives of those tortured kings whose stories had added the aspect of tragedy to some of the history plays, Shakespeare had found that the world of politics could serve as background to the story of an individual whose mind demanded isolation from his surroundings, and whose actions would effect a downfall as inevitable as his virtues were magnificent. The two years preceding *Troilus* saw Shakespeare's utilization of Roman politics for the scene of Brutus' individual tragedy. The fall of Julius Caesar, finished by the middle of the play, is patterned after the simple downward movement of Fortune's wheel—the pattern of almost all late medieval and early Tudor tragedies. But Shakespeare intended that his exploration of Brutus' constancy should hold the center of the drama; in *Julius Caesar* his refining hand turned attention in upon the mind of the hero himself. Roughly contemporary with this play were the romantic comedies *As You Like It* and *Twelfth Night,* each touched with a pervasive melancholy, each in its own way implying that only the truth of love can survive the vicissitudes of the world, the "rain [that] raineth every day." Perhaps a year before *Troilus* came *Hamlet,* in which the public and private responsibilities of the mind are probed with a range and precision that elude comment. It may be helpful to observe, however, that many of the problems that challenge Hamlet's mind are paralleled by those that confuse the Trojan princes and the Greek generals. In both *Hamlet* and *Troilus and Cressida,* the authority of law is opposed by individual desire or private principle; in both, the ultimate canon of morality is set against the honor, real or supposed, of the individual; and in both, the definition of honor, "rightly to be great," is strenuously argued by those who have most at stake.

In *Troilus and Cressida* Shakespeare tried for the first time to combine in dramatic terms a story of love with a story of public affairs. It is worth noting that in the major tragedies that follow, the personal fate of the hero is inextricably bound up in the world of the state, and that in *Troilus* Shakespeare made his first real study of the relationship between the pressures of the public world and the survival of love. Hamlet's uncle believed that "within the very flame of love" there lived a power which would destroy it, that, like goodness itself, it could not remain constant, but would grow "to a plurisy" and die in its own excess (*Hamlet,* 4.7)— a metaphor very similar to Ulysses' description of passion, the "universal wolf" that would "last eat up himself" (1.3.121, 124). Whatever Claudius' opinion, however, Shakespeare clearly believed that true love, untainted with destructive appetite, would not alter "when it alteration finds. . . . But [bear] it out even to the edge of doom" (Sonnet 116). These two statements articulate extremes that became the foundations for much of Shakespeare's thinking in the second half of his professional career; again and again he concerned himself with those forms of love that would survive all trials or succumb to the snares of the world. Always the process involved a growth of self-knowledge, and in *King Lear,* his most inclusive tragic statement, Shakespeare was able to show that after the greatest suffering might come the greatest achievement—a perception of constancy more powerful than any worldly reward or punishment; and that after such perception, death could come almost as a reward, as the final felicity.

Naturally, the creation of dramatic situations capable of sustaining this sort of action required a gradual revision of forms in which to work, and Shakespeare searched continually for the most appropriate modes of expression. That he moved from romantic comedy and history to tragedy, and from tragedy to romance, indicates a developing view of life and art; this development should not be divided into sharply limited chronological "periods," each one represented by a different kind of play. Nothing could be more misleading, for even in Shakespeare's earliest plays are individual lines and scenes as typical of his mature outlook as anything in the last romances. His metamorphosis of dramatic forms is more like Beethoven's progress toward the last piano sonatas and string quartets—a steady growth, a long series of experiments and finished monuments, none actually exclusive of the others, but attaining finally an absolute correspondence between idea and expression. Coming where it does in Shakespeare's development, *Troilus and Cressida* contains within it all the components of the playwright's most typical tragic pattern, but arranged in such a way as to prohibit the achievement possible in that form.

In 1601, probably about a year before the first performances of *Troilus,* Shakespeare's poem "The Phoenix and the Turtle" was published in *Love's Martyr,* a collection of allegorical and emblematic verse. The subject matter of this poem clarifies the nature of Shakespeare's thematic concerns in his play, and it is no accident that in both poem and play one senses the author's effort to shape difficult materials to his purpose. "The Phoenix and the Turtle" describes the remarkable union of the mythical Phoenix and the Turtle-dove, in which love was so complete that even Reason stands amazed at the sight. In this mating, we are told, "number . . . in love was slain," for two separate lovers became one, and "Property" itself—the defining essence of the individual thing—was "appalled."

> Property was thus appalled,
> That the self was not the same;
> Single nature's double name
> Neither two nor one was called.　　　　(37–40)

These two lovers, in themselves all "Beauty, truth, and rarity," do not survive their own union, but are consumed

"In a mutual flame," even as each finds absolute perfection in the other. The implication is that such absolute love cannot survive its own assault upon reason; its achievement is set forth as admirable and its inevitable passing as wonderful, but the poem also articulates the great sadness of such an event. It is a funeral dirge in which Reason, personified as the voice of admiration, composes the closing hymn of praise—a hymn, Shakespeare says specifically, "As chorus to their tragic scene."

Claudius' "too-much" of love, drowning itself in a "plurisy," may be equated with the self-cannibalism of appetite, as described by Ulysses; but these are a far cry from the admirable, yet sadly "tragic scene," which Shakespeare paints in "The Phoenix and the Turtle." Shakespeare articulated in this poem—perhaps for the first time in his career—what was to become his most powerful dramatic irony in plays still to come: that the purity of love in "the marriage of true minds," while stronger than any other human achievement, cannot survive in the material world; and, as he demonstrated about five years after *Troilus,* in the glorious conclusion to *Antony and Cleopatra,* such an achievement in love is inimical to that earthly order which must control the reasonable state. In this sense, the coolly efficient Octavius Caesar, in *Antony,* and the personified Reason, in "The Phoenix and the Turtle," both observe the same qualities of constancy in the dead lovers before them. The possession of these qualities was a basic criterion for tragedy, as Shakespeare must have understood the form at this time. The pure strains of love of Troilus for Cressida and of Antony for Cleopatra are, speaking quantitatively, the same; but a tragedy is the result of Antony's love, because he is as constant as Cleopatra's beauty is felicitous. However, "Property" in *Troilus and Cressida* cannot be "appalled" by "simple . . . so well compounded"; in this play no miraculous marriage of "Truth and Beauty" deserves the repose of death.

In its structural position in the play, Troilus' sight of Cressida, as she gives in to Diomedes, corresponds to the insight that carries the truly tragic hero toward his death; but what

Troilus sees, though the truth, runs counter to his ideal, and
to this ideal he is as constant as any genuinely tragic hero.
His vocabulary, as he tries to convince both himself and
Ulysses that what he has seen cannot actually have taken
place, is very similar to that of "The Phoenix and the
Turtle." "If there be rule in unity itself," he cries, "This was
not she" (5.2.138–39) — recalling the paradox in the poem
that "number" (i.e., that "one" cannot be "two") "was slain,"
that the lovers merged into one entity, yet preserved their
distinct essences. Building upon the conceit that there must
be two Cressidas — his own, faithfully waiting in Troy, and
this one, who is Diomedes' — he elaborates the most painful
truth in the play: that what has seemed glorious and
admirable, is not so.

> This she? No, this is Diomed's Cressida.
> If beauty have a soul, this is not she;
> If souls guide vows, if vows be sanctimonies,
> If sanctimony be the gods' delight,
> If there be rule in unity itself,
> This was not she. O madness of discourse,
> That cause sets up with and against itself:
> Bifold authority, where reason can revolt
> Without perdition, and loss assume all reason
> Without revolt. This is, and is not, Cressid. (134–43)

Shakespeare wanted to show the disruption of constancy
in both streams of action in the play — that of the love affair,
and that of the famous war. Troilus' view of Cressida in
Diomedes' arms does not give him that sublime lucidity of
the tragic hero, but tempts him instead toward nihilism; his
prayer, as the play closes, is that Troy's destruction be swift,
that the gods show their mercy by sending "brief plagues."
Similarly, the great order of government which is Ulysses'
ideal, and in which all men must assume their proper degree,
is shown to elude the Greek generals. Shakespeare never
maligns the ideal itself (it would be absurd to imagine that
the author of the English histories would do so!), but he
allows Thersites to remark how "that stale old mouse-eaten

dry cheese, Nestor, and that same dog-fox, Ulysses" have failed it:

> O'the t'other side, the policy of those crafty swearing rascals . . . is not proved worth a blackberry. They set me up, in policy, that mongrel cur, Ajax, against that dog of as bad a kind, Achilles; and now is the cur Ajax prouder than the cur Achilles, and will not arm today. Whereupon the Grecians begin to proclaim barbarism, and policy grows into an ill opinion. (5.4.9–18)

Many of the difficulties of this play in performance, as we have seen, occur because the dramatic rendering of inconstancy in love and in the state actually forces an inconstancy of character and a jarring sequence of events. To make the metamorphoses of love and political honor as striking as possible, Shakespeare first had to set forth both in their admirable condition. That Troilus' love and Ulysses' ideal polity come to nothing is not the result of satirical intention, but rather the requirement of the particular history Shakespeare chose to render dramatically. He always chose his plots carefully, and must have realized that the story of the lovers and the war contained the potential for tragedy, as he was beginning to understand it, but never achieved it. In *Antony and Cleopatra,* after all, he was to demonstrate how a "marriage of true minds," violently drawn together with physical and spiritual joy, would admit no impediments, even that of the Roman state; in *Troilus and Cressida,* he chose a plot full of impediments which are appallingly effective. The Trojan lover dotes upon his own ideal of faith as much as he dotes upon his faithless woman, and is blinded to a true perception of worth. His ringing question, "What's aught but as 'tis valued?" implies assessment by only one of two parties in love, for whatever price Troilus puts upon Cressida, he has yet to learn that she holds herself cheap. Similarly, that "policy grows into an ill opinion" in the Greek camp shows that its leaders have been insufficient to Ulysses' early description of divine and earthly order; and they, and Ulysses himself, have substituted machination—

Thersites' "policy"—for true statecraft. On stage, what begins as divine intelligence ends as a practical joke.

We must not forget that Shakespeare's Elizabethan audiences (public or private) probably would not have found the inconsistencies of *Troilus and Cressida* where we find them. In the retelling of a story so familiar, they would have been surprised, for example, that so much hope is engendered in the first part of the play for Cressida's constancy, and not that she proves unfaithful. Ulysses' "degree" speech, perhaps the *locus classicus* in modern study of the Elizabethan conception of the "Great Chain of Being," is the sort of speech ordinarily suggestive in Shakespeare of a different dramatic decorum; it explicitly defines an ideal which this play never renders in action.

All this Shakespeare must have realized. The incidents of the Troy story chosen for dramatization predicated disappointment in the love plot and a shambles of order in the story of the war; even if he planned to carry forward the story of Troy in the sequel, which many critics infer from Pandarus' epilogue, surely he knew that in this drama the materials he had chosen demanded an ending in which no realization of the ideal was possible. Moreover, he knew that although the sequence of events and partial characterizations of his history were basically appropriate to the "tragic scene," he would be dealing as well with incongruities of folly and affectation suggestive of comic decorum. Since his audience would be familiar with his fable, he could count on their awareness of traditional characters and events; but even though he did not strive for novelty, he must have wondered how the implicit ethical significance of his rendering would be received. Moreover, since the public nature of the state was the background for the action, he would have realized that he was combining, for the first time with equal importance, a romantic story with a historical story. Clearly he desired to indicate a parallel between the betrayal of love that ends the former and the disintegration of heroism that ends the latter. Shakespeare may have anticipated the intractable nature of some of his materials, and it is quite possible that, during its composition, he knew that *Troilus and Cressida* might turn out to be an imperfect play—but the experiment fascinated him, and it was necessary.

The dangers that can prevent the triumph of love—both external to it and within it—occupied his mind henceforth, but his genius as a practical man of the theater did not always prevent this interest from assuming proportions inappropriate to the play at hand. Just as Shylock's monstrous faith in himself had almost swamped the romantic action of *The Merchant of Venice,* Angelo's morbidly distorted concept of law and love in *Measure for Measure* (written three or four years after *Troilus*) was disproportionate to the romantic action surrounding it. Ultimately—but not until *Antony and Cleopatra* had shown him the way—Shakespeare discovered the dramatic form in which the persistent faith necessary for tragic achievement could be preserved in the living world, in which the ideal is made part of reality. The dying life in *Troilus and Cressida* is far from the world of romance, but the qualities of humanity and the grace of nature required to revivify men are so violently excluded from the fabric of the play, that these healing powers become more explicit for their absence. The characters of *Troilus* are unable to achieve them, but by implication we know what they must be.

Following an earlier formula for tragical action, Shakespeare created, in *Romeo and Juliet,* a hero and heroine whose hopes seem almost mechanically doomed; the truth and beauty of their faith stand no chance against the external accidents of the world, although their love never alters in purity. After *Romeo and Juliet,* Shakespeare slowly shifted his emphasis; the character's inner strength to withstand external impediments became more important than an arbitrary caprice of fate, and the cause of disaster or tragic achievement was shown thereafter to reside within the human personality itself. Such causes were never again only partially articulated. In *Troilus and Cressida* they are frighteningly explicit, and because of the experimental form of the play they appear to us brutal and even cynical. But Thersites' view of the world was never Shakespeare's. Never again was he to allow his audiences to witness such despair in the ability of men to achieve grace in love or death.

—DANIEL SELTZER
Harvard University

The History of
Troilus and Cressida

Priam, King of Troy
Hector
Troilus
Paris ⎫ his sons
Deiphobus
Helenus
Margarelon, a bastard son of Priam
Aeneas ⎫ Trojan commanders
Antenor
Calchas, a Trojan priest, taking part with the Greeks
Pandarus, uncle to Cressida
Agamemnon, the Greek general
Menelaus, his brother
Achilles
Ajax
Ulysses
Nestor ⎫ Greek commanders
Diomedes
Patroclus
Thersites, a deformed and scurrilous Greek
Alexander, servant to Cressida
Servant to Troilus
Servant to Paris
Servant to Diomedes
Helen, wife to Menelaus
Andromache, wife to Hector
Cassandra, daughter to Priam; a prophetess
Cressida, daughter to Calchas
Trojan and Greek Soldiers and Attendants

Scene: Troy, and the Greek camp before it]

A Never Writer, to an Ever Reader. News.

Eternal reader, you have here a new play, never staled with the stage, never clapperclawed with the palms of the vulgar, and yet passing full of the palm comical; for it is a birth of your brain°1 that never undertook anything comical vainly. And were but the vain names of comedies changed for the titles of commodities, or of plays for pleas, you should see all those grand censors, that now style them such vanities, flock to them for the main grace of their gravities—especially this author's comedies, that are so framed to the life that they serve for the most common commentaries of all the actions of our lives, showing such a dexterity and power of wit that the most displeased with plays are pleased with his comedies. And all such dull and heavy-witted worldlings as were never capable of the wit of a comedy, coming by report of them to his representations, have found that wit there that they never found in themselves and have parted better witted than they came, feeling an edge of wit set upon them more than ever they dreamed they had brain to grind it on. So much and such savored salt of wit is in his comedies that they seem, for their height of pleasure, to be born in that sea that brought forth Venus.° Amongst all

1 The degree sign ° indicates a footnote, which is keyed to the text by line number. Text references are printed in **boldface** type; the annotation follows in roman type.

4 **your brain** i.e., Shakespeare's brain   23 **Venus** (the Greek goddess Aphrodite, who, according to Hesiod, was born in ocean foam)

there is none more witty than this; and had I time I
25 would comment upon it, though I know it needs not,
for so much as will make you think your testern° well
bestowed, but for so much worth as even poor I know
to be stuffed in it. It deserves such a labor as well as the
30 best comedy in Terence or Plautus. And believe this,
that when he is gone and his comedies out of sale, you
will scramble for them and set up a new English Inqui-
sition. Take this for a warning, and at the peril of your
pleasure's loss, and judgment's, refuse not, nor like
35 this the less for not being sullied with the smoky breath
of the multitude; but thank fortune for the 'scape it hath
made amongst you, since by the grand possessors'°
wills I believe you should have prayed for them rather
than been prayed. And so I leave all such to be prayed
40 for, for the state of their wits' healths, that will not
praise it. *Vale.*

---

26 **testern** sixpence (slang) 37 **grand possessors** (presumably, the actor-
sharers of the King's Men, who may have tried to stop publication)

The History of Troilus and Cressida

[*Enter the Prologue, armed for battle.*]

In Troy there lies the scene. From isles of Greece
The princes orgulous,° their high blood chafed,
Have to the port of Athens sent their ships,
Fraught with the ministers and instruments
Of cruel war. Sixty and nine, that wore   5
Their crownets regal, from th' Athenian bay
Put forth toward Phrygia;° and their vow is made
To ransack Troy, within whose strong immures°
The ravished Helen, Menelaus' queen,
With wanton Paris sleeps—and that's the quarrel.   10
To Tenedos° they come,
And the deep-drawing barks do there disgorge
Their warlike fraughtage.° Now on Dardan° plains
The fresh and yet unbruisèd Greeks do pitch

Prologue 2 **orgulous** proud 7 **Phrygia** western Asia Minor 8 **immures** walls 11 **Tenedos** the port of Troy 13 **fraughtage** freight, i.e., soldiers 13 **Dardan** Trojan (after Dardanus, son of Zeus and the Pleiad Electra, and ancestor of Priam)

15   Their brave pavilions. Priam's six-gated city,
      Dardan, and Timbria, Helias, Chetas, Troien,
      And Antenonidus,° with massy staples
      And corresponsive and fulfilling° bolts,
      Sperr up° the sons of Troy.
20   Now expectation, tickling skittish° spirits,
      On one and other side, Troyan and Greek,
      Sets all on hazard. And hither am I come,
      A prologue armed,° but not in confidence
      Of author's pen or actor's voice, but suited°
25   In like conditions as our argument,°
      To tell you, fair beholders, that our play
      Leaps o'er the vaunt° and firstlings of those broils,
      Beginning in the middle, starting thence away
      To what may be digested in a play.
30   Like or find fault; do as your pleasures are;
      Now good or bad, 'tis but the chance of war.

16–17 **Dardan ... Antenonidus** (names of the gates of Troy)   18 **ful-filling** filling tightly   19 **Sperr up** shut up   20 **skittish** nervous   23 **armed** equipped for fight   24 **suited** dressed   25 **argument** subject   27 **vaunt** beginning

ACT 1

[Scene 1. *Within Troy.*]

Enter Pandarus and Troilus.

Troilus. Call here my varlet,° I'll unarm again.
    Why should I war without° the walls of Troy
    That find such cruel battle here within?
    Each Troyan that is master of his heart,
    Let him to field; Troilus, alas, hath none.   5

Pandarus. Will this gear° ne'er be mended?

Troilus. The Greeks are strong, and skillful to° their
    strength.
    Fierce to their skill, and to their fierceness valiant;
    But I am weaker than a woman's tear,
    Tamer than sleep, fonder° than ignorance,   10
    Less valiant than the virgin in the night,
    And skilless° as unpracticed infancy.

Pandarus. Well, I have told you enough of this. For
    my part, I'll not meddle nor make no farther. He
    that will have a cake out of the wheat must tarry   15
    the grinding.

1.1.1 **varlet** servant   2 **without** outside   6 **gear** business   7 **to** in addition to, in proportion to   10 **fonder** more unsophisticated, simpler 12 **skilless** inept, naïve

Troilus. Have I not tarried?

Pandarus. Ay, the grinding; but you must tarry the bolting.°

20 *Troilus.* Have I not tarried?

Pandarus. Ay, the bolting; but you must tarry the leavening.

Troilus. Still have I tarried.

Pandarus. Ay, to the leavening; but here's yet in the
25 word "hereafter" the kneading, the making of the cake, the heating the oven, and the baking. Nay, you must stay the cooling too, or ye may chance burn your lips.

Troilus. Patience herself, what goddess e'er she be,
30 Doth lesser blench° at suff'rance than I do.
At Priam's royal table do I sit,
And when fair Cressid comes into my thoughts—
So, traitor,° then she comes when she is thence.°

Pandarus. Well, she looked yesternight fairer than
35 ever I saw her look, or any woman else.

Troilus. I was about to tell thee, when my heart,
As wedgèd with a sigh, would rive° in twain,
Lest Hector or my father should perceive me—
I have, as when the sun doth light a-scorn,°
40 Buried this sigh in wrinkle of a smile;
But sorrow, that is couched in seeming gladness,
Is like that mirth fate turns to sudden sadness.

Pandarus. An° her hair were not somewhat darker
than Helen's—well, go to—there were no more
45 comparison between the women; but, for my part,
she is my kinswoman: I would not, as they term it,
praise her, but I would somebody had heard her

19 **bolting** sifting 30 **blench** flinch 33 **traitor** (a self-rebuke, for
suggesting that she is sometimes absent) 33 **then she comes when she
is thence** i.e., she returns immediately whenever she is absent 37 **rive**
split 39 **a-scorn** mockingly (?), grudgingly (?) 43 **An** if

talk yesterday, as I did. I will not dispraise your
sister Cassandra's wit, but— —

Troilus. O Pandarus! I tell thee, Pandarus,   *50*
    When I do tell thee, there my hopes lie drowned,
    Reply not in how many fathoms deep
    They lie indrenched. I tell thee I am mad
    In Cressid's love; thou answer'st she is fair,
    Pour'st in the open ulcer of my heart   *55*
    Her eyes, her hair, her cheek, her gait, her voice;
    Handlest in thy discourse, O, that her hand°
    In whose comparison all whites are ink,
    Writing their own reproach; to whose soft seizure°
    The cygnet's° down is harsh, and spirit° of sense   *60*
    Hard as the palm of plowman. This thou tell'st me,
    As true thou tell'st me, when I say I love her;
    But, saying thus, instead of oil and balm,
    Thou lay'st in every gash that love hath given me
    The knife that made it.   *65*

Pandarus. I speak no more than truth.

Troilus. Thou dost not speak so much.

Pandarus. Faith, I'll not meddle in it; let her be as
she is. If she be fair, 'tis the better for her; and she
be not, she has the mends° in her own hands.   *70*

Troilus. Good Pandarus, how now, Pandarus?

Pandarus. I have had my labor for my travail;° ill
thought on of her, and ill thought of you; gone between and between, but small thanks for my labor.

Troilus. What, art thou angry, Pandarus? What, with   *75*
me?

Pandarus. Because she's kin to me, therefore she's
not so fair as Helen. An she were not kin to me,

---

57 **that her hand** that hand of hers   59 **seizure** grasp   60 **cygnet's**
young swan's   60 **spirit** (the thin bodily substance believed to transmit
sense impressions through the nerves)   70 **mends** (1) remedies (2) cos-
metics   72 **travail** (punning on "travel" ["gone between and between"])

she would be as fair a'° Friday as Helen is on Sun-
80   day.° But what care I? I care not an she were a
blackamoor; 'tis all one to me.

Troilus. Say I she is not fair?

Pandarus. I do not care whether you do or no. She's
a fool to stay behind her father.° Let her to the
85   Greeks, and so I'll tell her the next time I see her.
For my part, I'll meddle nor make no more i' th'
matter.

Troilus. Pandarus——

Pandarus. Not I.

90   *Troilus.* Sweet Pandarus——

Pandarus. Pray you, speak no more to me. I will leave
all as I found it, and there an end.

                              Exit. Sound alarum.

Troilus. Peace, you ungracious clamors! Peace, rude
          sounds!
     Fools on both sides! Helen must needs be fair,
95   When with your blood you daily paint her thus.
     I cannot fight upon this argument;°
     It is too starved a subject for my sword.
     But Pandarus—O gods, how do you plague me!
     I cannot come to Cressid but by Pandar;
100 And he's as tetchy° to be wooed to woo
     As she is stubborn, chaste, against all suit.
     Tell me, Apollo, for thy Daphne's° love,
     What Cressid is, what Pandar, and what we.
     Her bed is India; there she lies, a pearl.
105 Between our Ilium° and where she resides
     Let it be called the wild and wand'ring flood,
     Ourself the merchant, and this sailing Pandar

---

79 **a'** on   79–80 **on Sunday** i.e., in her Sunday best   84 **father**
(Calchas, who had deserted to the Greeks)   96 **argument** theme   100
tetchy peevish   102 **Daphne** (the nymph who was changed into a bay
tree as she ran to escape Apollo)   105 **Ilium** (here, Priam's palace; generally, Troy [for Ilus, founder of the city, Priam's grandfather])

Our doubtful hope, our convoy and our bark.

Alarum. Enter Aeneas.

Aeneas. How now, Prince Troilus, wherefore not
　　afield?

Troilus. Because not there. This woman's answer
　　sorts,°　　　　　　　　　　　　　　　　　　*110*
For womanish it is to be from thence.
What news, Aeneas, from the field today?

Aeneas. That Paris is returnèd home, and hurt.

Troilus. By whom, Aeneas?

Aeneas.　　　　　　　　　　Troilus, by Menelaus.

Troilus. Let Paris bleed; 'tis but a scar to scorn:°　　*115*
Paris is gored with Menelaus' horn.°　　　　*Alarum.*

Aeneas. Hark what good sport is out of town today!

Troilus. Better at home, if "would I might" were
　　"may."
But to the sport abroad; are you bound thither?

Aeneas. In all swift haste.

Troilus.　　　　　　　　Come, go we then together.　　*120*

　　　　　　　　　　　　　　　　　　Exeunt.

110 **sorts** is appropriate　115 **but a scar to scorn** i.e., considering its
source, the kind of scar to be scorned　116 **horn** (of a cuckold)

[Scene 2. *Within Troy.*]

Enter Cressida and [Alexander,] her man.

Cressida. Who were those went by?

Man.   Queen Hecuba and Helen.

Cressida. And whither go they?

Man.   Up to the eastern tower,
Whose height commands as subject all the vale,
To see the battle. Hector, whose patience
5   Is as a virtue fixed, today was moved.
He chid Andromache, and struck his armorer,
And, like as there were husbandry° in war,
Before the sun rose he was harnessed° light,
And to the field goes he, where every flower
10   Did, as a prophet, weep what it foresaw
In Hector's wrath.

Cressida.   What was his cause of anger?

Man. The noise goes, this: there is among the Greeks
A lord of Troyan blood, nephew to Hector;
They call him Ajax.

Cressida.   Good; and what of him?

15   *Man.* They say he is a very man per se
And stands alone.

Cressida. So do all men unless they are drunk, sick,
or have no legs.

Man. This man, lady, hath robbed many beasts of
20   their particular additions.° He is as valiant as the

1.2.7 **husbandry** good management, thrift   8 **harnessed** armored   20
additions distinctive qualities, characteristics

lion, churlish as the bear, slow as the elephant; a
man into whom nature hath so crowded humors°
that his valor is crushed into folly, his folly sauced
with discretion. There is no man hath a virtue that
he hath not a glimpse° of, nor any man an attaint° 25
but he carries some stain of it. He is melancholy
without cause and merry against the hair.° He hath
the joints of everything, but everything so out of
joint that he is a gouty Briareus,° many hands and
no use, or purblind Argus,° all eyes and no sight. 30

Cressida. But how should this man that makes me
smile make Hector angry?

Man. They say he yesterday coped° Hector in the
battle and struck him down, the disdain and shame
whereof hath ever since kept Hector fasting and 35
waking.

Enter Pandarus.

Cressida. Who comes here?

Man. Madam, your uncle Pandarus.

Cressida. Hector's a gallant man.

Man. As may be in the world, lady. 40

Pandarus. What's that? What's that?

Cressida. Good morrow, uncle Pandarus.

Pandarus. Good morrow, cousin° Cressid. What do
you talk of? Good morrow, ~Alexander. How do
you, cousin? When were you at Ilium? 45

Cressida. This morning, uncle.

---

22 **humors** (bodily fluids which, in excess, were thought to cause emotional disorder) 25 **glimpse** momentary shining 25 **attaint** imputation of dishonor 27 **against the hair** contrary to natural tendency (cf.
"against the grain") 29 **Briareus** (a hundred-handed giant) 30
Argus (a herdsman with eyes covering his body) 33 **coped** engaged,
encountered 43 **cousin** (a term of familiarity; here, niece)

Pandarus. What were you talking of when I came? Was Hector armed and gone ere ye came to Ilium? Helen was not up, was she?

50 *Cressida*. Hector was gone, but Helen was not up.

Pandarus. E'en so, Hector was stirring early.

Cressida. That were we talking of, and of his anger.

Pandarus. Was he angry?

Cressida. So he says here.

55 *Pandarus*. True, he was so; I know the cause too. He'll lay about him today, I can tell them that; and there's Troilus will not come far behind him. Let them take heed of Troilus, I can tell them that too.

60 *Cressida*. What, is he angry too?

Pandarus. Who, Troilus? Troilus is the better man of the two.

Cressida. O Jupiter! There's no comparison.

Pandarus. What, not between Troilus and Hector? Do
65 you know a man if you see him?

Cressida. Ay, if I ever saw him before and knew him.

Pandarus. Well, I say Troilus is Troilus.

Cressida. Then you say as I say, for I am sure he is not Hector.

70 *Pandarus*. No, nor Hector is not Troilus in some degrees.°

Cressida. 'Tis just to each of them; he is himself.

Pandarus. Himself? Alas, poor Troilus, I would he were.°

70–71 **in some degrees** by some distance; in some (specific) ways (?)
73–74 **I would he were** i.e., I wish he were himself, and not in love

Cressida. So he is.   75

Pandarus. Condition,° I had gone barefoot to India.

Cressida. He is not Hector.

Pandarus. Himself? No, he's not himself. Would 'a°
were himself. Well, the gods are above; time must
friend or end. Well, Troilus, well, I would my heart   80
were in her body. No, Hector is not a better man
than Troilus.

Cressida. Excuse me.

Pandarus. He is elder.

Cressida. Pardon me, pardon me.   85

Pandarus. Th' other's not come to't;° you shall tell me
another tale when th' other's come to't. Hector shall
not have his will° this year.

Cressida. He shall not need it if he have his own.

Pandarus. Nor his qualities.   90

Cressida. No matter.

Pandarus. Nor his beauty.

Cressida. 'Twould not become him. His own's better.

Pandarus. You have no judgment, niece. Helen herself swore th' other day that Troilus, for a brown   95
favor°—for so 'tis, I must confess—not brown
neither— —

Cressida. No, but brown.

Pandarus. Faith, to say truth, brown and not brown.

Cressida. To say the truth, true and not true.   100

Pandarus. She praised his complexion above Paris.

Cressida. Why, Paris hath color enough.

76 **Condition** i.e., even if to bring that about   78 **'a** he   86 **come to't**
reached manhood   88 **will** (some editors emend to *wit*, i.e., intelligence)
95–96 **brown favor** dark complexion

Pandarus. So he has.

Cressida. Then Troilus should have too much. If she
105 praised him above, his complexion is higher than
his. He having color enough, and the other higher,
is too flaming a praise for a good complexion. I had
as lief Helen's golden tongue had commended
Troilus for a copper nose.

110 *Pandarus.* I swear to you, I think Helen loves him
better than Paris.

Cressida. Then she's a merry Greek° indeed.

Pandarus. Nay, I am sure she does. She came to him
th' other day into the compassed° window—and,
115 you know, he has not past three or four hairs on his
chin——

Cressida. Indeed, a tapster's arithmetic may soon
bring his particulars therein to a total.

Pandarus. Why, he is very young; and yet will he,
120 within three pound, lift as much as his brother
Hector.

Cressida. Is he so young a man, and so old a lifter?°

Pandarus. But to prove to you that Helen loves him,
she came and puts me her white hand to his cloven
125 chin——

Cressida. Juno have mercy; how came it cloven?

Pandarus. Why, you know 'tis dimpled; I think his
smiling becomes him better than any man in all
Phrygia.

130 *Cressida.* O, he smiles valiantly.

Pandarus. Does he not?

Cressida. O, yes, an 'twere a cloud in autumn.

112 **a merry Greek** i.e., one of frivolous or loose behavior (slang)   114
compassed bay   122 **so old a lifter** so experienced a thief (cf.
"shoplifter")

Pandarus. Why, go to then. But to prove to you that Helen loves Troilus——

Cressida. Troilus will stand° to the proof if you'll prove it so. 135

Pandarus. Troilus? Why, he esteems her no more than I esteem an addle° egg.

Cressida. If you love an addle egg as well as you love an idle head, you would eat chickens i' the shell. 140

Pandarus. I cannot choose but laugh to think how she tickled his chin. Indeed, she has a marvel's° white hand, I must needs confess.

Cressida. Without the rack.°

Pandarus. And she takes upon her to spy a white hair 145 on his chin.

Cressida. Alas poor chin, many a wart is richer.

Pandarus. But there was such laughing. Queen Hecuba laughed that her eyes ran o'er.

Cressida. With millstones. 150

Pandarus. And Cassandra laughed.

Cressida. But there was a more temperate fire under the pot of her eyes. Did her eyes run o'er too?

Pandarus. And Hector laughed.

Cressida. At what was all this laughing? 155

Pandarus. Marry,° at the white hair that Helen spied on Troilus' chin.

Cressida. An't had been a green hair, I should have laughed too.

Pandarus. They laughed not so much at the hair as at 160 his pretty answer.

135 **stand** (a bawdy pun; cf. Sonnet 151)   138 **addle** rotten   142 **marvel's** marvelous   144 **rack** torture   156 **Marry** (an interjection, from the oath, "By the Virgin Mary")

Cressida. What was his answer?

Pandarus. Quoth she, "Here's but two-and-fifty hairs
on your chin, and one of them is white."

165 *Cressida.* This is her question.

Pandarus. That's true, make no question of that.
"Two-and-fifty hairs," quoth he, "and one white.
That white hair is my father, and all the rest are
his sons." "Jupiter!" quoth she, "which of these
170 hairs is Paris, my husband?" "The forked° one,"
quoth he; "pluck't out, and give it him." But there
was such laughing, and Helen so blushed, and
Paris so chafed, and all the rest so laughed, that
it passed.

175 *Cressida.* So let it now, for it has been a great while
going by.

Pandarus. Well, cousin, I told you a thing yesterday;
think on't.

Cressida. So I do.

180 *Pandarus.* I'll be sworn 'tis true; he will weep you,
an° 'twere a man born in April.   *Sound a retreat.*

Cressida. And I'll spring up in his tears, an 'twere a
nettle against° May.

Pandarus. Hark, they are coming from the field. Shall
185 we stand up here and see them as they pass toward
Ilium? Good niece, do; sweet niece, Cressida.

Cressida. At your pleasure.

Pandarus. Here, here, here's an excellent place; here
we may see most bravely.° I'll tell you them all by
190 their names as they pass by, but mark Troilus above
the rest.

        Enter Aeneas [and passes across the stage].

170 **forked** (resembling a cuckold's horns [?])   181 **an** as if   183
against in advance of   189 **bravely** excellently

Cressida. Speak not so loud.

Pandarus. That's Aeneas. Is not that a brave° man?
He's one of the flowers of Troy, I can tell you. But
mark Troilus; you shall see anon.   195

Enter Antenor [and passes across the stage].

Cressida. Who's that?

Pandarus. That's Antenor. He has a shrewd wit, I can
tell you; and he's man good enough—he's one o'
the soundest judgments in Troy whosoever, and a
proper° man of person. When comes Troilus? I'll   200
show you Troilus anon. If he see me, you shall see
him nod at me.

Cressida. Will he give you the nod?°

Pandarus. You shall see.

Cressida. If he do, the rich shall have more.°   205

Enter Hector [and passes across the stage].

Pandarus. That's Hector, that, that, look you, that;
there's a fellow! Go thy way, Hector! There's a
brave man, niece. O brave Hector! Look how he
looks; there's a countenance! Is't not a brave man?

Cressida. O, a brave man.   210

Pandarus. Is 'a not? It does a man's heart good. Look
you what hacks are on his helmet. Look you yonder, do you see? Look you there. There's no jesting;
there's laying on, take't off who will,° as they say.
There be hacks!   215

Cressida. Be those with swords?

___

193 **brave** fine   200 **proper** handsome   203 **nod** (play on "noddy,"
simpleton)   205 **the rich shall have more** i.e., the fool shall become
more foolish   214 **take't off who will** i.e., whoever cares to say otherwise (to "lay on" and "take off" were common colloquial tags)

Pandarus. Swords, anything, he cares not; an the devil come to him, it's all one. By God's lid, it does one's heart good.

      Enter Paris [and passes across the stage].

220 Yonder comes Paris, yonder comes Paris. Look ye yonder, niece. Is't not a gallant° man too, is't not? Why, this is brave now. Who said he came hurt home today? He's not hurt. Why, this will do Helen's heart good now, ha? Would I could see
225 Troilus now. You shall see Troilus anon.

Cressida. Who's that?

      Enter Helenus [and passes across the stage].

Pandarus. That's Helenus. I marvel where Troilus is. That's Helenus. I think he went not forth today. That's Helenus.

230 *Cressida.* Can Helenus fight, uncle?

Pandarus. Helenus? No. Yes, he'll fight indifferent well. I marvel where Troilus is. Hark, do you not hear the people cry "Troilus"? Helenus is a priest.

Cressida. What sneaking fellow comes yonder?

      Enter Troilus [and passes across the stage].

235 *Pandarus.* Where? Yonder? That's Deiphobus. 'Tis Troilus! There's a man, niece, hem? Brave Troilus, the prince of chivalry!

Cressida. Peace, for shame, peace!

Pandarus. Mark him, note him. O brave Troilus!
240 Look well upon him, niece. Look you how his sword is bloodied, and his helm more hacked than Hector's—and how he looks, and how he goes. O

221 **gallant** (general term of praise, as "brave")

admirable youth! He never saw three-and-twenty.
Go thy way, Troilus, go thy way! Had I a sister
were a grace,° or a daughter a goddess, he should 245
take his choice. O admirable man! Paris? Paris is
dirt to him; and I warrant Helen, to change, would
give an eye to boot.

Enter Common Soldiers.

Cressida. Here comes more.

Pandarus. Asses, fools, dolts; chaff and bran, chaff 250
and bran; porridge after meat. I could live and die
in the eyes of Troilus. Ne'er look, ne'er look. The
eagles are gone; crows and daws, crows and daws.
I had rather be such a man as Troilus than Agamemnon and all Greece. 255

Cressida. There is amongst the Greeks Achilles, a
better man than Troilus.

Pandarus. Achilles? A drayman,° a porter, a very
camel.°

Cressida. Well, well. 260

Pandarus. "Well, well"? Why, have you any discretion, have you any eyes, do you know what a man
is? Is not birth, beauty, good shape, discourse,
manhood, learning, gentleness, virtue, youth, lib-
erality, and such like, the spice and salt that season 265
a man?

Cressida. Ay, a minced° man; and then to be baked
with no date in the pie, for then the man's date is
out.°

---

245 **grace** attendant goddess   258 **drayman** one who draws a cart
259 **camel** i.e., beast of burden   267 **minced** (1) mincing, affected (2)
overspiced (3) divided into parts beyond recognition   267–69 **then to
be baked ... out** (dates were a common ingredient in most pastries;
Cressida's pun implies that Troilus, as Pandarus compounds him, could
contain no substance and be of no interest, out of date)

270 *Pandarus.* You are such a woman a man knows not
   at what ward° you lie.

   Cressida. Upon my back, to defend my belly; upon
      my wit, to defend my wiles; upon my secrecy, to
      defend mine honesty;° my mask, to defend my
275   beauty; and you, to defend all these. And at all these
      wards I lie, at a thousand watches.°

   Pandarus. Say one of your watches.

   Cressida. Nay, I'll watch you for that; and that's one
      of the chiefest of them too. If I cannot ward what
280   I would not have hit, I can watch you for telling°
      how I took the blow; unless it swell past hiding,°
      and then it's past watching.

   Pandarus. You are such another!

                  Enter [Troilus'] Boy.

   Boy. Sir, my lord would instantly speak with you.

285 *Pandarus.* Where?

   Boy. At your own house. There he unarms him.

   Pandarus. Good boy, tell him I come.   [*Exit Boy.*]
      I doubt° he be hurt. Fare ye well, good niece.

   Cressida. Adieu, uncle.

290 *Pandarus.* I will be with you, niece, by and by.

   Cressida. To bring,° uncle.

   Pandarus. Ay, a token from Troilus.

---

271 **ward** position of defense in swordplay 274 **honesty** chastity
276 **watches** periods of the night 280 **watch you for telling** i.e., to
make certain you do not tell 281 **swell past hiding** (Cressida thus
completes her ribald play on words) 288 **doubt** suspect that, fear that
291 **To bring** (an idiomatic intensifier, now obsolete, meaning roughly,
"indeed" or "with a vengeance"; Cressida says, with mild sarcasm, "yes,
I am sure you will," although Pandarus picks up the word in its normal
verbal sense)

Cressida. By the same token, you are a bawd.
                                    Exit Pandarus.
Words, vows, gifts, tears, and love's full sacrifice
He offers in another's enterprise;   *295*
But more in Troilus thousandfold I see
Than in the glass of Pandar's praise may be.
Yet hold I off. Women are angels, wooing;°
Things won are done, joy's soul lies in the doing.
That she° beloved knows nought that knows not   *300*
    this:
Men prize the thing ungained more than it is;°
That she was never yet, that ever knew
Love got° so sweet as when desire did sue.
Therefore this maxim out of love° I teach:
Achievement is command; ungained, beseech.°   *305*
Then, though my heart's content firm love doth
    bear,
Nothing of that shall from mine eyes appear.   *Exit.*

[Scene 3. *The Greek camp.*]

*Sennet.° Enter Agamemnon, Nestor, Ulysses, Dio-
    medes, Menelaus, with others.*

Agamemnon. Princes,
    What grief hath set these jaundies° o'er your
        cheeks?
    The ample proposition that hope makes
    In all designs begun on earth below
    Fails in the promised largeness. Checks and disas-   *5*
        ters

---

298 **wooing** while being wooed   300 **That she** that woman   301 **it is**
its value   303 **got** i.e., by men   304 **out of love** from love's teaching
305 **Achievement . . . beseech** when men achieve love, they command;
while still trying to gain it, they will beg   1.3.s.d. **Sennet** (a trumpet call
announcing specific personages in a procession)   2 **jaundies** jaundice
(an obsolete plural)

Grow in the veins of actions highest reared,
As knots, by the conflux° of meeting sap,
Infects the sound pine and diverts his grain
Tortive and errant° from his course of growth.
10   Nor, princes, is it matter new to us
That we come short of our suppose° so far
That after seven years' siege yet Troy walls stand;
Sith every action that hath gone before,
Whereof we have record, trial did draw
15   Bias and thwart,° not answering the aim
And that unbodied figure of the thought
That gave't surmisèd shape. Why then, you princes,
Do you with cheeks abashed° behold our works
And call them shames, which are indeed nought
    else
20   But the protractive° trials of great Jove
To find persistive constancy in men?
The fineness of which metal is not found
In Fortune's love; for then, the bold and coward,
The wise and fool, the artist° and unread,
25   The hard and soft, seem all affined° and kin.
But, in the wind and tempest of her frown,
Distinction, with a broad and powerful fan,
Puffing at all, winnows the light away,
And what hath mass or matter by itself
30   Lies rich in virtue and unmingled.°

Nestor. With due observance of thy godlike seat,
    Great Agamemnon, Nestor shall apply°
    Thy latest words. In the reproof° of chance
    Lies the true proof of men. The sea being smooth,
35   How many shallow bauble boats dare sail
    Upon her patient breast, making their way
    With those of nobler bulk?

---

7 **conflux** flowing together   9 **Tortive and errant** twisted and wandering   11 **suppose** anticipation   15 **Bias and thwart** to one side and crosswise   18 **cheeks abashed** i.e., faces turned aside in confusion and shame   20 **protractive** extended   24 **artist** scholar   25 **affined** in affinity, related   30 **unmingled** unmixed with other essences   32 **apply** show examples of (as in a rhetorical exercise)   33 **reproof** rebuff

But let the ruffian Boreas° once enrage
The gentle Thetis,° and anon behold
The strong-ribbed bark through liquid mountains 40
cut,
Bounding between the two moist elements
Like Perseus' horse,° where's then the saucy boat,
Whose weak untimbered sides but even now
Corrivaled greatness? Either to harbor fled,
Or made a toast° for Neptune. Even so 45
Doth valor's show° and valor's worth divide
In storms of fortune. For in her ray and brightness
The herd hath more annoyance by the breese°
Than by the tiger; but when the splitting wind
Makes flexible the knees of knotted oaks, 50
And flies fled under shade, why then the thing of
courage,
As roused with rage, with rage doth sympathize,°
And with an accent tuned in selfsame key
Returns° to chiding fortune.

Ulysses.   Agamemnon,
Thou great commander, nerves° and bone of 55
Greece,
Heart of our numbers, soul and only sprite,°
In whom the tempers and the minds of all
Should be shut up,° hear what Ulysses speaks.
Besides th' applause and approbation
The which [*to Agamemnon*], most mighty for thy 60
place and sway,
[*to Nestor*] And thou most reverend for thy
stretched-out life,
I give to both your speeches—which were such
As Agamemnon and the hand of Greece
Should hold up high in brass; and such again

---

38 **Boreas** (the north wind) 39 **Thetis** (a sea maiden, Achilles'
mother, but here personifying the sea) 42 **Perseus' horse** (Pegasus,
the winged horse) 45 **toast** (a piece of toast was usually soaked in
wine) 46 **show** outward appearance 48 **breese** gadfly 52 **sympathize** becomes similar to 54 **Returns** replies 55 **nerves** sinews 56
sprite spirit 58 **shut up** gathered in

65   As venerable Nestor, hatched in silver,°
     Should with a bond of air, strong as the axletree
     On which heaven rides, knit all the Greekish ears
     To his experienced tongue—yet let it please both,
     Thou great, and wise, to hear Ulysses speak.

70   *Agamemnon.* Speak, Prince of Ithaca; and be't of less
       expect
     That matter needless, of importless burden,
     Divide thy lips than we are confident,
     When rank Thersites opes his mastic° jaws,
     We shall hear music, wit, and oracle.

75   *Ulysses.* Troy, yet upon his basis, had been down,
     And the great Hector's sword had lacked a master,
     But for these instances.°
     The specialty of rule° hath been neglected;
     And look, how many Grecian tents do stand
80   Hollow upon this plain, so many hollow factions.
     When that the general is not like the hive
     To whom the foragers shall all repair,
     What honey is expected?° Degree being vizarded,°
     Th' unworthiest shows as fairly in the mask.
85   The heavens themselves, the planets, and this center
     Observe degree, priority, and place,
     Insisture,° course, proportion, season, form,
     Office, and custom, in all line of order.
     And therefore is the glorious planet Sol°
90   In noble eminence enthroned and sphered
     Amidst the other;° whose med'cinable eye
     Corrects the influence° of evil planets,

---

65 **hatched in silver** (referring to the silver lines in his hair)   73 **mastic** abusive, scourging (sometimes emended to "mastiff")   77 **instances** reasons   78 **The specialty of rule** the particular organization of ruling, the distinction of rights in a chain of authority   81–83 **When ... expected** i.e., when the endeavors of the general populace are not similar to those of the agent which rules them, and to which they are responsible, what profit can be expected? (?); when the ruling general is dissimilar in kind to the soldiers in his army, what profit, etc. (?)   83 **Degree being vizarded** the hierarchy of authority being hidden   87 **Insisture** regularity of position   89 **Sol** the sun   91 **other** others   92 **influence** astrological effect

And posts, like the commandment of a king,
Sans check, to good and bad. But when the planets
In evil mixture° to disorder wander,   *95*
What plagues, and what portents, what mutiny,
What raging of the sea, shaking of earth,
Commotion in the winds, frights, changes, horrors,
Divert and crack, rend and deracinate°
The unity and married calm of states   *100*
Quite from their fixure? O, when degree is shaked,
Which is the ladder of all high designs,
The enterprise is sick. How could communities,
Degrees in schools, and brotherhoods in cities,
Peaceful commerce from dividable shores,   *105*
The primogenity° and due of birth,
Prerogative of age, crowns, scepters, laurels,
But by degree, stand in authentic place?
Take but degree away, untune that string,
And hark what discord follows. Each thing meets   *110*
In mere oppugnancy.° The bounded waters
Should lift their bosoms higher than the shores
And make a sop° of all this solid globe;
Strength should be lord of imbecility,°
And the rude son should strike his father dead;   *115*
Force should be right, or rather right and wrong—
Between whose endless jar° justice resides—
Should lose their names, and so should justice too.
Then everything include itself in power,°
Power into will, will into appetite,   *120*
And appetite, an universal wolf,
So doubly seconded with will and power,
Must make perforce an universal prey
And last eat up himself. Great Agamemnon,
This chaos, when degree is suffocate,   *125*
Follows the choking.
And this neglection of degree it is

---

95 **evil mixture** unlucky or malignant relationship (astrological) 99
deracinate uproot 106 **primogenity** right of the eldest son to succeed
to his father's estate 111 **mere oppugnancy** total strife 113 **sop**
pulp 114 **imbecility** i.e., weakness 117 **jar** discord 119 **include
itself in power** enclose itself within power, i.e., become power

That by a pace goes backward with a purpose
It hath to climb.° The general's disdained
130 By him one step below, he by the next,
That next by him beneath; so every step,
Exampled by the first pace that is sick
Of his superior, grows to an envious fever
Of pale and bloodless emulation;°
135 And 'tis this fever that keeps Troy on foot,
Not her own sinews. To end a tale of length,
Troy in our weakness stands, not in her strength.

Nestor. Most wisely hath Ulysses here discovered
The fever whereof all our power is sick.

Agamemnon. The nature of the sickness found,
140   Ulysses,
What is the remedy?

Ulysses. The great Achilles, whom opinion crowns
The sinew and the forehand of our host,
Having his ear full of his airy fame,
145 Grows dainty of° his worth, and in his tent
Lies mocking our designs. With him Patroclus
Upon a lazy bed the livelong day
Breaks scurril jests,
And with ridiculous and silly action
150 (Which, slanderer, he imitation° calls)
He pageants° us. Sometime, great Agamemnon,
Thy topless deputation° he puts on,
And, like a strutting player, whose conceit
Lies in his hamstring,° and doth think it rich
155 To hear the wooden dialogue° and sound
'Twixt his stretched footing° and the scaffoldage,°

127–29 **And this neglection . . . climb** this neglect of hierarchy causes a
step toward disintegration each time an attempt is made to climb upward
134 **emulation** rivalry   145 **dainty of** finicky about   149–50 **silly
action . . . imitation** (Ulysses contrasts such charades with true imitation
to the life, presumably the goal of the excellent actor)   151 **pageants**
mimics   152 **topless deputation** unlimited office   153–54 **conceit
Lies in his hamstring** imagination lies in the tendon of his leg   155
wooden dialogue i.e., the thumps of heavy footfalls on the wooden stage
floor   156 **stretched footing** absurdly long strides   156 **scaffoldage**
scaffold, stage

Such to-be-pitied and o'erwrested seeming°
He acts thy greatness in; and when he speaks,
'Tis like a chime a-mending,° with terms un-
　　squared,°
Which, from the tongue of roaring Typhon°
　　dropped,　　　　　　　　　　　　　　　　　　160
Would seem hyperboles. At this fusty° stuff
The large Achilles, on his pressed bed lolling,
From his deep chest laughs out a loud applause,
Cries, "Excellent! 'tis Agamemnon right.
Now play me Nestor; hem, and strike thy beard,　165
As he being drest° to some oration."
That's done, as near as the extremest ends
Of parallels, as like as Vulcan and his wife,°
Yet god Achilles still cries, "Excellent!
'Tis Nestor right. Now play him me,° Patroclus,　170
Arming to answer in a night alarm."
And then, forsooth, the faint defects of age
Must be the scene of mirth; to cough and spit,
And with a palsy fumbling on his gorget,°
Shake in and out the rivet. And at this sport　　175
Sir Valor dies; cries, "O, enough, Patroclus,
Or give me ribs of steel; I shall split all
In pleasure of my spleen!"° And in this fashion
All our abilities, gifts, natures, shapes,
Severals and generals° of grace exact,　　　　　180
Achievements, plots, orders, preventions,
Excitements to the field or speech for truce,
Success or loss, what is or is not, serves
As stuff for these two to make paradoxes.°

---

157 **o'erwrested seeming** overstrained impersonation　159 **chime
a-mending** (1) chime being repaired (2) dissonant combination of sounds
just following the ringing of many chimes (?)　159 **unsquared** inappropriate　160 **roaring Typhon** (a monster with serpents' heads and a
tremendous voice)　161 **fusty** stale, second-rate　166 **drest** carefully
prepared for, addressed　168 **Vulcan and his wife** (Vulcan, god of the
smithy and forge, was depicted as sooty, and was lame besides; his
"wife" was Venus, who cuckolded him with Mars)　170 **me** i.e., for me
174 **gorget** throat armor　178 **spleen** (supposed the seat of the emotions of anger and hilarity)　180 **Severals and generals** individual and
general qualities　184 **paradoxes** absurdities

185 *Nestor.* And in the imitation of these twain,
        Who, as Ulysses says, opinion crowns
        With an imperial voice, many are infect.
        Ajax is grown self-willed, and bears his head
        In such a rein,° in full as proud a place
190   As broad Achilles; keeps his tent like him;
        Makes factious feasts; rails on our state of war,
        Bold as an oracle, and sets Thersites,
        A slave whose gall° coins slanders like a mint,
        To match us in comparisons with dirt,
195   To weaken and discredit our exposure,
        How rank° soever rounded in with danger.

        Ulysses. They tax° our policy and call it cowardice,
        Count wisdom as no member of the war,
        Forestall prescience,° and esteem no act
200   But that of hand. The still and mental parts
        That do contrive how many hands shall strike
        When fitness° calls them on, and know by measure
        Of their observant toil the enemies' weight—
        Why, this hath not a finger's dignity.
205   They call this bed-work, mapp'ry,° closet war;
        So that the ram that batters down the wall,
        For the great swinge° and rudeness of his poise,
        They place before his hand that made the engine,
        Or those that with the fineness of their souls
210   By reason guide his execution.

        Nestor. Let this be granted, and Achilles' horse°
        Makes many Thetis' sons.   *Tucket.°*

Agamemnon. What trumpet? Look, Menelaus.

Menelaus. From Troy.

---

189 **In such a rein** i.e., so high   193 **gall** (the source of bile, which was
thought to produce rancor and abuse)   196 **rank** densely, abundantly
197 **tax** criticize   199 **Forestall prescience** discount foresight   202
fitness readiness   205 **mapp'ry** map work   207 **swinge** impetus,
whirling force   211 **Achilles' horse** (either literally, or collectively, for
his soldiers, the Myrmidons)   212s.d. **Tucket** trumpet call

Enter Aeneas.

Agamemnon. What would you 'fore our tent?   *215*

Aeneas. Is this great Agamemnon's tent, I pray you?

Agamemnon. Even this.

Aeneas. May one that is a herald and a prince
  Do a fair message to his kingly eyes?°

Agamemnon. With surety stronger than Achilles' arm   *220*
  'Fore all the Greekish heads, which with one voice
  Call Agamemnon head and general.

Aeneas. Fair leave and large security. How may
  A stranger to those most imperial looks
  Know them from eyes of other mortals?

Agamemnon.   How?   *225*

Aeneas. Ay.
  I ask, that I might waken reverence,
  And bid the cheek be ready with a blush
  Modest as morning when she coldly eyes
  The youthful Phoebus.°   *230*
  Which is that god in office, guiding men?
  Which is the high and mighty Agamemnon?

Agamemnon. This Troyan scorns us, or the men of
    Troy
  Are ceremonious courtiers.

Aeneas. Courtiers as free, as debonair, unarmed,   *235*
  As bending° angels; that's their fame in peace.
  But when they would seem soldiers, they have galls,
  Good arms, strong joints, true swords—and, great
    Jove's accord,°
  Nothing so full of heart. But peace, Aeneas;
  Peace, Troyan; lay thy finger on thy lips.   *240*
  The worthiness of praise distains° his worth,

---

219 **to his kingly eyes** i.e., in his presence   230 **Phoebus** Phoebus
Apollo (the sun god)   236 **bending** bowing   238 **Jove's accord** i.e.,
with Jove on their side   241 **distains** sullies

If that the praised himself bring the praise forth.
But what the repining enemy commends,
That breath fame blows; that praise, sole pure,
    transcends.

Agamemnon. Sir, you of Troy, call you yourself
245   Aeneas?

Aeneas. Ay, Greek, that is my name.

Agamemnon. What's your affair, I pray you?

Aeneas. Sir, pardon; 'tis for Agamemnon's ears.

Agamemnon. He hears nought privately that comes
    from Troy.

250 *Aeneas.* Nor I from Troy come not to whisper him.
I bring a trumpet to awake his ear,
To set his seat on the attentive bent,°
And then to speak.

Agamemnon.   Speak frankly as the wind;
It is not Agamemnon's sleeping hour.
255 That thou shalt know, Troyan, he is awake,
He tells thee so himself.

Aeneas.   Trumpet, blow loud,
Send thy brass voice through all these lazy tents;
And every Greek of mettle, let him know,
What Troy means fairly shall be spoke aloud.
                                        Sound trumpet.
260   We have, great Agamemnon, here in Troy
A prince called Hector—Priam is his father—
Who in this dull and long-continued truce
Is rusty grown. He bade me take a trumpet,°
And to this purpose speak: kings, princes, lords,
265   If there be one among the fair'st of Greece
That holds his honor higher than his ease,
That seeks his praise more than he fears his peril,
That knows his valor and knows not his fear,
That loves his mistress more than in confession

252 **To ... bent** i.e., to make him, and his place of government, pay
attention   263 **trumpet** i.e., a trumpeter in attendance

With truant vows to her own lips he loves,°   270
And dare avow her beauty and her worth
In other arms than hers°—to him this challenge;
Hector, in view of Troyans and of Greeks,
Shall make it good, or do his best to do it;
He hath a lady wiser, fairer, truer,   275
Than ever Greek did compass in his arms;
And will tomorrow with his trumpet call,
Midway between your tents and walls of Troy,
To rouse a Grecian that is true in love.
If any come, Hector shall honor him;   280
If none, he'll say in Troy when he retires,
The Grecian dames are sunburnt° and not worth
The splinter of a lance. Even so much.

Agamemnon. This shall be told our lovers, Lord
Aeneas;
If none of them have soul in such a kind,   285
We left them all at home. But we are soldiers;
And may that soldier a mere recreant prove,
That means not, hath not, or is not in love!
If then one is, or hath, or means to be,
That one meets Hector; if none else, I am he.   290

Nestor. Tell him of Nestor, one that was a man
When Hector's grandsire sucked. He is old now,
But if there be not in our Grecian host
A nobleman that hath one spark of fire
To answer for his love, tell him from me,   295
I'll hide my silver beard in a gold beaver,°
And in my vantbrace° put my withered brawns,°
And, meeting him, will tell him that my lady
Was fairer than his grandam, and as chaste
As may be in the world. His youth in flood,   300
I'll prove this truth with my three drops of blood.

269–70 **That loves ... lips he loves,** i.e., one that loves his mistress
even more than the false oaths of lip service (?); more than enough to
swear false vows that he loves her (?)   272 **In other arms than hers**
i.e., with weapons   282 **sunburnt** dark (for the Elizabethans, ugly)
296 **beaver** movable face guard of a helmet   297 **vantbrace** armor fitting the forearm   297 **brawns** arm (or leg) muscles (an obsolete plural)

Aeneas. Now heavens forfend such scarcity of youth!

Ulysses. Amen.

[*Agamemnon.*] Fair Lord Aeneas, let me touch your
    hand;
305   To our pavilion shall I lead you first.
      Achilles shall have word of this intent;
      So shall each lord of Greece, from tent to tent.
      Yourself shall feast with us before you go,
      And find the welcome of a noble foe.
                    Exeunt. Manent° Ulysses and Nestor.

310 *Ulysses.* Nestor.

Nestor. What says Ulysses?

Ulysses. I have a young conception in my brain;
      Be you my time to bring it to some shape.°

Nestor. What is't?

315 *Ulysses.* This 'tis:
      Blunt wedges rive hard knots; the seeded pride
      That hath to this maturity blown up
      In rank Achilles, must or now be cropped
      Or, shedding,° breed a nursery of like evil
320   To overbulk us all.

Nestor.   Well, and how?

Ulysses. This challenge that the gallant Hector sends,
      However it is spread in general name,
      Relates in purpose only to Achilles.

Nestor. True, the purpose is perspicuous as substance
325   Whose grossness little characters sum up;°
      And, in the publication, make no strain°
      But that Achilles, were his brain as barren
      As banks of Libya—though, Apollo knows,
      'Tis dry enough—will with great speed of judgment,

309s.d. **Manent** (they) remain   312–13 **I have … some shape** i.e., I
have the beginning of an idea; let me develop it as you listen   319 **shed-
ding** i.e., scattering seed   325 **Whose grossness … sum up** whose
large size can be defined by small figures   326 **make no strain** you
may be sure

Ay with celerity, find Hector's purpose   330
Pointing on him.

Ulysses. And wake him to the answer, think you?

Nestor. Why, 'tis most meet. Who may you else op-
    pose
That can from Hector bring his honor off,
If not Achilles? Though't be a sportful combat,   335
Yet in the trial much opinion° dwells;
For here the Troyans taste our dear'st repute
With their fin'st palate;° and trust to me, Ulysses,
Our imputation shall be oddly poised
In this vild action.° For the success,   340
Although particular, shall give a scantling°
Of good or bad unto the general;°
And in such indexes, although small pricks
To their subsequent volumes,° there is seen
The baby figure of the giant mass   345
Of things to come at large. It is supposed
He that meets Hector issues from our choice;
And choice, being mutual act of all our souls,
Makes merit her election,° and doth boil,
As 'twere from forth us all, a man distilled   350
Out of our virtues—who miscarrying,
What heart receives from hence a conquering part,
To steel a strong opinion to themselves;
Which entertained, limbs are his° instruments,
In no less working than are swords and bows   355
Directive by the limbs.

Ulysses. Give pardon to my speech. Therefore 'tis
    meet
Achilles meet not Hector. Let us, like merchants,
First show foul wares, and think perchance they'll
    sell;

336 **opinion** reputation   337–38 **taste ... palate** put our most valued
reputation to the test of their most careful, sensitive observation
339–40 **Our ... action** our reputation shall be unequally balanced in
this trivial action   341 **scantling** sample   342 **general** (1) general
view (2) entire army   343–44 **small ... volumes** small markings compared to the great significance to follow   349 **election** criteria for
choice   354 **his** i.e., of the strong opinion

360   If not, the luster of the better shall exceed
By showing the worse first. Do not consent
That ever Hector and Achilles meet;
For both our honor and our shame in this
Are dogged with two strange followers.°

Nestor. I see them not with my old eyes; what are
365   they?

Ulysses. What glory our Achilles shares from Hector,
Were he not proud, we all should share with him.
But he already is too insolent,
And it were better parch in Afric sun
370   Than in the pride and salt° scorn of his eyes,
Should he 'scape Hector fair. If he were foiled,
Why then we do our main opinion° crush
In taint of° our best man. No, make a lott'ry;
And by device let blockish Ajax draw
375   The sort° to fight with Hector; among ourselves
Give him allowance for the better man,
For that will physic the great Myrmidon°
Who broils° in loud applause, and make him fall
His crest that prouder than blue Iris° bends.
380   If the dull brainless Ajax comes safe off,
We'll dress him up in voices; if he fail,
Yet go we under our opinion still
That we have better men. But, hit or miss,
Our project's life this shape of sense assumes:
385   Ajax employed plucks down Achilles' plumes.

Nestor. Now, Ulysses, I begin to relish thy advice,
And I will give a taste thereof forthwith
To Agamemnon. Go we to him straight.
Two curs shall tame each other; pride alone
390   Must tarre° the mastiffs on, as 'twere a bone.

Exeunt.

364 **followers** consequences   370 **salt** bitter   372 **our main opinion** the mainstay of our reputation   373 **In taint of** to the loss of, with the shame of   375 **sort** lot   377 **the great Myrmidon** (Achilles, whose father, Peleus, had subjects called Myrmidons)   378 **broils** bakes; i.e., suns himself   379 **Iris** (the rainbow)   390 **tarre** incite, provoke

ACT 2

[Scene 1. *The Greek camp*.]

Enter Ajax and Thersites.

Ajax. Thersites!

Thersites. Agamemnon, how if he had boils—full, all over, generally?

Ajax. Thersites!

Thersites. And those boils did run?—say so—did not   5
the general run then? Were not that a botchy core?°

Ajax. Dog!

Thersites. Then would come some matter from him. I see none now.

Ajax. Thou bitch-wolf's son, canst thou not hear?   10
Feel then.   *Strikes him.*

Thersites. The plague of Greece upon thee, thou mongrel beef-witted lord!

Ajax. Speak then, thou vinewed'st leaven,° speak. I will beat thee into handsomeness.   15

2.1.6 **botchy core** erupted boil   14 **vinewed'st leaven** most mildewed dough

Thersites. I shall sooner rail thee into wit and holi-
ness; but I think thy horse will sooner con° an
oration than thou learn a prayer without book.°
Thou canst strike, canst thou? A red murrain° o'
20   thy jade's° tricks!

Ajax. Toadstool, learn me° the proclamation.

Thersites. Dost thou think I have no sense, thou
strikest me thus?

Ajax. The proclamation!

25   *Thersites.* Thou art proclaimed fool, I think.

Ajax. Do not, porpentine,° do not; my fingers itch.

Thersites. I would thou didst itch from head to foot;
an I had the scratching of thee, I would make thee
the loathsomest scab in Greece. When thou art
30   forth in the incursions,° thou strikest as slow as another.

Ajax. I say, the proclamation!

Thersites. Thou grumblest and railest every hour on
Achilles, and thou art as full of envy at his great-
35   ness as Cerberus° is at Proserpina's° beauty, ay,
that thou bark'st at him.

Ajax. Mistress Thersites!

Thersites. Thou shouldst strike him.

Ajax. Cobloaf!°

40   *Thersites.* He would pun° thee into shivers with his
fist, as a sailor breaks a biscuit.

Ajax. You whoreson cur!   [*Beating him.*]

---

17 **con** memorize   18 **without book** by heart   19 **red murrain** (form
of plague manifested in red skin eruptions)   20 **jade's** nag's   21 **learn
me** find out for me   26 **porpentine** porcupine   30 **incursions** battle
raids, attacks   35 **Cerberus** (the monstrous watchdog of Hades)   35
Proserpina (a beautiful goddess carried off by Pluto to the underworld)
39 **Cobloaf** a badly baked, crusty loaf of bread   40 **pun** pound

Thersites. Do, do.

Ajax. Thou stool for a witch!

Thersites. Ay, do, do, thou sodden-witted lord! thou   45
hast no more brain than I have in mine elbows;
an asinico° may tutor thee. Thou scurvy-valiant
ass, thou art here but to thrash Troyans, and thou
art bought and sold° among those of any wit like
a barbarian slave. If thou use to beat me, I will   50
begin at thy heel, and tell what thou art by inches,
thou thing of no bowels,° thou!

Ajax. You dog!

Thersites. You scurvy lord!

Ajax. You cur!   [*Beating him.*]   55

Thersites. Mars his° idiot! Do, rudeness; do, camel;
do, do.

Enter Achilles and Patroclus.

Achilles. Why, how now, Ajax, wherefore do you
thus? How now, Thersites, what's the matter, man?

Thersites. You see him there? Do you?   60

Achilles. Ay, what's the matter?

Thersites. Nay, look upon him.

Achilles. So I do. What's the matter?

Thersites. Nay, but regard him well.

Achilles. "Well"—why so I do.   65

Thersites. But yet you look not well upon him; for,
whosomever° you take him to be, he is Ajax.

Achilles. I know that, fool.

---

47 **asinico** ass, simpleton   49 **bought and sold** i.e., made fun of   52
bowels mercy (the bowels were thought to be the source of compassion)
56 **Mars his** Mars's   67 **whosomever** whomsoever

Thersites. Ay, but that fool° knows not himself.

70   *Ajax.* Therefore I beat thee.

Thersites. Lo, lo, lo, lo, what modicums of wit he ut-
utters! His evasions have ears thus long.° I have
bobbed his brain more than he has beat my bones.
I will buy nine sparrows for a penny, and his pia
75   mater° is not worth the ninth part of a sparrow.
This lord, Achilles, Ajax, who wears his wit in his
belly and his guts in his head, I'll tell you what I
say of him.

Achilles. What?

80   *Thersites.* I say, this Ajax— —
                    [*Ajax threatens to strike him.*]

Achilles. Nay, good Ajax.

Thersites. Has not so much wit— —
                    [*Ajax threatens again to strike him.*]

Achilles. Nay, I must hold you.

Thersites. As will stop the eye of Helen's needle, for
85   whom he comes to fight.

Achilles. Peace, fool!

Thersites. I would have peace and quietness, but the
fool will not—he there, that he. Look you there.

Ajax. O thou damned cur, I shall— —

90   *Achilles.* Will you set° your wit to a fool's?

Thersites. No, I warrant you; the fool's will shame it.

Patroclus. Good words, Thersites.

Achilles. What's the quarrel?

---

69 **that fool** (as though Achilles had said "I know that fool") 72 **thus
long** i.e., as long as those of an ass   74–75 **pia mater** i.e., brain (literally, the membrane covering the brain)   90 **set** match

Ajax. I bade the vile owl go learn me the tenor of the
  proclamation, and he rails upon me.   *95*

Thersites. I serve thee not.

Ajax. Well, go to, go to.

Thersites. I serve here voluntary.

Achilles. Your last service was suff'rance, 'twas not
  voluntary; no man is beaten voluntary. Ajax was   *100*
  here the voluntary, and you as under an impress.°

Thersites. E'en so. A great deal of your wit, too, lies
  in your sinews, or else there be liars. Hector shall
  have a great catch if he knock out either of your
  brains. 'A were as good crack a fusty nut with no   *105*
  kernel.

Achilles. What, with me too, Thersites?

Thersites. There's Ulysses and old Nestor, whose wit
  was moldy ere your grandsires had nails on their
  toes, yoke you like draft oxen and make you plow   *110*
  up the wars.

Achilles. What, what?

Thersites. Yes, good sooth. To, Achilles! To, Ajax!
  To— —°

Ajax. I shall cut out your tongue.   *115*

Thersites. 'Tis no matter, I shall speak as much as
  thou afterwards.

Patroclus. No more words, Thersites; peace!

Thersites. I will hold my peace when Achilles' brach°
  bids me, shall I?   *120*

Achilles. There's for you, Patroclus.

Thersites. I will see you hanged like clotpoles,° ere

---

101 **impress** (pun on impressment, compulsory military service)
113–14 **To, Achilles! To, Ajax! To** (imitation of the shouts of a driver,
urging on his horses)   119 **brach** bitch   122 **clotpoles** blockheads

I come any more to your tents. I will keep where
there is wit stirring and leave the faction of fools.
Exit.

125 *Patroclus.* A good riddance.

Achilles. Marry, this, sir, is proclaimed through all
    our host:
That Hector, by the fifth hour° of the sun,
Will, with a trumpet, 'twixt our tents and Troy
Tomorrow morning call some knight to arms
130 That hath a stomach,° and such a one that dare
Maintain—I know not what; 'tis trash. Farewell.

Ajax. Farewell? Who shall answer him?

Achilles. I know not. 'Tis put to lott'ry. Otherwise,
He knew his man.

        [*Exeunt Achilles and Patroclus.*]

135 *Ajax.* O, meaning you? I will go learn more of it.
Exit.

[Scene 2. *Troy; Priam's palace.*]

Enter Priam, Hector, Troilus, Paris, and Helenus.

Priam. After so many hours, lives, speeches spent,
Thus once again says Nestor from the Greeks:
"Deliver Helen, and all damage else,
As honor, loss of time, travail, expense,
Wounds, friends, and what else dear that is con-
5   sumed
In hot digestion of this cormorant° war,
Shall be struck off." Hector, what say you to't?

---

127 **fifth hour** i.e., eleven in the morning . 130 **stomach** temperament
or relish (here, for chivalric achievement) 2.2.6 **cormorant** ravenous,
rapacious

Hector. Though no man lesser fears the Greeks than
   I,
    As far as toucheth my particular,°
    Yet, dread Priam,   *10*
    There is no lady of more softer bowels,°
    More spongy to suck in the sense of fear,
    More ready to cry out, "Who knows what follows?"
    Than Hector is. The wound of peace is surety,°
    Surety secure; but modest doubt is called   *15*
    The beacon of the wise, the tent° that searches
    To the bottom of the worst. Let Helen go.
    Since the first sword was drawn about this question,
    Every tithe soul, 'mongst many thousand dismes,°
    Hath been as dear as Helen. I mean, of ours.   *20*
    If we have lost so many tenths of ours
    To guard a thing not ours nor worth to us,
    Had it our name, the value of one ten,°
    What merit's in that reason which denies
    The yielding of her up?

Troilus.   Fie, fie, my brother!   *25*
    Weigh you the worth and honor of a king
    So great as our dread father in a scale
    Of common ounces? Will you with counters° sum
    The past proportion of his infinite,°
    And buckle in a waist most fathomless°   *30*
    With spans° and inches so diminutive
    As fears and reasons? Fie, for godly shame!

Helenus. No marvel, though you bite so sharp at reasons,
    You are so empty of them. Should not our father

---

9 **my particular** me, personally   11 **of more softer bowels** more
averse to violence   14 **The wound of peace is surety** peace is endan-
gered by a sense of safety 16 **tent** (roll of absorbent material, for
cleaning or probing wounds) 19 **Every ... dismes** every tenth soul,
among many thousand tens (?); every soul taken by war as its tenth among
many thousand such tenths (?) 23 **one ten** i.e., one in ten 28 **coun-
ters** pieces of worthless metal used for computation 29 **The past ...
infinite** i.e., his infinite greatness which is past all measurement 30
fathomless i.e., immeasurable 31 **spans** (units of measure averaging
nine inches)

35   Bear the great sway of his affairs with reason,
Because your speech hath none that tell him so?

Troilus. You are for dreams and slumbers, brother priest;
You fur your gloves with reason.° Here are your reasons:
You know an enemy intends you harm;
40   You know a sword employed is perilous,
And reason flies the object° of all harm.
Who marvels then, when Helenus beholds
A Grecian and his sword, if he do set
The very wings of reason to his heels
45   And fly like chidden Mercury from Jove,
Or like a star disorbed?° Nay, if we talk of reason,
Let's shut our gates and sleep! Manhood and honor
Should have hare-hearts, would they but fat their thoughts
With this crammed° reason. Reason and respect
50   Make livers° pale and lustihood deject.

Hector. Brother, she is not worth what she doth cost
The keeping.

Troilus.   What's aught but as 'tis valued?

Hector. But value dwells not in particular will.°
It holds his° estimate and dignity°
55   As well wherein 'tis precious of itself
As in the prizer.° 'Tis mad idolatry
To make the service greater than the god;
And the will dotes that is attributive°
To what infectiously itself affects,
60   Without some image of th' affected merit.°

---

38 **You fur your gloves with reason** i.e., you use reason as a comfortable word with which to decorate your speech, much as fur lines gloves   41 **object** (here, presentation, sight)   46 **disorbed** thrown from its sphere   49 **crammed** filled to excess, doughy   50 **livers** (thought to be the seats of passions)   53 **particular will** the individual's inclination   54 **his** its   54 **dignity** value   56 **prizer** appraiser   58 **attributive** dependent, subservient   59–60 **To what . . . merit** to what it, to its own infection, desires, with no objective perception of the worth of the thing desired

Troilus. I take today a wife, and my election
  Is led on in the conduct of my will—°
  My will enkindled by mine eyes and ears,
  Two traded° pilots 'twixt the dangerous shores
  Of will and judgment. How may I avoid,   65
  Although my will distaste what it elected,
  The wife I chose? There can be no evasion
  To blench° from this and to stand firm by honor.
  We turn not back the silks upon the merchant
  When we have soiled them, nor the remainder
    viands   70
  We do not throw in unrespective sieve°
  Because we now are full. It was thought meet
  Paris should do some vengeance on the Greeks.
  Your breath with full consent bellied his sails;
  The seas and winds, old wranglers, took a truce   75
  And did him service; he touched the ports desired,
  And for an old aunt° whom the Greeks held captive
  He brought a Grecian queen, whose youth and
    freshness
  Wrinkles Apollo's and makes pale the morning.
  Why keep we her? The Grecians keep our aunt.   80
  Is she worth keeping? Why, she is a pearl
  Whose price hath launched above a thousand ships
  And turned crowned kings to merchants.
  If you'll avouch 'twas wisdom Paris went—
  As you must needs, for you all cried, "Go, go"—   85
  If you'll confess he brought home worthy prize—
  As you must needs, for you all clapped your hands
  And cried, "Inestimable!"—why do you now
  The issue of your proper wisdoms rate,°
  And do a deed that never Fortune did: 90
  Beggar the estimation° which you prized

61–62 **I take ... my will—** (Troilus is setting forth, rhetorically, an
example to prove his point; whatever he may be thinking, he is not
announcing, of course, his approaching liaison with Cressida) 64
traded experienced 68 **blench** shrink 71 **unrespective sieve** common receptacle 77 **aunt** (Hesione, Priam's sister and Ajax's mother,
married to Telamon; another son was Teucer, greatest archer among the
Greeks) 89 **The issue ... rate** condemn the result of your own judgments 91 **estimation** thing esteemed

Richer than sea and land? O theft most base,
That we have stol'n what we do fear to keep!
But thieves unworthy of a thing so stol'n,
95   That in their country did them that disgrace°
We fear to warrant° in our native place.

Enter Cassandra raving with her hair about her ears.

Cassandra. Cry, Troyans, cry!

Priam.   What noise? What shriek
   is this?

Troilus. 'Tis our mad sister.° I do know her voice.

Cassandra. Cry, Troyans!

100 *Hector.* It is Cassandra.

Cassandra. Cry, Troyans, cry! Lend me ten thousand
   eyes,
   And I will fill them with prophetic tears.

Hector. Peace, sister, peace!

Cassandra. Virgins and boys, mid-age and wrinkled
   eld,
105 Soft infancy, that nothing canst but cry,
   Add to my clamors! Let us pay betimes
   A moiety° of that mass of moan to come.
   Cry, Troyans, cry! Practice your eyes with tears!
   Troy must not be, nor goodly Ilion stand;
110 Our firebrand° brother, Paris, burns us all.
   Cry, Troyans, cry! A Helen and a woe!
   Cry, cry! Troy burns, or else let Helen go.   *Exit.*

Hector. Now, youthful Troilus, do not these high
   strains
   Of divination in our sister work
115 Some touches of remorse? Or is your blood

95 **disgrace** i.e., the abduction of Helen 96 **warrant** justify by
defense 98 **our mad sister** (when Cassandra refused Apollo's love, he
destroyed his former gift of prophecy by causing her never to be
believed) 107 **moiety** part 110 **firebrand** (Hecuba dreamed she was
delivered of a firebrand when Paris was born)

So madly hot that no discourse of reason,
Nor fear of bad success in a bad cause,
Can qualify° the same?

Troilus.   Why, brother Hector,
We may not think the justness of each act
Such and no other than event° doth form it,   120
Nor once deject the courage of our minds
Because Cassandra's mad. Her brainsick raptures°
Cannot distaste° the goodness of a quarrel
Which hath our several honors all engaged
To make it gracious. For my private part,   125
I am no more touched than all Priam's sons;
And Jove forbid there should be done amongst us
Such things as might offend the weakest spleen°
To fight for and maintain.

Paris. Else might the world convince° of levity   130
As well my undertakings as your counsels;
But I attest the gods, your full consent
Gave wings to my propension° and cut off
All fears attending on so dire a project.
For what, alas, can these my single arms?   135
What propugnation° is in one man's valor
To stand the push and enmity of those
This quarrel would excite? Yet, I protest,
Were I alone to pass° the difficulties,
And had as ample power as I have will,   140
Paris should ne'er retract what he hath done
Nor faint in the pursuit.

Priam.   Paris, you speak
Like one besotted on your sweet delights.
You have the honey still, but these the gall;
So to be valiant is no praise at all.   145

Paris. Sir, I propose not merely to myself

118 **qualify** moderate   120 **event** outcome   122 **brainsick raptures**
fits of prophecy   123 **distaste** make distasteful   128 **spleen** temper,
temperament   130 **convince** convict   133 **propension** inclination
136 **propugnation** defense   139 **pass** suffer, undergo

The pleasure such a beauty brings with it;
But I would have the soil of her fair rape°
Wiped off in honorable keeping her.
150 What treason were it to the ransacked° queen,
Disgrace to your great worths, and shame to me,
Now to deliver her possession up
On terms of base compulsion! Can it be
That so degenerate a strain as this
155 Should once set footing in your generous° bosoms?
There's not the meanest spirit on our party
Without a heart to dare or sword to draw
When Helen is defended, nor none so noble
Whose life were ill bestowed or death unfamed
160 Where Helen is the subject. Then, I say,
Well may we fight for her whom we know well
The world's large spaces cannot parallel.

Hector. Paris and Troilus, you have both said well,
And on the cause and question now in hand
165 Have glozed°—but superficially: not much
Unlike young men, whom Aristotle thought
Unfit to hear moral° philosophy.
The reasons you allege do more conduce
To the hot passion of distempered blood
170 Than to make up a free determination
'Twixt right and wrong; for pleasure and revenge
Have ears more deaf than adders° to the voice
Of any true decision. Nature craves
All dues be rendered to their owners. Now,
175 What nearer debt in all humanity
Than wife is to the husband? If this law
Of nature be corrupted through affection,°
And that great minds, of partial° indulgence

---

148 **rape** carrying off   150 **ransacked** carried off   155 **generous** nobly born (therefore magnanimous)   165 **glozed** commented, glossed   167 **moral** (Aristotle wrote "political" [*Nicomachean Ethics*, 1.3], but the use of "moral" here is paralleled in Erasmus, Bacon, and many other contemporary translations and commentaries; the two words were roughly interchangeable in sixteenth-century terminology)   172 **more deaf than adders** (cf. Psalm 58:4–5)   177 **affection** appetite   178 **partial** biased, favoring

To their benumbèd° wills, resist the same,
There is a law in each well-ordered nation   180
To curb those raging appetites that are
Most disobedient and refractory.
If Helen, then, be wife to Sparta's king,
As it is known she is, these moral laws
Of nature and of nations speak aloud   185
To have her back returned. Thus to persist
In doing wrong extenuates° not wrong,
But makes it much more heavy. Hector's opinion
Is this in way of truth. Yet ne'ertheless,
My spritely° brethren, I propend° to you   190
In resolution to keep Helen still;
For 'tis a cause that hath no mean dependence
Upon our joint and several° dignities.

Troilus. Why, there you touched the life of our design!
Were it not glory that we more affected   195
Than the performance of our heaving spleens,°
I would not wish a drop of Troyan blood
Spent more in her defense. But, worthy Hector,
She is a theme of honor and renown,
A spur to valiant and magnanimous deeds,   200
Whose present courage may beat down our foes
And fame in time to come canonize us;
For I presume brave Hector would not lose
So rich advantage of a promised glory
As smiles upon the forehead of this action   205
For the wide world's revenue.

Hector.   I am yours,
You valiant offspring of great Priamus.
I have a roisting° challenge sent amongst
The dull and factious nobles of the Greeks
Will strike amazement to their drowsy spirits.   210
I was advertised° their great general slept

---

179 **benumbèd** paralyzed (by affection and appetite)   187 **extenuates**
lessens   190 **spritely** spirited   190 **propend** incline   193 **joint and
several** collective and individual   196 **heaving spleens** angry passions
208 **roisting** noisy, clamorous   211 **advertised** informed

Whilst emulation° in the army crept;
This, I presume, will wake him.   *Exeunt.*

[Scene 3. *The Greek camp; near Achilles' tent.*]

Enter Thersites solus.

Thersites. How now, Thersites? What, lost in the
labyrinth of thy fury? Shall the elephant Ajax carry
it° thus? He beats me, and I rail at him. O worthy
satisfaction! Would it were otherwise—that I could
5 beat him, whilst he railed at me. 'Sfoot,° I'll learn
to conjure and raise devils, but I'll see° some issue
of my spiteful execrations. Then there's Achilles, a
rare enginer.° If Troy be not taken till these two
undermine it, the walls will stand till they fall of
10 themselves. O thou great thunder-darter of Olym-
pus, forget that thou art Jove, the king of gods;
and, Mercury, lose all the serpentine craft of thy
caduceus,° if ye take not that little, little, less than
little wit from them that they have; which short-
15 armed ignorance itself knows is so abundant scarce
it will not in circumvention deliver a fly from a
spider, without drawing their massy irons and
cutting the web. After this, the vengeance on the
whole camp! Or, rather, the Neapolitan bone-ache,°
20 for that, methinks, is the curse depending on those
that war for a placket.° I have said my prayers,
and devil Envy say "Amen." What ho, my Lord
Achilles!

212 **emulation** envious rivalry (see 1.3.134)   2.3.2–3 **carry it** carry it
off, come out on top   5 **'Sfoot** (an oath; "God's foot")   6 **but I'll see**
rather than not see   8 **enginer** (a soldier in a company used for ditch
digging, tunneling, and otherwise undermining the battlements of an
enemy camp)   13 **caduceus** (Mercury's staff, twined with serpents)
19 **Neapolitan bone-ache** syphilis   21 **placket** opening in a petticoat
(used obscenely, with anatomical suggestion)

Enter Patroclus.

Patroclus. Who's there? Thersites? Good Thersites, come in and rail.   25

Thersites. If I could 'a' rememb'red a gilt counterfeit, thou wouldst not have slipped° out of my contemplation. But it is no matter; thyself upon thyself! The common curse of mankind, folly and ignorance, be thine in great revenue. Heaven bless°   30 thee from a tutor, and discipline come not near thee. Let thy blood° be thy direction till thy death. Then, if she that lays thee out says thou art a fair corse,° I'll be sworn and sworn upon't she never shrouded any but lazars.° Amen. Where's Achilles?   35

Patroclus. What, art thou devout? Wast thou in prayer?

Thersites. Ay, the heavens hear me!

Patroclus. Amen.

Enter Achilles.

Achilles. Who's there?   40

Patroclus. Thersites, my lord.

Achilles. Where? Where? O, where? Art thou come? Why, my cheese, my digestion,° why hast thou not served thyself in to my table so many meals? Come, what's Agamemnon?   45

Thersites. Thy commander, Achilles. Then tell me, Patroclus, what's Achilles?

Patroclus. Thy lord, Thersites. Then tell me, I pray thee, what's thyself?

---

27 **slipped** (pun on "slip," a counterfeit coin of brass, covered with silver or gold) 30 **bless** i.e., save 32 **blood** passion 34 **corse** corpse 35 **lazars** lepers (with decayed bodies) 43 **my cheese, my digestion** (cheese served as the final course of a meal was thought to aid digestion)

50 *Thersites*. Thy knower, Patroclus. Then tell me, Pa-
     troclus, what art thou?

Patroclus. Thou must tell that knowest.

Achilles. O tell, tell.

Thersites. I'll decline° the whole question. Agamem-
55   non commands Achilles, Achilles is my lord, I am
     Patroclus' knower, and Patroclus is a fool.

Patroclus. You rascal!

Thersites. Peace, fool! I have not done.

Achilles. He is a privileged man.° Proceed, Thersites.

60 *Thersites*. Agamemnon is a fool, Achilles is a fool,
     Thersites is a fool, and, as aforesaid, Patroclus is a
     fool.

Achilles. Derive this; come.

Thersites. Agamemnon is a fool to offer° to command
65   Achilles, Achilles is a fool to be commanded of
     Agamemnon, Thersites is a fool to serve such a
     fool, and this Patroclus is a fool positive.

Patroclus. Why am I a fool?

Thersites. Make that demand of the Creator; it suffices
70   me thou art. Look you, who comes here?

*Enter Agamemnon, Ulysses, Nestor, Diomedes, Ajax,
          and Calchas.*

Achilles. Patroclus, I'll speak with nobody. Come in
     with me, Thersites.   *Exit.*

Thersites. Here is such patchery,° such juggling, and
     such knavery. All the argument is a whore and a
75   cuckold, a good quarrel to draw emulous° factions

---

54 **decline** run through (in the grammatical sense, as to decline a noun)
59 **He is a privileged man** (in the sense that the railing of a professional
jester or fool was "allowed")   64 **offer** attempt   73 **patchery** roguery
75 **emulous** jealous

and bleed to death upon. Now, the dry serpigo° on
the subject, and war and lechery confound all!

> [*Exit.*]

Agamemnon. Where is Achilles?

Patroclus. Within his tent, but ill-disposed, my lord.

Agamemnon. Let it be known to him that we are here.   80
He shent° our messengers, and we lay by
Our appertainments,° visiting of him.
Let him be told so, lest perchance he think
We dare not move° the question of our place
Or know not what we are.

Patroclus.   I shall so say to him.   85

> [*Exit.*]

Ulysses. We saw him at the opening of his tent. He is
not sick.

Ajax. Yes, lion-sick, sick of proud heart. You may
call it melancholy if you will favor the man; but,
by my head, 'tis pride. But why, why? Let him show   90
us a cause. A word, my lord.

> [*Takes Agamemnon aside.*]

Nestor. What moves Ajax thus to bay at him?

Ulysses. Achilles hath inveigled his fool from him.

Nestor. Who, Thersites?

Ulysses. He.   95

Nestor. Then will Ajax lack matter, if he have lost his
argument.°

Ulysses. No, you see, he is his argument that has his
argument, Achilles.

Nestor. All the better. Their fraction° is more our   100

---

76 **serpigo** a quickly spreading skin disease, with eruptions   81 **shent**
rebuked   82 **appertainments** rights of rank   84 **move** raise   97
argument subject matter   100 **fraction** fracture, break

wish than their faction.° But it was a strong com-
posure° a fool could disunite.

Ulysses. The amity that wisdom knits not, folly may
easily untie.

Enter Patroclus.

105   Here comes Patroclus.

Nestor. No Achilles with him?

Ulysses. The elephant hath joints, but none for courtesy. His legs are legs for necessity, not for flexure.°

Patroclus. Achilles bids me say he is much sorry
110   If anything more than your sport and pleasure
Did move your greatness and this noble state°
To call upon him. He hopes it is no other
But, for your health and your digestion sake,
An after-dinner's breath.°

Agamemnon.   Hear you, Patroclus.
115   We are too well acquainted with these answers;
But his evasion, winged thus swift with scorn,
Cannot outfly our apprehensions.°
Much attribute he hath, and much the reason
Why we ascribe it to him; yet all his virtues,
120   Not virtuously on his own part beheld,°
Do in our eyes begin to lose their gloss—
Yea, like fair fruit in an unwholesome dish,
Are like to rot untasted. Go and tell him
We come to speak with him; and you shall not sin
125   If you do say we think him overproud
And underhonest,° in self-assumption greater
Than in the note of judgment,° and worthier than
    himself

Here tend the savage strangeness° he puts on,
Disguise the holy strength of their command,
And underwrite in an observing kind   .130
His humorous predominance;° yea, watch
His pettish lunes,° his ebbs and flows, as if
The passage and whole carriage of this action
Rode on his tide. Go tell him this; and add
That, if he overhold° his price so much,   135
We'll none of him; but let him, like an engine°
Not portable, lie under this report:
"Bring action hither, this cannot go to war."
A stirring dwarf we do allowance° give
Before a sleeping giant. Tell him so.   140

Patroclus. I shall, and bring his answer presently.
                                            [*Exit.*]

Agamemnon. In second voice we'll not be satisfied;
We come to speak with him. Ulysses, enter you.
                                    Exit Ulysses.

Ajax. What is he more than another?

Agamemnon. No more than what he thinks he is.   145

Ajax. Is he so much? Do you not think he thinks
himself a better man than I am?

Agamemnon. No question.

Ajax. Will you subscribe his thought, and say he is?

Agamemnon. No, noble Ajax; you are as strong, as .150
valiant, as wise, no less noble, much more gentle,
and altogether more tractable.

Ajax. Why should a man be proud? How doth pride
grow? I know not what pride is.

128 **tend the savage strangeness** wait upon the rude aloofness   129–31
Disguise ... predominance allow to be hidden the divine authority of
their command, and, in a form of acquiescence, subscribe to his eccentric
notion of superiority   132 **pettish lunes** capricious variations (like the
changes of the moon)   135 **overhold** overvalue   136 **engine** mechan-
ical contrivance (here, military)   139 **allowance** praise

155 *Agamemnon.* Your mind is the clearer and your vir-
　　tues the fairer. He that is proud eats up himself.
　　Pride is his own glass,° his own trumpet, his own
　　chronicle; and whatever praises itself but in the
　　deed, devours the deed in the praise.

　　　　　　　　Enter Ulysses.

160 *Ajax.* I do hate a proud man as I hate the engend'r-
　　ing of toads.

　　Nestor. [*Aside*] And yet he loves himself. Is't not
　　strange?

　　Ulysses. Achilles will not to the field tomorrow.

　　Agamemnon. What's his excuse?

165 *Ulysses.*　　　　　　　　　He doth rely on none,
　　But carries on the stream of his dispose°
　　Without observance or respect of any,
　　In will peculiar and in self-admission.°

　　Agamemnon. Why will he not upon our fair request
170　　Untent his person and share th'air with us?

　　Ulysses. Things small as nothing, for request's sake
　　　　only,°
　　He makes important. Possessed he is with great-
　　　　ness,
　　And speaks not to himself but with a pride
　　That quarrels at self-breath.° Imagined worth
175　　Holds in his blood such swoln and hot discourse
　　That 'twixt his mental and his active parts
　　Kingdomed° Achilles in commotion rages
　　And batters down himself. What should I say?

---

157 **glass** mirror　166 **dispose** inclination　168 **In … self-admission**
i.e., with will exclusively his own and with self-approval　171 **for
request's sake only** only because requested　174 **That quarrels at
self-breath** that quarrels with speech itself　177 **Kingdomed** i.e., as
though Achilles were himself a kingdom engaged in civil strife

He is so plaguy proud that the death-tokens° of it
Cry "No recovery."

Agamemnon.   Let Ajax go to him.   *180*
Dear lord, go you and greet him in his tent;
'Tis said he holds you well, and will be led
At your request a little from himself.

Ulysses. O Agamemnon, let it not be so!
We'll consecrate the steps that Ajax makes   *185*
When they go from Achilles. Shall the proud lord
That bastes his arrogance with his own seam°
And never suffers matter of the world
Enter his thoughts, save such as doth revolve
And ruminate himself—shall he be worshiped   *190*
Of that we hold an idol more than he?
No, this thrice-worthy and right valiant lord
Shall not so stale his palm,° nobly acquired,
Nor, by my will, assubjugate° his merit,
As amply titled as Achilles' is,   *195*
By going to Achilles.
That were to enlard his fat-already pride,
And add more coals to Cancer° when he burns
With entertaining great Hyperion.°
This lord go to him! Jupiter forbid,   *200*
And say in thunder, "Achilles, go to him."

Nestor. [*Aside*] O, this is well. He rubs the vein° of
him.

Diomedes. [*Aside*] And how his silence drinks up his
applause!

Ajax. If I go to him, with my armèd fist
I'll pash° him o'er the face.   *205*

Agamemnon. O, no! You shall not go.

---

179 **death-tokens** external symptoms of the plague preceding death
187 **seam** grease, fat   193 **stale his palm** detract from his glory   194
assubjugate debase   198 **Cancer** i.e., summer, which begins under this
sign of the zodiac   199 **Hyperion** the sun   202 **vein** mood   205
pash bash

Ajax. An he be proud with me, I'll pheese° his pride.
Let me go to him.

Ulysses. Not for the worth that hangs upon our quarrel.

210 *Ajax.* A paltry, insolent fellow!

Nestor. [*Aside*] How he describes himself!

Ajax. Can he not be sociable?

Ulysses. [*Aside*] The raven chides blackness.

Ajax. I'll let his humor's blood.°

215 *Agamemnon.* [*Aside*] He will be the physician that
should be the patient.

Ajax. An all men were of my mind— —

Ulysses. [*Aside*] Wit would be out of fashion.

Ajax. 'A° should not bear it so, 'a should eat swords
220 first! Shall pride carry it?

Nestor. [*Aside*] An 'twould, you'd carry half.

Ulysses. [*Aside*] 'A would have ten shares.

Ajax. I will knead him; I'll make him supple.

Nestor. [*Aside*] He's not yet through° warm. Force°
225 him with praises; pour in, pour, his ambition is dry.

Ulysses. [*To Agamemnon*] My lord, you feed too
much on this dislike.

Nestor. Our noble general, do not do so.

Diomedes. You must prepare to fight without Achilles.

Ulysses. Why, 'tis this naming of him does him harm.
230 Here is a man—but 'tis before his face;
I will be silent.

---

207 **pheese** settle the business of   214 **let his humor's blood** i.e., cure
him by letting blood, thus decreasing the strength of Achilles' humor, his
mood of pride   219 **'A** he   224 **through** thoroughly   224 **Force**
stuff

Nestor.   Wherefore should you so?
  He is not emulous,° as Achilles is.

Ulysses. Know the whole world, he is as valiant— —

Ajax. A whoreson dog, that shall palter° with us thus!
  Would he were a Troyan!   235

Nestor. What a vice were it in Ajax now— —

Ulysses. If he were proud— —

Diomedes. Or covetous of praise— —

Ulysses. Ay, or surly borne— —

Diomedes. Or strange, or self-affected!°   240

Ulysses. Thank the heavens, lord, thou art of sweet
    composure;
  Praise him that gat° thee, she that gave thee suck;
  Famed be thy tutor, and thy parts of nature
  Thrice-famed beyond, beyond all erudition;°
  But he that disciplined thine arms to fight,   245
  Let Mars divide eternity in twain
  And give him half; and, for thy vigor,
  Bull-bearing Milo° his addition° yield
  To sinewy Ajax. I will not praise thy wisdom,
  Which, like a bourn, a pale,° a shore, confines   250
  Thy spacious and dilated parts. Here's Nestor,
  Instructed by the antiquary times,°
  He must, he is, he cannot but be wise;
  But pardon, father Nestor, were your days
  As green as Ajax, and your brain so tempered,   255
  You should not have the eminence of him,
  But be as Ajax.

---

232 **emulous** jealously competitive   234 **palter** play shifty games,
dodge   240 **strange, or self-affected** haughty, or self-centered   242
gat begat   243–44 **thy parts . . . erudition** your natural attributes three
times more famous (i.e., than your tutor), even more famous than all
learning itself   248 **Milo** (a famous Greek athlete, said to have carried a
bull upon his shoulders for forty yards)   248 **addition** title, i.e., "Bull-
bearing"   250 **a bourn, a pale** a boundary, a fence   252 **Instructed
by the antiquary times** i.e., his wisdom learned from olden times, all the
years of his old age

Ajax.   Shall I call you father?

Nestor. Ay, my good son.

Diomedes.   Be ruled by him, Lord Ajax.

Ulysses. There is no tarrying here; the hart Achilles
260   Keeps thicket. Please it our great general
  To call together all his state° of war;
  Fresh kings are come to Troy. Tomorrow,
  We must with all our main° of power stand fast.
  And here's a lord—come knights from east to west,
265   And cull their flower, Ajax shall cope the best.

Agamemnon. Go we to council. Let Achilles sleep;
  Light boats sail swift, though greater hulks draw
    deep.   · ·   *Exeunt*.

261 **state** noblemen in council   263 **main** might

ACT 3

[Scene 1. *Troy; Priam's palace.*]

Music sounds within. Enter Pandarus and a Servant.

Pandarus. Friend you, pray you a word. Do you not follow the young Lord Paris?

Servant. Ay, sir, when he goes before me.

Pandarus. You depend° upon him, I mean.

Servant. Sir, I do depend upon the Lord.　　　　5

Pandarus. You depend upon a notable gentleman; I must needs praise him.

Servant. The Lord be praised!

Pandarus. You know me, do you not?

Servant. Faith, sir, superficially.　　　　10

Pandarus. Friend, know me better. I am the Lord Pandarus.

Servant. I hope I shall know your honor better.

Pandarus. I do desire it.

3.1.4 **depend** i.e., serve, in a position of dependence

15   *Servant.* You are in the state of grace.°

      Pandarus. Grace?° Not so, friend. Honor and lord-
         ship are my titles. What music is this?

      Servant. I do but partly know, sir. It is music in
         parts.°

20   *Pandarus.* Know you the musicians?

      Servant. Wholly, sir.

      Pandarus. Who play they to?

      Servant. To the hearers, sir.

      Pandarus. At whose pleasure, friend?

25   *Servant.* At mine, sir, and theirs that love music.

      Pandarus. Command, I mean, friend.

      Servant. Who shall I command, sir?

      Pandarus. Friend, we understand not one another. I
         am too courtly, and thou too cunning. At whose
30   request do these men play?

      Servant. That's to't, indeed, sir. Marry, sir, at the re-
         quest of Paris, my lord, who is there in person;
         with him the mortal Venus, the heartblood of
         beauty, love's invisible soul.

35   *Pandarus.* Who? My cousin Cressida?

      Servant. No, sir, Helen. Could not you find out that
         by her attributes?

      Pandarus. It should seem, fellow, that thou hast not
         seen the Lady Cressid. I come to speak with
40   Paris from the Prince Troilus. I will make a com-

---

15 **You ... grace** (pretending that Pandarus meant that he desired his
own honor to be better; also, perhaps, the servant is hinting for a gratuity)
16 **Grace** (the courtly title of a duke, etc.)   18–19 **music in parts**
music containing several vocal or instrumental parts in counterpoint

plimental assault upon him, for my business seethes.°

Servant. Sodden business! There's a stewed° phrase, indeed.

    Enter Paris and Helen [with courtiers].

Pandarus. Fair be to you, my lord, and to all this fair 45 company. Fair desires in all fair measure fairly guide them. Especially to you, fair queen, fair thoughts be your fair pillow.

Helen. Dear lord, you are full of fair words.

Pandarus. You speak your fair pleasure, sweet queen. 50 Fair prince, here is good broken music.°

Paris. You have broke it, cousin; and, by my life, you shall make it whole again; you shall piece it out with a piece of your performance. Nell, he is full of harmony. 55

Pandarus. Truly, lady, no.

Helen. O, sir!

Pandarus. Rude,° in sooth; in good sooth, very rude.

Paris. Well said, my lord. Well, you say so in fits.°

Pandarus. I have business to my lord, dear queen. My 60 lord, will you vouchsafe me a word?

Helen. Nay, this shall not hedge us out. We'll hear you sing, certainly.

Pandarus. Well, sweet queen, you are pleasant with me. But, marry, thus, my lord: my dear lord and 65 most esteemed friend, your brother Troilus— —

---

42 **seethes** boils, i.e., demands immediate attention   43 **stewed** (1) boiled (2) pertaining to stews, or brothels (?)   51 **broken music** music the parts for which are written for different solo instruments, or groups of different instruments   58 **Rude** unpolished, rough   59 **fits** sections or divisions of a song (perhaps Paris means, "you say so only at times")

Helen. My Lord Pandarus, honey-sweet lord——

Pandarus. Go to, sweet queen, go to—commends himself most affectionately to you.

70 *Helen.* You shall not bob° us out of our melody. If you do, our melancholy upon your head!

Pandarus. Sweet queen, sweet queen, that's a sweet queen, i' faith.

Helen. And to make a sweet lady sad is a sour offense.

75 *Pandarus.* Nay, that shall not serve your turn; that shall it not, in truth, la. Nay, I care not for such words; no, no. And, my lord, he desires you that, if the king call for him at supper, you will make his excuse.

80 *Helen.* My Lord Pandarus——

Pandarus. What says my sweet queen, my very, very sweet queen?

Paris. What exploit's in hand? Where sups he tonight?

Helen. Nay, but my Lord——

85 *Pandarus.* What says my sweet queen? My cousin will fall out with you.°

Helen. You must not know where he sups.

Paris. I'll lay my life, with my disposer° Cressida.

Pandarus. No, no; no such matter; you are wide.°
90 Come, your disposer is sick.

Paris. Well, I'll make excuse.

Pandarus. Ay, good my lord. Why should you say Cressida? No, your poor disposer's sick.

Paris. I spy.

---

70 **bob** cheat   85–86 **My cousin . . . you** (Pandarus lightly pretends that Paris, his "cousin," will become jealous if Helen continues to flirt with him, Pandarus)   88 **disposer** i.e., she who rules him (Paris jokingly uses an excessively gallant term)   89 **wide** wide of the mark

Pandarus. You spy? What do you spy? Come, give 95
me an instrument now, sweet queen.

Helen. Why, this is kindly done.

Pandarus. My niece is horribly in love with a thing
you have, sweet queen.°

Helen. She shall have it, my lord, if it be not my Lord 100
Paris.

Pandarus. He? No, she'll none of him; they two are
twain.°

Helen. Falling in, after falling out, may make them
three.° 105

Pandarus. Come, come, I'll hear no more of this. I'll
sing you a song now.

Helen. Ay, ay, prithee. Now by my troth, sweet lord,
thou hast a fine forehead.

Pandarus. Ay, you may, you may.° 110

Helen. Let thy song be love. This love will undo us all.
O Cupid, Cupid, Cupid!

Pandarus. Love! Ay, that it shall, i' faith.

Paris. Ay, good now, "Love, love, nothing but love."

Pandarus. In good troth, it begins so: [*Sings.*] 115
Love, love, nothing but love, still love still more!
For, O, love's bow shoots buck and doe.
The shaft confounds not that° it wounds,
But tickles still the sore.°
These lovers cry, O ho! they die! 120
Yet that which seems the wound to kill

98–99 **My niece is . . . sweet queen** i.e., Cressida loves, or would love to
have, a sexual partner such as Paris is to Helen   103 **twain** at odds,
have nothing in common   104–05 **Falling in . . . them three** (Helen's
bawdy joke picks up the train of thought begun by Pandarus)   110 **you
may,** i.e., have your joke   118 **confounds not that** does not distress
because   119 **sore** wound (perhaps a pun on the term for a buck in his
fourth year)

Doth turn O ho! to Ha, ha, he!
So dying love lives still.
O ho! a while, but Ha, ha, ha!
125 O ho! groans out for Ha, ha, ha!—Heigh ho!

Helen. In love, i' faith, to the very tip of the nose.

Paris. He eats nothing but doves, love, and that breeds
hot blood, and hot blood begets hot thoughts, and
hot thoughts beget hot deeds, and hot deeds is love.

130 *Pandarus.* Is this the generation of love—hot blood,
hot thoughts, and hot deeds? Why, they are vipers.
Is love a generation of vipers?° Sweet lord, who's
a-field today?

Paris. Hector, Deiphobus, Helenus, Antenor, and all
135 the gallantry of Troy. I would fain have armed
today, but my Nell would not have it so. How
chance my brother Troilus went not?

Helen. He hangs the lip at something. You know all,
Lord Pandarus.

140 *Pandarus.* Not I, honey-sweet queen. I long to hear
how they sped° today. You'll remember your
brother's excuse?

Paris. To a hair.°

Pandarus. Farewell, sweet queen.

145 *Helen.* Commend me to your niece.

Pandarus. I will, sweet queen. [*Exit.*] *Sound a retreat.*

Paris. They're come from the field. Let us to Priam's
hall
To greet the warriors. Sweet Helen, I must woo you
To help unarm our Hector. His stubborn buckles,
150 With these your white enchanting fingers touched,
Shall more obey than to the edge of steel

132 **a generation of vipers** (cf. Matthew 3:7)   141 **how they sped** i.e.,
the results of their action   143 **To a hair** (does Paris jokingly recall
Troilus' "pretty answer" about the hairs on his chin [see 1.2.169–71]?)

Or force of Greekish sinews. You shall do more
Than all the island kings° — disarm great Hector.

Helen. 'Twill make us proud to be his servant, Paris;
Yea, what he shall receive of us in duty   *155*
Gives us more palm in beauty than we have,
Yea, overshines ourself.

Paris. Sweet, above thought I love thee.   *Exeunt*.

[Scene 2. *Within Troy*.]

Enter Pandarus and Troilus' Man.

Pandarus. How now, where's thy master? At my
cousin Cressida's?

Man. No, sir; he stays for you to conduct him thither.

Enter Troilus.

Pandarus. O, here he comes. How now, how now?

Troilus. Sirrah, walk off.   [*Exit Man*.]   *5*

Pandarus. Have you seen my cousin?

Troilus. No, Pandarus. I stalk about her door
Like a strange soul upon the Stygian° banks
Staying for waftage.° O, be thou my Charon,°
And give me swift transportance to those fields   *10*
Where I may wallow in the lily beds
Proposed° for the deserver. O gentle Pandar,
From Cupid's shoulder pluck his painted wings,
And fly with me to Cressid.

153 **island kings** i.e., kings of the Grecian islands 3.2.8 **Stygian**
(from Styx, the principal river of the underworld) 9 **waftage** passage
across water 9 **Charon** (ferryman of the dead, across the Styx to
Hades) 12 **Proposed** promised

15 *Pandarus.* Walk here i' th' orchard. I'll bring her
     straight.   *Exit Pandarus.*

Troilus. I am giddy; expectation whirls me round.
     Th' imaginary relish is so sweet
     That it enchants my sense. What will it be
20   When that the wat'ry° palates taste indeed
     Love's thrice-repurèd° nectar? Death, I fear me,
     Sounding° destruction, or some joy too fine,
     Too subtle, potent, tuned too sharp in sweetness
     For the capacity of my ruder° powers.
25   I fear it much; and I do fear besides
     That I shall lose distinction° in my joys,
     As doth a battle, when they charge on heaps
     The enemy flying.

                    Enter Pandarus.

Pandarus. She's making her ready; she'll come
30   straight; you must be witty° now. She does so blush,
     and fetches her wind so short as if she were frayed
     with a spirit.° I'll fetch her. It is the prettiest vil-
     lain;° she fetches her breath as short as a new-
     ta'en sparrow.   *Exit Pandarus.*

35 *Troilus.* Even such a passion doth embrace my bosom.
     My heart beats thicker than a feverous pulse,
     And all my powers do their bestowing° lose,
     Like vassalage° at unawares encount'ring
     The eye of majesty.

                    Enter Pandarus and Cressida.

40 *Pandarus.* Come, come, what need you blush? Shame's
     a baby. Here she is now; swear the oaths now to

---

20 **wat'ry** watering (cf. mouth "watering" with appetite)   21 **thrice-
repurèd** distilled again and again (i.e., to extract the purest essence)   22
Sounding swooning   24 **ruder** physical   26 **distinction** ability to distinguish   30 **be witty** be alert, have your wits about you   31–32
frayed with a spirit frightened by a ghost   32–33 **villain** (here a term
of endearment)   37 **bestowing** proper use   38 **vassalage** vassals

her that you have sworn to me. What! Are you
gone again? You must be watched ere you be made
tame,° must you? Come your ways, come your
ways; an you draw backward, we'll put you i' the   45
fills.° Why do you not speak to her? Come, draw
this curtain,° and let's see your picture. Alas the
day, how loath you are to offend daylight! An
'twere dark, you'd close° sooner. So, so; rub on,
and kiss the mistress.° How now, a kiss in fee-   50
farm!° Build there, carpenter; the air is sweet.
Nay, you shall fight your hearts out ere I part you.
The falcon as the tercel, for all the ducks i' the
river.° Go to, go to.

Troilus. You have bereft me of all words, lady.   55

Pandarus. Words pay no debts, give her deeds; but
she'll bereave you o' the deeds too if she call your
activity in question. What, billing again? Here's "In
witness whereof the parties interchangeably"° —
Come in, come in. I'll go get a fire.   [*Exit.*]   60

Cressida. Will you walk in, my lord?

Troilus. O Cressid, how often have I wished me thus!

Cressida. Wished, my lord? The gods grant—O my
lord!

Troilus. What should they grant? What makes this   65
pretty abruption?° What too curious° dreg espies
my sweet lady in the fountain of our love?

43–44 **watched ere you be made tame** i.e., prodded on until made sub-
missive (a hawk was tamed by "watching" it, i.e., keeping it constantly
awake) 46 **fills** shafts (of a cart) 47 **curtain** i.e., her veil 49 **close**
move together 49–50 **rub ... mistress** (terms from bowling, where
"to rub" was to meet obstacles in the way of the small object-ball, called
the "mistress"; bowls are still said "to kiss" when they touch gently)
50–51 **a kiss in fee-farm** i.e., a long kiss (a fee-farm was a grant of
lands in perpetuity) 53–54 **The falcon ... river** i.e., I will bet on the
falcon (the term applied only to the female of the species) against the
tercel (the male) to bring down any game 58–59 **"In witness ...
interchangeably"** (a legal formula, usually ending with the words "have
set their hands and seals") 66 **abruption** breaking off 66 **too curious** overly cautious, anxious, or inquisitive

Cressida. More dregs than water, if my fears have eyes.

70 *Troilus.* Fears make devils of cherubins; they never see truly.

Cressida. Blind fear, that seeing reason leads, finds safer footing than blind reason stumbling without fear. To fear the worst oft cures the worse.

75 *Troilus.* O, let my lady apprehend no fear; in all Cupid's pageant there is presented no monster.°

Cressida. Nor nothing monstrous neither?

Troilus. Nothing but our undertakings when we vow to weep seas, live in fire, eat rocks, tame tigers,
80 thinking it harder for our mistress to devise imposition enough than for us to undergo any difficulty imposed. This is the monstruosity in love, lady, that the will is infinite and the execution confined; that the desire is boundless and the act a slave to
85 limit.

Cressida. They say all lovers swear more performance than they are able, and yet reserve an ability that they never perform, vowing more than the perfection of ten and discharging less than the
90 tenth part of one. They that have the voice of lions and the act of hares—are they not monsters?

Troilus. Are there such? Such are not we. Praise us as we are tasted,° allow us as we prove; our head shall go bare till merit crown it. No perfection in
95 reversion° shall have a praise in present; we will not name desert before his birth, and, being born, his addition shall be humble.° Few words to fair faith. Troilus shall be such to Cressid, as what envy

75–76 **apprehend ... no monster** (Troilus refers to some type of dramatic allegory such as Cupid might be depicted as "presenting," or the emblematic characters, such as Fear, in pageants or court masques)　93 **tasted** tested　95 **reversion** right or anticipation of future possession　97 **his addition shall be humble** it shall be given no high or pompous titles

can say worst shall be a mock for his truth, and
what truth can speak truest not truer than Troilus.° *100*

Cressida. Will you walk in, my lord?

Enter Pandarus.

Pandarus. What, blushing still? Have you not done
talking yet?

Cressida. Well, uncle, what folly I commit, I dedicate
to you. *105*

Pandarus. I thank you for that. If my lord get a boy
of you, you'll give him me. Be true to my lord;
if he flinch, chide me for it.

Troilus. You know now your hostages: your uncle's
word and my firm faith. *110*

Pandarus. Nay, I'll give my word for her too. Our
kindred, though they be long ere they be wooed,
they are constant being won. They are burrs, I can
tell you; they'll stick where they are thrown.

Cressida. Boldness comes to me now and brings me
heart. *115*
Prince Troilus, I have loved you night and day
For many weary months.

Troilus. Why was my Cressid then so hard to win?

Cressida. Hard to seem won; but I was won, my lord,
With the first glance that ever—pardon me; *120*
If I confess much you will play the tyrant.
I love you now, but, till now, not so much
But I might master it. In faith, I lie;
My thoughts were like unbridled children grown
Too headstrong for their mother. See, we fools! *125*
Why have I blabbed? Who shall be true to us
When we are so unsecret to ourselves?

98–100 **as what envy ... Troilus** so that the worst malice can do is
sneer at his constancy, and even the best truth that truth can speak will
not be truer than Troilus

But, though I loved you well, I wooed you not;
And yet, good faith, I wished myself a man,
130   Or that we women had men's privilege
Of speaking first. Sweet, bid me hold my tongue,
For in this rapture I shall surely speak
The thing I shall repent. See, see! Your silence,
Cunning in dumbness, from my weakness draws
135   My very soul of counsel.° Stop my mouth.

Troilus. And shall, albeit sweet music issues thence.

Pandarus. Pretty, i'faith.

Cressida. My lord, I do beseech you, pardon me;
'Twas not my purpose thus to beg a kiss.
140   I am ashamed. O heavens, what have I done?
For this time will I take my leave, my lord.

Troilus. Your leave, sweet Cressid?

Pandarus. Leave! An you take leave till tomorrow
morning— —

Cressida. Pray you, content you.

145 *Troilus.*   What offends you, lady?

Cressida. Sir, mine own company.

Troilus. You cannot shun yourself.

Cressida. Let me go and try.
I have a kind of self resides with you;
150   But an unkind self, that itself will leave
To be another's fool.° I would be gone.
Where is my wit? I know not what I speak.

Troilus. Well know they what they speak that speak
so wisely.

Cressida. Perchance, my lord, I show more craft than
love,
155   And fell so roundly° to a large° confession

---

135 **very soul of counsel** inmost thoughts and secrets   151 **fool** dupe
155 **roundly** frankly, openly   155 **large** unrestrained

To angle for your thoughts. But you are wise,
Or else you love not, for to be wise and love
Exceeds man's might;° that dwells with gods above.

Troilus. O that I thought it could be in a woman—
As, if it can, I will presume in you—　　　　　*160*
To feed for aye her lamp and flames of love;
To keep her constancy in plight and youth,°
Outliving beauty's outward,° with a mind
That doth renew swifter than blood decays;
Or that persuasion could but thus convince me　　*165*
That my integrity and truth to you
Might be affronted° with the match and weight
Of such a winnowed° purity in love:
How were I then uplifted! But, alas,
I am as true as truth's simplicity,　　　　　*170*
And simpler than the infancy of truth.

Cressida. In that I'll war with you.

Troilus.　　　　　　　　O virtuous fight,
When right with right wars who shall be most right!
True swains in love shall in the world to come
Approve° their truth by Troilus. When their rhymes,　*175*
Full of protest, of oath and big compare,
Wants similes, truth tired with iteration,
"As true as steel, as plantage to the moon,°
As sun to day, as turtle° to her mate,
As iron to adamant,° as earth to the center,"　　*180*
Yet, after all comparisons of truth,
As truth's authentic author to be cited,
"As true as Troilus" shall crown up the verse
And sanctify the numbers.°

156–58 **But you are wise … man's might** i.e., you are reasonable,
which means you are not in love, for no man can follow reason and love
at the same time　162 **in plight and youth** as it was when it was
plighted, and as fresh　163 **beauty's outward** external, transitory
beauty　167 **affronted** confronted, i.e., equaled　168 **winnowed** i.e.,
distilled　175 **Approve** attest　178 **plantage to the moon** (the moon
was thought to influence plantage, or vegetation)　179 **turtle** turtledove
(an emblem of eternally faithful love)　180 **adamant** the lodestone
(magnetic)　184 **numbers** metrical verses

Cressida.   Prophet may you be!
185   If I be false or swerve a hair from truth,
       When time is old and hath forgot itself,
       When waterdrops have worn the stones of Troy,
       And blind oblivion swallowed cities up,
       And mighty states characterless° are grated
190   To dusty nothing, yet let memory,
       From false to false among false maids in love,
       Upbraid my falsehood! When they've said, "As false
       As air, as water, wind or sandy earth,
       As fox to lamb, as wolf to heifer's calf,
195   Pard to the hind,° or stepdame to her son,"
       Yea, let them say, to stick the heart of falsehood,
       "As false as Cressid."

Pandarus. Go to, a bargain made. Seal it, seal it; I'll
       be the witness. Here I hold your hand, here my
200   cousin's. If ever you prove false one to another,
       since I have taken such pains to bring you to-
       gether, let all pitiful goers-between be called to the
       world's end after my name; call them all Pandars.
       Let all constant men be Troiluses, all false women
205   Cressids, and all brokers-between Pandars! Say,
       "Amen."

Troilus. Amen.

Cressida. Amen.

Pandarus. Amen. Whereupon I will show you a cham-
210   ber which bed,° because° it shall not speak of your
       pretty encounters, press it to death. Away!
                         Exeunt [*Troilus and Cressida*].
       And Cupid grant all tongue-tied maidens here
       Bed, chamber, Pandar to provide this gear!   *Exit.*

---

189 **characterless** without an identifying mark   195 **Pard to the hind**
leopard to the doe   210 **which bed** the bed in which   210 **because** (1)
for the reason that (normal usage) (2) in order that (?)

[Scene 3. *The Greek camp.*]

*Enter Ulysses, Diomedes, Nestor, Agamemnon, [Mene-
laus, Ajax, and] Calchas. Flourish [of trumpets.]*

Calchas. Now, princes, for the service I have done,
   Th' advantage of the time prompts me aloud
   To call for recompense. Appear it to mind
   That through the sight° I bear in things to come,
   I have abandoned Troy, left my possession,   5
   Incurred a traitor's name, exposed myself,
   From certain and possessed conveniences,
   To doubtful fortunes, sequest'ring° from me all
   That time, acquaintance, custom, and condition
   Made tame° and most familiar to my nature;   10
   And here, to do you service, am become
   As new into the world, strange, unacquainted.
   I do beseech you, as in way of taste,°
   To give me now a little benefit
   Out of those many registered in promise,   15
   Which, you say, live to come in my behalf.

Agamemnon. What wouldst thou of us, Troyan? Make
   demand.

Calchas. You have a Troyan prisoner, called Antenor,
   Yesterday took; Troy holds him very dear.
   Oft have you—often have you thanks therefor—   20
   Desired my Cressid in right great exchange,°
   Whom Troy hath still° denied; but this Antenor

3.3.4 **sight** i.e., foresight   8 **sequest'ring** putting aside   10 **tame**
familiar, comfortable   13 **taste** foretaste   21 **right great exchange**
exchange for someone sufficiently great   22 **still** always

I know is such a wrest° in their affairs
That their negotiations all must slack,
25 Wanting his manage; and they will almost
Give us a prince of blood, a son of Priam,
In change of him. Let him be sent, great princes,
And he shall buy my daughter; and her presence
Shall quite strike off all service I have done
In most accepted° pain.

30 *Agamemnon.*   Let Diomedes bear him,
And bring us Cressid hither; Calchas shall have
What he requests of us. Good Diomed,
Furnish you fairly, for this interchange.
Withal bring word if Hector will tomorrow
35 Be answered in his challenge. Ajax is ready.

Diomedes. This shall I undertake, and 'tis a burden
Which I am proud to bear.   *Exit [with Calchas].*

Achilles and Patroclus stand in their tent.°

Ulysses. Achilles stands i' th' entrance of his tent.
Please it our general pass strangely° by him,
40 As if he were forgot; and, princes all,
Lay negligent and loose regard upon him.
I will come last. 'Tis like he'll question me
Why such unplausive° eyes are bent, why turned,
on him.
If so, I have derision medicinable
45 To use between your strangeness and his pride,
Which his own will shall have desire to drink.
It may do good; pride hath no other glass
To show° itself but pride, for supple knees
Feed arrogance and are the proud man's fees.

50 *Agamemnon.* We'll execute your purpose, and put on
A form of strangeness as we pass along.
So do each lord, and either greet him not

23 **wrest** a key used for tuning stringed instruments (i.e., the influence of
harmony in Trojan discussions)   30 **accepted** cheerfully endured   37
s.d. **stand in their tent** i.e., appear and stand in the entrance of their tent
39 **strangely** aloofly   43 **unplausive** disapproving   48 **show** mirror

Or else disdainfully, which shall shake him more
Than if not looked on. I will lead the way.

Achilles. What comes the general to speak with me?   55
  You know my mind; I'll fight no more 'gainst Troy.

Agamemnon. What says Achilles? Would he aught
  with us?

Nestor. Would you, my lord, aught with the general?

Achilles. No.

Nestor. Nothing, my lord.   60

Agamemnon. The better.

Achilles. Good day, good day.

Menelaus. How do you? How do you?

Achilles. What, does the cuckold scorn me?

Ajax. How now, Patroclus?   65

Achilles. Good morrow, Ajax.

Ajax. Ha?

Achilles. Good morrow.

Ajax. Ay, and good next day too.   *Exeunt.*

Achilles. What mean these fellows? Know they not
  Achilles?   70

Patroclus. They pass by strangely. They were used to
      bend,
  To send their smiles before them to Achilles,
  To come as humbly as they used to creep
  To holy altars.

Achilles.   What, am I poor of late?
  'Tis certain, greatness, once fall'n out with fortune,   75
  Must fall out with men too. What the declined is
  He shall as soon read in the eyes of others
  As feel in his own fall; for men, like butterflies,

Show not their mealy° wings but to the summer,
80   And not a man, for being simply man,
Hath any honor, but honor for those honors
That are without° him, as place, riches, and favor,
Prizes of accident as oft as merit;
Which when they fall, as being slippery standers,
85   The love that leaned on them as slippery too,
Doth one pluck down another, and together
Die in the fall. But 'tis not so with me;
Fortune and I are friends. I do enjoy
At ample point° all that I did possess,
90   Save these men's looks—who do, methinks, find out
Something not worth in me such rich beholding
As they have often given. Here is Ulysses;
I'll interrupt his reading.
How now, Ulysses.

Ulysses.   Now, great Thetis' son.

Achilles. What are you reading?

95   *Ulysses.*   A strange fellow here
Writes me that man, how dearly ever parted,°
How much in having, or without or in,°
Cannot make boast to have that which he hath,
Nor feels not what he owes but by reflection;°
100 As when his virtues aiming upon others
Heat them, and they retort that heat again
To the first giver.

Achilles.   This is not strange, Ulysses.
The beauty that is borne here in the face
The bearer knows not, but commends itself
105 To others' eyes; nor doth the eye itself,
That most pure spirit of sense, behold itself,
Not going from itself; but eye to eye opposed

---

79 **mealy** powdery 82 **without** external to 89 **At ample point** in full measure, in every way 96 **how dearly ever parted** however excellently endowed by nature 97 **How much . . . or in** however much in possession, whether externally or internally 99 **Nor feels . . . by reflection** and understands what he himself possesses (**owes** = "owns") only as it is reflected

Salutes each other with each other's form;
For speculation° turns not to itself
Till it hath traveled and is married there   *110*
Where it may see itself. This is not strange at all.

Ulysses. I do not strain at the position°—
  It is familiar—but at the author's drift;
  Who in his circumstance° expressly proves
  That no man is the lord of anything—   *115*
  Though in and of him there be much consisting°—
  Till he communicate his parts to others.
  Nor doth he of himself know them for aught
  Till he behold them formèd in th' applause
  Where they're extended;° who,° like an arch, rever-
    b'rate   *120*
  The voice again, or, like a gate of steel
  Fronting the sun, receives and renders back
  His figure and his heat. I was much rapt in this,
  And apprehended here immediately
  Th' unknown Ajax.   *125*
  Heavens, what a man is there! A very horse,
  That has he knows not what. Nature, what things
    there are
  Most abject in regard and dear in use!°
  What things again most dear in the esteem
  And poor in worth! Now shall we see tomorrow,   *130*
  An act that very chance doth throw upon him:
  Ajax renowned. O heavens, what some men do,
  While some men leave to do!
  How some men creep in° skittish° Fortune's hall,
  Whiles others play the idiots in her eyes!   *135*
  How one man eats into another's pride,
  While pride is fasting in his wantonness!°
  To see these Grecian lords—why, even already

---

109 **speculation** power of sight   112 **position** i.e., that of the writer
whom Ulysses paraphrases above   114 **circumstance** detailed discussion   116 **Though . . . consisting** although much exists in him and also
because of him   120 **Where they're extended** in which his natural
attributes are noised abroad   120 **who** which   128 **Most . . . use** most
despised and yet invaluable   134 **in** into   134 **skittish** i.e., unreliable
137 **his wantonness** its own self-satisfaction

They clap the lubber Ajax on the shoulder,
140   As if his foot were on brave Hector's breast,
And great Troy shrinking.

Achilles. I do believe it; for they passed by me
As misers do by beggars, neither gave to me
Good word nor look. What, are my deeds forgot?

145 *Ulysses.* Time hath, my lord, a wallet at his back,
Wherein he puts alms for oblivion,
A great-sized monster of ingratitudes.
Those scraps are good deeds past, which are de-
voured
As fast as they are made, forgot as soon
150   As done. Perseverance, dear my lord,
Keeps honor bright. To have done, is to hang
Quite out of fashion, like a rusty mail°
In monumental mock'ry. Take the instant° way;
For honor travels in a strait so narrow
155   Where one but goes abreast. Keep, then, the path;
For emulation hath a thousand sons
That one by one pursue. If you give way,
Or hedge aside from the direct forthright,°
Like to an ent'red tide they all rush by
160   And leave you hindmost;
Or, like a gallant horse fall'n in first rank,
Lie there for pavement to the abject rear,°
O'errun and trampled on. Then what they do in
present,
Though less than yours in past, must o'ertop yours.
165   For time is like a fashionable host,
That slightly shakes his parting guest by the hand,
And with his arms outstretched, as he would fly,
Grasps in the comer. The welcome ever smiles,
And farewell goes out sighing. Let not virtue seek
170   Remuneration for the thing it was. For beauty, wit,
High birth, vigor of bone, desert in service,

152 **mail** piece of armor 153 **instant** most immediate 158 **direct
forthright** course of action clearly at hand, the path straight ahead 162
the abject rear the miserable, degraded members of the rear (as in a
military charge or parade)

Love, friendship, charity, are subjects all
To envious and calumniating time.
One touch of nature° makes the whole world kin,
That all with one consent praise newborn gauds,°　175
Though they are made and molded of things past,
And give to dust that is a little gilt
More laud than gilt o'erdusted.°
The present eye praises the present object.
Then marvel not, thou great and complete man,　180
That all the Greeks begin to worship Ajax;
Since things in motion sooner catch the eye
Than what stirs not. The cry° went once on thee,
And still it might, and yet it may again,
If thou wouldst not entomb thyself alive　185
And case° thy reputation in thy tent;
Whose glorious deeds, but in these fields of late,
Made emulous missions° 'mongst the gods them-
　　selves
And drave great Mars to faction.°

Achilles.　　　　　　　　　　　　Of this my privacy
I have strong reasons.

Ulysses.　　　　　　　　But 'gainst your privacy　190
The reasons are more potent and heroical.
'Tis known, Achilles, that you are in love
With one of Priam's daughters.°

Achilles. Ha! Known!

Ulysses. Is that a wonder?　195
The providence° that's in a watchful state
Knows almost every grain of Pluto's° gold
Finds bottom in th' uncomprehensive° deeps,

---

174 **One touch of nature** a natural inclination, common to all men (to praise according to superficial values)　175 **gauds** toys, trifles　178 **More laud than gilt o'erdusted** more praise than gold covered with dust　183 **cry** public opinion　186 **case** encase　188 **emulous missions** competitive and jealous warfare (the gods took sides in the Trojan war, fighting among themselves)　189 **to faction** to become a partisan　193 **one of Priam's daughters** (Polyxena)　196 **providence** careful and timely understanding　197 **Pluto's** (Shakespeare's error for Plutus, god of wealth; Pluto was god of the underworld)　198 **uncomprehensive** unfathomable

Keeps place° with thought, and almost, like the gods,
200 Do thoughts unveil in their dumb cradles.
There is a mystery—with whom relation°
Durst never meddle—in the soul of state,
Which hath an operation more divine
Than breath or pen can give expressure to.
205 All the commerce that you have had with Troy
As perfectly is ours as yours, my lord;
And better would it fit Achilles much
To throw down Hector than Polyxena.
But it must grieve young Pyrrhus° now at home,
210 When fame shall in our islands sound her trump,
And all the Greekish girls shall tripping sing,
"Great Hector's sister did Achilles win,
But our great Ajax bravely beat down him."
Farewell, my lord; I as your lover speak;
215 The fool slides o'er the ice that you should break.
                                                    [*Exit.*]

Patroclus. To this effect, Achilles, have I moved you.
A woman impudent and mannish grown
Is not more loathed than an effeminate man
In time of action. I stand condemned for this;
220 They think my little stomach to the war
And your great love to me restrains you thus.
Sweet, rouse yourself; and the weak wanton Cupid
Shall from your neck unloose his amorous fold
And, like a dewdrop from the lion's mane,
Be shook to air.

225 *Achilles.*   Shall Ajax fight with Hector?

Patroclus. Ay, and perhaps receive much honor by him.

Achilles. I see my reputation is at stake.
My fame is shrewdly gored.°

---

199 **Keeps place** keeps up, runs parallel   201 **relation** open statement
209 **Pyrrhus** (Achilles' son, also called Neoptolemus)   228 **shrewdly gored** sorely wounded

Patroclus.   O, then, beware!
Those wounds heal ill that men do give themselves.
Omission to do what is necessary   230
Seals a commission to a blank of danger°
And danger, like an ague, subtly taints°
Even then when they sit idly in the sun.

Achilles. Go call Thersites hither, sweet Patroclus.
I'll send the fool to Ajax and desire him   235
T' invite the Troyan lords after the combat
To see us here unarmed. I have a woman's° longing,
An appetite that I am sick withal,
To see great Hector in his weeds° of peace,
To talk with him and to behold his visage,   240
Even to my full of view.°

Enter Thersites.

A labor saved!

Thersites. A wonder!

Achilles. What?

Thersites. Ajax goes up and down the field, asking
for himself.°   245

Achilles. How so?

Thersites. He must fight singly tomorrow with Hector,
and is so prophetically proud of an heroical cudgel-
ing that he raves in saying nothing.

Achilles. How can that be?   250

Thersites. Why, he stalks up and down like a pea-
cock—a stride and a stand; ruminates like an

---

231 **Seals ... danger** i.e., binds one to confront unnamed danger (royal
officers sometimes carried blank warrants for arrest, already bearing the
commissioning seal of authority, which could be filled in as necessary)
232 **taints** infects 237 **woman's** i.e., pregnant woman's (?) 239
weeds apparel 240–41 **to behold ... view** (since in full armor
Hector's face would have been hidden behind the closed beaver of his
helmet) 244–45 **asking for himself** (here "Ajax" is probably a pun on
a jakes, i.e., a privy)

hostess that hath no arithmetic but her brain to set
down her reckoning; bites his lip with a politic
255 regard,° as who should say, "There were wit in
this head an 'twould out"; and so there is, but it
lies as coldly in him as fire in a flint, which will not
show without knocking. The man's undone forever, for if Hector break not his neck i' the combat,
260 he'll break't himself in vainglory. He knows not
me. I said, "Good morrow, Ajax"; and he replies,
"Thanks, Agamemnon." What think you of this
man that takes me for the general? He's grown a
very land-fish, languageless, a monster. A plague of
265 opinion! A man may wear it on both sides like
a leather jerkin.°

Achilles. Thou must be my ambassador to him, Thersites.

Thersites. Who, I? Why, he'll answer nobody. He pro-
270 fesses not answering. Speaking is for beggars; he
wears his tongue in's arms. I will put on° his
presence; let Patroclus make demands to me, you
shall see the pageant of Ajax.

Achilles. To him, Patroclus. Tell him I humbly desire
275 the valiant Ajax to invite the most valorous Hector
to come unarmed to my tent, and to procure safe-
conduct for his person of the magnanimous and
most illustrious, six-or-seven-times-honored cap-
tain-general of the Grecian army, Agamemnon, et
280 cetera. Do this.

Patroclus. Jove bless great Ajax!

Thersites. Hum.

Patroclus. I come from the worthy Achilles——

Thersites. Ha!

285 *Patroclus*. Who most humbly desires you to invite
Hector to his tent——

254–55 **politic regard** expression of shrewd judgment 266 **jerkin**
close-fitting jacket 271 **put on** imitate

Thersites. Hum!

Patroclus. And to procure safe-conduct from Agamemnon.

Thersites. Agamemnon?   290

Patroclus. Ay, my lord.

Thersites. Ha!

Patroclus. What say you to't?

Thersites. God b'wi'you, with all my heart.

Patroclus. Your answer, sir.   295

Thersites. If tomorrow be a fair day, by eleven of the
clock it will go one way or other; howsoever, he
shall pay for me ere he has me.

Patroclus. Your answer, sir.

Thersites. Fare ye well, with all my heart.   300

Achilles. Why, but he is not in this tune, is he?

Thersites. No, but out of tune thus. What music will
be in him when Hector has knocked out his brains,
I know not; but I am sure none, unless the fiddler
Apollo get his sinews to make catlings° on.   305

Achilles. Come, thou shalt bear a letter to him
straight.

Thersites. Let me bear another to his horse, for that's
the more capable° creature.

Achilles. My mind is troubled, like a fountain stirred,   310
And I myself see not the bottom of it.
               [*Exeunt Achilles and Patroclus.*]

Thersites. Would the fountain of your mind were clear
again, that I might water an ass at it! I had rather
be a tick in a sheep than such a valiant ignorance.
                                              [*Exit.*]

305 **catlings** strings of catgut   309 **capable** intelligent

ACT 4

[Scene 1. *Within Troy.*]

*Enter, at one door, Aeneas [with a torch;] at
  another, Paris, Deiphobus, Antenor, Diomed the
  Grecian, [and others,] with torches.*

Paris. See, ho! Who is that there?

Deiphobus.   It is the Lord Aeneas.

Aeneas. Is the prince there in person?
  Had I so good occasion to lie long
  As you, Prince Paris, nothing but heavenly business
5 Should rob my bedmate of my company.

Diomedes. That's my mind too. Good morrow, Lord
  Aeneas.

Paris. A valiant Greek, Aeneas; take his hand.
  Witness the process° of your speech, wherein
  You told how Diomed, a whole week by days,°
  Did haunt you in the field.

10 *Aeneas.*   Health to you, valiant sir,
  During all question of the gentle truce;°

4.1.8 **process** gist, drift   9 **by days** day by day   11 **question of the
gentle truce** i.e., intercourse made possible by the truce

But when I meet you armed, as black defiance
As heart can think or courage execute.

Diomedes. The one and other Diomed embraces.
Our bloods are now in calm, and, so long, health!   *15*
But when contention and occasion° meet,
By Jove, I'll play the hunter for thy life
With all my force, pursuit, and policy.°

Aeneas. And thou shalt hunt a lion that will fly
With his face backward. In humane gentleness,
Welcome to Troy. Now, by Anchises'° life,   *20*
Welcome indeed! By Venus' hand° I swear,
No man alive can love in such a sort
The thing he means to kill more excellently.

Diomedes. We sympathize.° Jove, let Aeneas live,   *25*
If to my sword his fate be not the glory,
A thousand complete courses of the sun!
But, in mine emulous honor, let him die
With every joint a wound, and that tomorrow!

Aeneas. We know each other well.   *30*

Diomedes. We do, and long to know each other worse.

Paris. This is the most despiteful gentle greeting,
The noblest hateful love, that e'er I heard of.
What business, lord, so early?

Aeneas. I was sent for to the king; but why, I know
not.   *35*

Paris. His purpose meets you; it was to bring this
Greek
To Calchas' house, and there to render him,
For the enfreed Antenor, the fair Cressid.
Let's have your company; or, if you please,
Haste there before us. I constantly° do think—   *40*
Or rather call my thought a certain knowledge—
My brother Troilus lodges there tonight.

16 **occasion** opportunity   18 **policy** cunning   21 **Anchises** (Aeneas'
father)   22 **Venus' hand** (Diomedes was supposed to have wounded
Venus, Aeneas' mother, in the hand)   25 **sympathize** have the same
feeling   40 **constantly** firmly

Rouse him and give him note of our approach,
With the whole quality° wherefore. I fear
We shall be much unwelcome.

45 *Aeneas.*   That I assure you.
Troilus had rather Troy were borne to Greece
Than Cressid borne from Troy.

Paris.   There is no help.
The bitter disposition of the time
Will have it so. On, lord; we'll follow you.

50 *Aeneas.* Good morrow, all.   *Exit Aeneas.*

Paris. And tell me, noble Diomed; faith, tell me true,
Even in the soul of sound good-fellowship,
Who, in your thoughts, deserves fair Helen best,
Myself or Menelaus?

Diomedes.   Both alike.
55 He merits well to have her that doth seek her,
Not making any scruple of her soilure,
With such a hell of pain and world of charge;°
And you as well to keep her that defend her,
Not palating° the taste of her dishonor,
60 With such a costly loss of wealth and friends.
He, like a puling cuckold, would drink up
The lees and dregs of a flat tamèd piece;°
You, like a lecher, out of whorish loins
Are pleased to breed out your inheritors.
65 Both merits poised,° each weighs nor less nor more;
But he as he, the heavier for a whore.°

Paris. You are too bitter to your countrywoman.

Diomedes. She's bitter to her country! Hear me,
Paris—

---

44 **quality** occasion, explanation   57 **charge** cost   59 **Not palating**
insensible to   62 **flat tamèd piece** (1) cask of wine opened so long that
the wine has gone flat (2) woman so promiscuous that she can no longer
excite or be excited sexually   65 **poised** weighed   66 **But he . . . a
whore** (1) but he, i.e., Menelaus, as heavy as his small merit may be, plus
the weight of the whore who is, after all, his legal possession (?); (2) but
he, whoever wins her, heavier only by the weight of a whore (to be
"light" was to be morally loose) (?)

For every false drop in her bawdy veins
A Grecian's life hath sunk; for every scruple°   70
Of her contaminated carrion weight
A Troyan hath been slain. Since she could speak,
She hath not given so many good words breath
As for her Greeks and Troyans suffered death.

Paris. Fair Diomed, you do as chapmen° do,   75
Dispraise the thing that you desire to buy;
But we in silence hold this virtue well,
We'll not commend what we intend to sell.°
Here lies our way.   *Exeunt.*

[Scene 2. *Within Troy; Calchas' house.*]

Enter Troilus and Cressida.

Troilus. Dear, trouble not yourself; the morn is cold.

Cressida. Then, sweet my lord, I'll call mine uncle
     down;
He shall unbolt the gates.

Troilus.   Trouble him not;
To bed, to bed. Sleep kill° those pretty eyes,
And give as soft attachment° to thy senses   5
As infants' empty of all thought!

Cressida.   Good morrow then.

Troilus. I prithee now, to bed.

Cressida.   Are you aweary of me?

Troilus. O Cressida! But that the busy day,

---

70 **scruple** (the smallest possible unit of weight)· 75 **chapmen**
hawkers of cheap wares   78 **We'll not . . . to sell** i.e., we'll not practice
the seller's tricks although you practice the buyer's (Paris does not imply
that Helen is for sale)   4.2.4 **kill** overpower   5 **attachment** seizure

Waked by the lark, hath roused the ribald crows,
10   And dreaming night will hide our joys no longer,
I would not from thee.

Cressida.   Night hath been too brief.

Troilus. Beshrew the witch! With venomous wights°
        she stays
    As tediously as hell, but flies the grasps of love
    With wings more momentary-swift than thought.
    You will catch cold and curse me.

15 *Cressida.*   Prithee, tarry;
    You men will never tarry.
    O foolish Cressid! I might have still held off,
    And then you would have tarried. Hark, there's one
        up.

Pandarus. (Within) What's all the doors open here?

20 *Troilus.* It is your uncle.

Cressida. A pestilence on him! Now will he be mock-
        ing.
    I shall have such a life.

Enter Pandarus.

Pandarus. How now, how now! How go maidenheads?
    Here, you maid, where's my cousin Cressid?

Cressida. Go hang yourself, you naughty mocking
25   uncle.
    You bring me to do°—and then you flout me too.

Pandarus. To do what? To do what? Let her say what.
    What have I brought you to do?

Cressida. Come come; beshrew your heart! You'll
        ne'er be good,
30   Nor suffer others.

Pandarus. Ha, ha! Alas, poor wretch! A poor capòc-

---

12 **venomous wights** malignant witches (or, simply, evil creatures)
26 **do** (used sometimes in obscene sense)

chia!° Hast not slept tonight? Would he not, a
naughty man, let it sleep? A bugbear° take him!

Cressida. Did not I tell you? Would he were knocked
   i' the head!   *One knocks.*
Who's that at door? Good uncle, go and see.   35
My lord, come you again into my chamber.
You smile and mock me, as if I meant naughtily.

Troilus. Ha, ha!

Cressida. Come, you are deceived, I think of no such
   thing.   *Knock.*
How earnestly they knock! Pray you, come in.   40
I would not for half Troy have you seen here.
                    Exeunt [*Troilus and Cressida*].

Pandarus. Who's there? What's the matter? Will you
beat down the door? How now, what's the matter?

[*Enter Aeneas.*]

Aeneas. Good morrow, lord, good morrow.

Pandarus. Who's there? My Lord Aeneas! By my
   troth,   45
I knew you not. What news with you so early?

Aeneas. Is not Prince Troilus here?

Pandarus. Here? What should he do here?

Aeneas. Come, he is here, my lord. Do not deny him.
It doth import° him much to speak with me.   50

Pandarus. Is he here, say you? 'Tis more than I know,
I'll be sworn. For my own part, I came in late.
What should he do here?

Aeneas. Who!° Nay, then. Come, come, you'll do him
wrong ere you are ware. You'll be so true to him, to   55

31–32 **capocchia** simpleton   33 **bugbear** hobgoblin   50 **doth import**
is important to   54 **Who!** (an exclamation of impatience; sometimes as
to call "stop!" to a horse)

be false to him. Do not you know of him, but yet
go fetch him hither; go.

Enter Troilus.

Troilus. How now, what's the matter?

Aeneas. My lord, I scarce have leisure to salute you,
60   My matter is so rash.° There is at hand
      Paris your brother, and Deiphobus,
      The Grecian Diomed, and our Antenor
      Delivered to us; and for him forthwith,
      Ere the first sacrifice, within this hour,
65   We must give up to Diomedes' hand
      The Lady Cressida.

Troilus.   Is it so concluded?

Aeneas. By Priam, and the general state° of Troy.
      They are at hand and ready to effect it.

Troilus. How my achievements mock me!
70   I will go meet them. And, my Lord Aeneas,
      We met by chance; you did not find me here.

Aeneas. Good, good, my lord; the secrets° of nature
      Have not more gift in taciturnity.
                          Exeunt [Troilus and Aeneas].

Pandarus. Is't possible? No sooner got but lost? The
75   devil take Antenor! The young prince will go mad.
      A plague upon Antenor! I would they had broke 's
      neck!

Enter Cressida.

Cressida. How now? What's the matter? Who was
      here?

80 *Pandarus.* Ah, ah!

Cressida. Why sigh you so profoundly? Where's my

---

60 **rash** urgent   67 **general state** noblemen in council   72 **secrets**
most unknown parts

lord? Gone? Tell me, sweet uncle, what's the matter?

Pandarus. Would I were as deep under the earth as
I am above!   *85*

Cressida. O the gods! What's the matter?

Pandarus. Pray thee, get thee in. Would thou hadst
ne'er been born! I knew thou wouldst be his death.
O poor gentleman! A plague upon Antenor!

Cressida. Good uncle, I beseech you on my knees,   *90*
what's the matter?

Pandarus. Thou must be gone, wench, thou must be
gone; thou art changed° for Antenor. Thou must
to thy father and be gone from Troilus. 'Twill be
his death; 'twill be his bane;° he cannot bear it.   *95*

Cressida. O you immortal gods! I will not go.

Pandarus. Thou must.

Cressida. I will not, uncle. I have forgot my father;
I know no touch of consanguinity°—
No kin, no love, no blood, no soul so near me   *100*
As the sweet Troilus. O you gods divine,
Make Cressid's name the very crown of falsehood
If ever she leave Troilus! Time, force, and death,
Do to this body what extremes you can;
But the strong base and building of my love   *105*
Is as the very center of the earth,
Drawing all things to it. I will go in and weep——

Pandarus. Do, do.

Cressida. —Tear my bright hair, and scratch my
     praisèd cheeks,
Crack my clear voice with sobs, and break my   *110*
     heart
With sounding Troilus. I will not go from Troy.
                         Exeunt.

---

93 **changed** exchanged   95 **bane** poison, destruction   99 **no touch of
consanguinity** no sense of relationship

[Scene 3. *Within Troy; near Calchas' house.*]

Enter Paris, Troilus, Aeneas, Deiphobus, Antenor,
Diomedes.

Paris. It is great morning,° and the hour prefixed
    For her delivery to this valiant Greek
    Comes fast upon. Good my brother Troilus,
    Tell you the lady what she is to do,
    And haste her to the purpose.

5 *Troilus.*   Walk into her house.
    I'll bring her to the Grecian presently;°
    And to his hand when I deliver her,
    Think it an altar, and thy brother Troilus
    A priest there off'ring to it his own heart.

10 *Paris.* I know what 'tis to love;
    And would, as I shall pity, I could help.
    Please you walk in, my lords.   *Exeunt.*

[Scene 4. *Within Troy; Calchas' house.*]

Enter Pandarus and Cressida.

Pandarus. Be moderate, be moderate.

Cressida. Why tell you me of moderation?
    The grief is fine, full, perfect, that I taste,
    And violenteth° in a sense as strong

4.3.1 **great morning** broad daylight **6 presently** immediately
4.4.4 **violenteth** rages

As that which causeth it. How can I moderate it?　*5*
If I could temporize with my affections,
Or brew it to a weak and colder palate,°
The like allayment could I give my grief.
My love admits no qualifying dross;°
No more my grief, in such a precious loss.　*10*

Enter Troilus.

Pandarus. Here, here, here he comes. Ah, sweet ducks!

Cressida. O Troilus! Troilus!

Pandarus. What a pair of spectacles° is here! Let me embrace too. "O heart," as the goodly saying is—　*15*
　O heart, heavy heart,
　Why sigh'st thou without breaking?
where he answers again,
　Because thou canst not ease thy smart
　By friendship nor by speaking.　*20*
There was never a truer rhyme. Let us cast away nothing, for we may live to have need of such a verse. We see it, we see it. How now, lambs!

Troilus. Cressid, I love thee in so strained° a purity,
That the blest gods, as angry with my fancy,°　*25*
More bright in zeal than the devotion which
Cold lips blow to their deities, take thee from me.

Cressida. Have the gods envy?

Pandarus. Ay, ay, ay, ay, 'tis too plain a case.

Cressida. And is it true that I must go from Troy?　*30*

Troilus. A hateful truth.

Cressida. 　　　　　　　What, and from Troilus too?

Troilus. From Troy and Troilus.

Cressida. 　　　　　　　Is't possible?

---

7 **palate** taste　9 **qualifying dross** moderating impurity　14 **spectacles** (a pun)　24 **strained** distilled, filtered　25 **fancy** love

Troilus. And suddenly, where injury of chance°
Puts back leave-taking, justles roughly by
35 All time of pause, rudely beguiles our lips
Of all rejoindure,° forcibly prevents
Our locked embrasures, strangles our dear vows
Even in the birth of our own laboring breath.
We two, that with so many thousand sighs
40 Did buy each other, must poorly sell ourselves
With the rude brevity and discharge of one.
Injurious time now with a robber's haste
Crams his rich thievery up, he knows not how;
As many farewells as be stars in heaven,
45 With distinct breath and consigned kisses to them,°
He fumbles° up into a loose adieu,
And scants us with a single famished kiss,
Distasted° with the salt of broken tears.

Aeneas. (*Within*) My lord, is the lady ready?

50 *Troilus.* Hark! You are called. Some say the Genius°
Cries so to him that instantly must die.
Bid them have patience; she shall come anon.

Pandarus. Where are my tears? Rain, to lay this wind,
or my heart will be blown up by the root! [*Exit.*]

Cressida. I must, then, to the Grecians?

55 *Troilus.*   No remedy.

Cressida. A woeful Cressid 'mongst the merry Greeks!
When shall we see again?

Troilus. Hear me, love. Be thou but true of heart— —

Cressida. I true! How now! What wicked deem° is
this?

60 *Troilus.* Nay, we must use expostulation kindly,

33 **injury of chance** injurious accident 36 **rejoindure** reunion
45 **With distinct ... to them** with the words of each farewell and the
kisses which ratify each of them 46 **fumbles** wraps clumsily 48 **Distasted** the taste (of the kiss) ruined 50 **Genius** guardian spirit 59
deem thought

For it is parting from us.°
I speak not "be thou true" as fearing thee,
For I will throw my glove° to Death himself
That there's no maculation° in thy heart;
But "be thou true," say I, to fashion in   65
My sequent protestation:° be thou true,
And I will see thee.

Cressida. O, you shall be exposed, my lord, to dangers
As infinite as imminent; but I'll be true.

Troilus. And I'll grow friend with danger. Wear this
    sleeve.   70

Cressida. And you this glove. When shall I see you?

Troilus. I will corrupt the Grecian sentinels,
To give thee nightly visitation.
But yet, be true.

Cressida.   O heavens! "Be true" again!

Troilus. Hear why I speak it, love.   75
The Grecian youths are full of quality;°
They're loving,° well composed with gift of nature,
And swelling o'er with arts and exercise.°
How novelty may move, and parts with person,°
Alas! A kind of godly jealousy—   80
Which, I beseech you, call a virtuous sin—
Makes me afeared.

Cressida.   O heavens, you love me not!

Troilus. Die I a villain then!
In this I do not call your faith in question
So mainly as my merit. I cannot sing,   85

60–61 **Nay, we ... from us** we must be gentle in all remonstrance, for
we are now saying good-bye   63 **throw my glove** give challenge
64 **maculation** taint, blemish (i.e., disloyalty)   65–66 **to fashion in ...
sequent protestation** as introduction for my own promise to follow
76 **quality** qualities   77 **loving** adept in the arts of love   78 **arts and
exercise** talents both in theory and practice   79 **parts with person** specific qualities and talents, combined with personal charm

Nor heel the high lavolt,° nor sweeten talk,
Nor play at subtle games—fair virtues all,
To which the Grecians are most prompt and preg-
          nant;°
But I can tell that in each grace of these
90   There lurks a still and dumb-discoursive° devil
That tempts most cunningly. But be not tempted.

Cressida. Do you think I will?

Troilus. No!
But something may be done that we will not;
95   And sometimes we are devils to ourselves
When we will tempt the frailty of our powers,
Presuming on their changeful potency.°

Aeneas. (Within) Nay, good my lord!

Troilus.   Come, kiss; and
          let us part.

Paris. (Within) Brother Troilus!

Troilus.   Good brother, come
          you hither;
100   And bring Aeneas and the Grecian with you.

Cressida. My lord, will you be true?

Troilus. Who? I? Alas, it is my vice, my fault.
Whiles others fish with craft for great opinion,°
I with great truth catch° mere simplicity;
105   Whilst some with cunning gild their copper crowns,
With truth and plainness I do wear mine bare.
Fear not my truth; the moral° of my wit
Is "plain and true"—there's all the reach of it.

          [*Enter Aeneas, Paris, Antenor, Deiphobus and*
                              Diomedes.]

Welcome, Sir Diomed. Here is the lady

86 **the high lavolt** (the lavolt was a dance for two persons, requiring
many high steps and bounds)   88 **pregnant** ready, fully able   90
dumb-discoursive articulate even in silence   97 **changeful potency**
power which may alter to failure   103 **opinion** reputation   104 **catch**
achieve; i.e., achieve a reputation for   107 **moral** maxim

Which for Antenor we deliver you.   *110*
At the port,° lord, I'll give her to thy hand,
And by the way possess° thee what she is.
Entreat° her fair; and, by my soul, fair Greek,
If e'er thou stand at mercy of my sword,
Name Cressid, and thy life shall be as safe   *115*
As Priam is in Ilion.

Diomedes.   Fair Lady Cressid,
So please you, save the thanks this prince expects.
The luster in your eye, heaven in your cheek,
Pleads your fair usage; and to Diomed
You shall be mistress, and command him wholly.   *120*

Troilus. Grecian, thou dost not use me courteously,
To shame the seal of my petition° to thee
In praising her. I tell thee, lord of Greece,
She is as far high-soaring o'er thy praises
As thou unworthy to be called her servant.   *125*
I charge thee use her well, even for my charge;°
For, by the dreadful Pluto, if thou dost not,
Though the great bulk Achilles be thy guard,
I'll cut thy throat.

Diomedes.   O, be not moved, Prince Troilus.
Let me be privileged by my place and message   *130*
To be a speaker free. When I am hence,
I'll answer to my lust;° and know you, lord,
I'll nothing do on charge. To her own worth
She shall be prized; but that you say "be't so,"
I speak it in my spirit and honor, "no."   *135*

Troilus. Come, to the port. I'll tell thee, Diomed,
This brave° shall oft make thee to hide thy head.
Lady, give me your hand, and, as we walk,
To our own selves bend we our needful talk.
               [*Exeunt Troilus, Cressida, and Diomedes.*]
                                   Sound trumpet.

---

111 **port** gate (of the city)   112 **possess** inform   113 **Entreat** treat
122 **To shame the seal of my petition** to disdain the worth of my charge
and promise   126 **even for my charge** simply because I say so   132
answer to my lust do as I please   137 **brave** boast

Paris. Hark! Hector's trumpet.

Aeneas.   How have we spent this
140   morning!
        The prince must think me tardy and remiss,
        That swore to ride before him to the field.

Paris. 'Tis Troilus' fault. Come, come, to field with
        him.

Deiphobus. Let us make ready straight.

145 *Aeneas*. Yea, with a bridegroom's fresh alacrity,
        Let us address° to tend on Hector's heels.
        The glory of our Troy doth this day lie
        On his fair worth and single chivalry.   *Exeunt*.

                [Scene 5. *The Greek camp*.]

        *Enter Ajax, armed; Achilles, Patroclus, Agamemnon,
            Menelaus, Ulysses, Nestor, Calchas, &c.*

Agamemnon. Here art thou in appointment° fresh and
        fair,
        Anticipating time. With starting° courage,
        Give with thy trumpet a loud note to Troy,
        Thou dreadful Ajax, that the appallèd air
5   May pierce the head of the great combatant
        And hale him hither.

Ajax.   Thou, trumpet,° there's my
        purse.
        Now crack thy lungs, and split thy brazen pipe.
        Blow, villain, till thy spherèd bias° cheek
        Outswell the colic of puffed Aquilon!°

146 **address** prepare   4.5.1 **appointment** equipment and apparel
2 **starting** active, prompt   6 **trumpet** trumpeter   8 **bias** puffed-out
9 **the colic of puffed Aquilon** the north wind, distended as if by colic

Come, stretch thy chest, and let thy eyes spout
   blood;   10
Thou blow'st for Hector.   [*Trumpet sounds.*]

Ulysses. No trumpet answers.

Achilles.   'Tis but early days.°

Agamemnon. Is not yond Diomed with Calchas'
   daughter?

Ulysses. 'Tis he, I ken the manner of his gait;
He rises on the toe. That spirit of his   15
In aspiration lifts him from the earth.

   [*Enter Diomedes, with Cressida.*]

Agamemnon. Is this the Lady Cressid?

Diomedes.   Even she.

Agamemnon. Most dearly welcome to the Greeks,
   sweet lady.

Nestor. Our general doth salute you with a kiss.

Ulysses. Yet is the kindness but particular.°   20
'Twere better she were kissed in general.°

Nestor. And very courtly counsel. I'll begin.
So much for Nestor.

Achilles. I'll take that winter° from your lips, fair
   lady.
Achilles bids you welcome.   25

Menelaus. I had good argument for kissing once.

Patroclus. But that's no argument for kissing now;
For thus popped Paris in his hardiment,°
And parted thus you and your argument.°

Ulysses. O, deadly gall, and theme of all our scorns,   30

---

12 **days** in the day 20 **particular** single 21 **in general** (1) by the
general (2) universally 24 **that winter** i.e., Nestor's kiss (cold from
old age) 28 **hardiment** boldness 29 **argument** i.e., Helen

For which we lose our heads to gild his horns.

Patroclus. The first was Menelaus' kiss; this, mine.
Patroclus kisses you.

Menelaus.   O, this is trim.

Patroclus. Paris and I kiss evermore for him.

35 *Menelaus*. I'll have my kiss, sir. Lady, by your leave.

Cressida. In kissing, do you render or receive?

Patroclus. Both take and give.

Cressida.   I'll make my match to
   live,°
The kiss you take is better than you give;
Therefore no kiss.

40 *Menelaus*. I'll give you boot;° I'll give you three for
   one.

Cressida. You are an odd° man; give even, or give
   none.

Menelaus. An odd man, lady? Every man is odd.

Cressida. No, Paris is not, for you know 'tis true
   That you are odd and he is even with you.

Menelaus. You fillip° me o' the head.

45 *Cressida*.   No, I'll be sworn.

Ulysses. It were no match, your nail against his
   horn.°
May I, sweet lady, beg a kiss of you?

Cressida. You may.

Ulysses.   I do desire it.

Cressida.   Why, beg then.

37 **I'll ... match to live** I'll bet my life   40 **boot** odds   41 **odd** i.e.,
single and singular   45 **fillip** tap   46 **It ... horn** your nail, in tapping,
would be no match for his hard cuckold's horn

Ulysses. Why, then, for Venus' sake, give me a kiss,
When Helen is a maid again, and his.   50

Cressida. I am your debtor; claim it when 'tis due.

Ulysses. Never's my day, and then a kiss of you.

Diomedes. Lady, a word. I'll bring you to your father.
[*Exeunt Diomedes and Cressida.*]

Nestor. A woman of quick sense.

Ulysses.   Fie, fie upon her!°
There's language in her eye, her cheek, her lip;   55
Nay, her foot speaks. Her wanton spirits look out
At every joint and motive° of her body.
O, these encounterers, so glib of tongue,
That give a coasting welcome ere it comes,°
And wide unclasp the tables° of their thoughts   60
To every ticklish reader, set them down
For sluttish spoils of opportunity°
And daughters of the game.°

*Flourish. Enter all of Troy [Hector, Paris, Aeneas,
Helenus, Troilus, and Attendants].*

All. The Troyans' trumpet.°

Agamemnon.   Yonder comes the troop.

Aeneas. Hail, all the state of Greece. What shall be
done   65
To him that victory commands? Or do you purpose
A victor shall be known? Will you the knights
Shall to the edge of all extremity
Pursue each other, or shall they be divided°

54 **Fie, fie upon her!** (Ulysses' exclamation does not imply disagreement with Nestor's observation; the following nine lines elaborate "quick sense") 57 **motive** moving part 59 **a coasting welcome ere it comes** a sidelong, flirtatious greeting before being greeted 60 **tables** tablets 62 **sluttish spoils of opportunity** harlots who yield at every opportunity 63 **daughters of the game** whores 64 **The Troyans' trumpet** (in the theater, this line becomes a pun on "strumpet") 69 **divided** i.e., separated during the fight

70   By any voice or order of the field?
      Hector bade ask.

Agamemnon.   Which way would Hector have it?

Aeneas. He cares not; he'll obey conditions.

Achilles. 'Tis done like Hector; but securely° done,
      A little proudly, and great deal misprising
      The knight opposed.

75 *Aeneas.*   If not Achilles, sir.
      What is your name?

Achilles.   If not Achilles, nothing.

Aeneas. Therefore Achilles; but, whate'er, know this:
      In the extremity of great and little,
      Valor and pride excel themselves in Hector;
80   The one almost as infinite as all,
      The other blank as nothing. Weigh him well;
      And that which looks like pride is courtesy.
      This Ajax is half made of Hector's blood,°
      In love whereof half Hector stays at home;
85   Half heart, half hand, half Hector comes to seek
      This blended knight, half Troyan, and half Greek.

Achilles. A maiden° battle, then? O, I perceive you.

            [*Enter Diomedes.*]

Agamemnon. Here is Sir Diomed. Go, gentle knight,
      Stand by our Ajax. As you and Lord Aeneas
90   Consent upon the order of their fight,
      So be it; either to the uttermost,
      Or else a breath.° The combatants being kin
      Half stints their strife before their strokes begin.
                  [*Ajax and Hector enter the lists.*]

Ulysses. They are opposed already.

---

73 **securely** overconfidently   83 **Hector's blood** (see note to 2.2.77)
87 **maiden** bloodless (as of novices or men in training, who do not
intend to kill)   92 **breath** exercise

Agamemnon. What Troyan is that same that looks so
    heavy?°   *95*

Ulysses. The youngest son of Priam, a true knight,
    Not yet mature, yet matchless; firm of word,
    Speaking in deeds and deedless in his tongue,°
    Not soon provoked, nor being provoked soon
    calmed;
    His heart and hand both open and both free,°   *100*
    For what he has he gives, what thinks he shows;
    Yet gives he not till judgment guide his bounty,
    Nor dignifies an impare thought° with breath;
    Manly as Hector, but more dangerous;
    For Hector, in his blaze of wrath, subscribes   *105*
    To tender objects,° but he in heat of action
    Is more vindicative than jealous love.
    They call him Troilus, and on him erect
    A second hope as fairly built as Hector.
    Thus says Aeneas, one that knows the youth   *110*
    Even to his inches,° and with private soul°
    Did in great Ilion thus translate him to me.
                    Alarum. [*Hector and Ajax fight.*]

Agamemnon. They are in action.

Nestor. Now, Ajax, hold thine own!

Troilus.   Hector, thou
    sleep'st; awake thee!

Agamemnon. His blows are well disposed.° There,
    Ajax!   *115*

Diomedes. You must no more.   *Trumpets cease.*

Aeneas.   Princes, enough, so please
    you.

---

95 **heavy** heavyhearted 98 **deedless in his tongue** free of boasts
100 **free** generous 103 **impare thought** (1) ill-considered thought
(2) thought unequal to the dignity of his character 105–06 **sub-
scribes/To tender objects** grants merciful terms to the defenseless 111
Even to his inches i.e., from head to toe 111 **with private soul** in confidence 115 **well disposed** well aimed, well placed

Ajax. I am not warm yet; let us fight again.

Diomedes. As Hector pleases.

Hector. Why, then will I no more.
Thou art, great lord, my father's sister's son,
120 A cousin-german to great Priam's seed;
The obligation of our blood forbids
A gory emulation 'twixt us twain.
Were thy commixtion° Greek and Troyan so
That thou couldst say, "This hand is Grecian all,
125 And this is Troyan; the sinews of this leg
All Greek, and this all Troy; my mother's blood
Runs on the dexter° cheek, and this sinister°
Bounds in my father's," by Jove multipotent,°
Thou shouldst not bear from me a Greekish member
Wherein my sword had not impressure made
130 Of our rank feud. But the just gods gainsay
That any drop thou borrow'dst from thy mother,
My sacred aunt, should by my mortal sword
Be drained! Let me embrace thee, Ajax—
135 By him that thunders,° thou hast lusty arms;
Hector would have them fall upon him thus.°
Cousin, all honor to thee!

Ajax. I thank thee, Hector;
Thou art too gentle and too free a man.
I came to kill thee, cousin, and bear hence
140 A great addition earnèd in thy death.

Hector. Not Neoptolemus° so mirable,°
On whose bright crest Fame with her loud'st
"Oyes"°
Cries, "This is he!" could promise to himself
A thought of added honor torn from Hector.

---

123 **commixtion** composition 127 **dexter** right 127 **sinister** left
128 **multipotent** of many powers 135 **him that thunders** i.e., Jove
(Zeus) 136 **thus** i.e., embracing him 141 **Neoptolemus** (this name
probably applies here to Achilles himself, and not to his son, Pyrrhus)
141 **mirable** wonderful 142 **Oyes** cries beginning the proclamations
of heralds or sessions of a court

Aeneas. There is expectance here from both the sides,   *145*
    What further you will do.

Hector.   We'll answer it.
    The issue° is embracement. Ajax, farewell.

Ajax. If I might in entreaties find success—
    As seld° I have the chance—I would desire
    My famous cousin to our Grecian tents.   *150*

Diomedes. 'Tis Agamemnon's wish; and great Achilles
    Doth long to see unarmed the valiant Hector.

Hector. Aeneas, call my brother Troilus to me,
    And signify° this loving interview
    To the expecters of our Troyan part.°   *155*
    Desire them home.° Give me thy hand, my cousin;
    I will go eat with thee and see your knights.

    [*Agamemnon and the rest approach them.*]

Ajax. Great Agamemnon comes to meet us here.

Hector. The worthiest of them tell me name by name;
    But for Achilles, my own searching eyes   *160*
    Shall find him by his large and portly size.

Agamemnon. Worthy all arms [*embraces him*], as wel-
      come as to one
    That would be rid of such an enemy—
    But that's no welcome. Understand more clear,
    What's past and what's to come is strewed with
      husks   *165*
    And formless ruin of oblivion;
    But in this extant° moment, faith and troth,
    Strained purely from all hollow bias-drawing,°
    Bids thee, with most divine integrity,
    From heart of very heart, great Hector, welcome. *170*

---

147 **issue** result, outcome   149 **seld** seldom   154 **signify** expound,
explain   155 **the expecters of our Troyan part** those on our side, the
Trojans, awaiting news   156 **Desire them home** ask them to go home
167 **extant** present   168 **all hollow bias-drawing** all fruitless and tor-
tuous dealings (in the course of the war, as in the course given by the bias
of a bowl in bowling)

Hector. I thank thee, most imperious Agamemnon.

Agamemnon. [*To Troilus*] My well-famed lord of Troy, no less to you.

Menelaus. Let me confirm my princely brother's greeting.
You brace of warlike brothers, welcome hither.

Hector. Who must we answer?

175 *Aeneas.*   The noble Menelaus.

Hector. O, you, my lord? By Mars his gauntlet, thanks!
Mock not that I affect th' untraded° oath;
Your quondam° wife swears still by Venus' glove.
She's well, but bade me not commend her to you.

Menelaus. Name her not now, sir; she's a deadly
180   theme.

Hector. O, pardon! I offend.

Nestor. I have, thou gallant Troyan, seen thee oft,
Laboring for destiny,° make cruel way
Through ranks of Greekish youth; and I have seen thee,
185 As hot as Perseus, spur thy Phrygian steed,
Despising many forfeits and subduements,°
When thou hast hung° thy advancèd sword i' th' air,
Not letting it decline on the declinèd,
That I have said to some my standers-by,
190 "Lo, Jupiter is yonder, dealing life!"°
And I have seen thee pause and take thy breath,

177 **untraded** unusual, unfamiliar (Hector, apologizing for what might appear to be an affected oath, gives his reason for using it in the following line, in which he completes a satirical reference to Menelaus and Helen by alluding to the liaison between Mars and Venus) 178 **quondam** former   183 **Laboring for destiny** working in behalf of destiny, i.e., causing destined deaths   186 **Despising many forfeits and subduements** ignoring or disdaining those already vanquished, whose lives were forfeit   187 **hung** held suspended   190 **dealing life** dispensing life (as a god might do by not causing death)

When that a ring of Greeks have shraped° thee in,
Like an Olympian wrestling. This have I seen;
But this thy countenance, still° locked in steel,
I never saw till now. I knew thy grandsire,°   195
And once fought with him. He was a soldier good;
But, by great Mars, the captain of us all,
Never like thee. O, let an old man embrace thee;
And, worthy warrior, welcome to our tents.

Aeneas. 'Tis the old Nestor.   200

Hector. Let me embrace thee, good old chronicle,
That hast so long walked hand in hand with time.
Most reverend Nestor, I am glad to clasp thee.

Nestor. I would my arms could match thee in conten-
    tion,
As they contend with thee in courtesy.   205

Hector. I would they could.

Nestor. Ha,
By this white beard, I'd fight with thee tomorrow.
Well, welcome, welcome. I have seen the time——

Ulysses. I wonder now how yonder city stands,   210
When we have here her base and pillar by us.

Hector. I know your favor,° Lord Ulysses, well.
Ah, sir, there's many a Greek and Troyan dead,
Since first I saw yourself and Diomed
In Ilion, on your Greekish embassy.   215

Ulysses. Sir, I foretold you then what would ensue.
My prophecy is but half his journey yet;
For yonder walls, that pertly front your town,
Yon towers, whose wanton tops do buss° the clouds,
Must kiss their own feet.

Hector.   I must not believe you.   220
There they stand yet, and modestly I think,

192 **shraped** trapped   194 **still** always   195 **grandsire** (Laomedon,
the builder of Troy)   212 **favor** face, features   219 **buss** kiss

The fall of every Phrygian stone will cost
A drop of Grecian blood. The end crowns all,
And that old common arbitrator, Time,
Will one day end it.

225 *Ulysses*.   So to him we leave it.
Most gentle and most valiant Hector, welcome.
After the general, I beseech you next
To feast with me and see me at my tent.

Achilles. I shall forestall thee, Lord Ulysses, thou!
230 Now, Hector, I have fed mine eyes on thee;
I have with exact view perused thee, Hector,
And quoted° joint by joint.

Hector.   Is this Achilles?

Achilles. I am Achilles.

Hector. Stand fair,° I pray thee; let me look on thee.

Achilles. Behold thy fill.

235 *Hector*.   Nay, I have done already.

Achilles. Thou art too brief. I will the second time,
As I would buy thee, view thee limb by limb.

Hector. O, like a book of sport thou'lt read me o'er;
But there's more in me than thou understand'st.
240 Why dost thou so oppress me with thine eye?

Achilles. Tell me, you heavens, in which part of his
body
Shall I destroy him, whether there, or there, or
there?
That I may give the local wound a name,
And make distinct the very breach whereout
245 Hector's great spirit flew. Answer me, heavens!

Hector. It would discredit the blessed gods, proud man,
To answer such a question. Stand again.
Think'st thou to catch my life so pleasantly°

232 **quoted** made exact mental note, scrutinized   234 **Stand fair** stand
openly, face me   248 **pleasantly** casually, merrily

As to prenominate in nice conjecture°
Where thou wilt hit me dead?

Achilles. I tell thee, yea. 250

Hector. Wert thou an oracle to tell me so,
I'd not believe thee. Henceforth guard thee well,
For I'll not kill thee there, nor there, nor there;
But, by the forge that stithied° Mars his helm,
I'll kill thee everywhere, yea, o'er and o'er. 255
You wisest Grecians, pardon me this brag.
His insolence draws folly from my lips;
But I'll endeavor deeds to match these words,
Or may I never——

Ajax. Do not chafe thee, cousin;
And you, Achilles, let these threats alone, 260
Till accident or purpose bring you to't.
You may have every day enough of Hector,
If you have stomach.° The general state,° I fear,
Can scarce entreat you to be odd° with him.

Hector. I pray you, let us see you in the field. 265
We have had pelting° wars since you refused
The Grecians' cause.

Achilles. Dost thou entreat° me, Hector?
Tomorrow do I meet thee, fell° as death;
Tonight all friends.

Hector. Thy hand upon that match.

Agamemnon. First, all you peers of Greece, go to my
tent; 270
There in the full convive° we. Afterwards,
As Hector's leisure and your bounties shall
Concur together, severally° entreat him
To taste your bounties. Let the trumpets blow,

---

249 **prenominate in nice conjecture** name beforehand in detailed
conjecture   254 **stithied** forged   263 **stomach** inclination, relish   263
general state commanders in council   264 **odd** at odds, engaged in
combat   266 **pelting** paltry, petty   267 **entreat** invite   268 **fell** fierce
271 **convive** feast   273 **severally** individually

275   That this great soldier may his welcome know.
                    Exeunt [all except Troilus and Ulysses].

     Troilus. My Lord Ulysses, tell me, I beseech you,
          In what place of the field doth Calchas keep?°

     Ulysses. At Menelaus' tent, most princely Troilus.
          There Diomed doth feast with him tonight—
280   Who neither looks upon the heaven nor earth,
          But gives all gaze and bent of amorous view
          On the fair Cressid.

     Troilus. Shall I, sweet lord, be bound to you so much,
          After we part from Agamemnon's tent,
          To bring me thither?

285 *Ulysses.*   You shall command me, sir.
          But gentle tell me, of what honor was
          This Cressida in Troy? Had she no lover there
          That wails her absence?

     Troilus. O, sir, to such as boasting show their scars
290   A mock is due. Will you walk on, my lord?
          She was beloved, she loved; she is, and doth;
          But still sweet love is food for fortune's tooth.
                                      Exeunt.

277 **keep** dwell

ACT 5

[Scene 1. *The Greek camp.*]

Enter Achilles and Patroclus.

Achilles. I'll heat his blood with Greekish wine to-
night,
Which with my scimitar I'll cool tomorrow.
Patroclus, let us feast him to the height.

Enter Thersites.

Patroclus. Here comes Thersites.

Achilles.   How now, thou cur of
envy!
Thou crusty batch° of nature, what's the news?   5

Thersites. Why, thou picture of what thou seemest,°
and idol of idiot-worshipers, here's a letter for thee.

Achilles. From whence, fragment?

Thersites. Why, thou full dish of fool, from Troy.

10 *Patroclus.* Who keeps the tent now?°

Thersites. The surgeon's box or the patient's wound.°

Patroclus. Well said, adversity, and what needs these tricks?

Thersites. Prithee, be silent, boy; I profit not by thy
15 talk. Thou art said to be Achilles' male varlet.

Patroclus. Male varlet, you rogue! What's that?

Thersites. Why, his masculine whore. Now, the rotten
diseases of the south,° the guts-griping ruptures,
catarrhs, loads o' gravel in the back, lethargies,
20 cold palsies,° raw eyes, dirt-rotten livers, wheez-
ing lungs, bladders full of imposthume,° sciaticas,
lime-kilns° i'the palm, incurable bone-ache, and
the riveled° fee-simple of the tetter,° and the like,
take and take again such preposterous discoveries!°

25 *Patroclus.* Why, thou damnable box of envy, thou,
what means thou to curse thus?

Thersites. Do I curse thee?

Patroclus. Why, no, you ruinous butt,° you whoreson
indistinguishable° cur, no.

30 *Thersites.* No? Why art thou then exasperate, thou
idle immaterial skein of sleave silk,° thou green
sarcenet° flap for a sore eye, thou tassel of a
prodigal's purse, thou? Ah, how the poor world is

---

10 **Who keeps the tent now?** (Thersites can no longer taunt Achilles for
refusing to leave his tent)   11 **The surgeon's . . . wound** (from the play
on "tent," a surgeon's probe for wounds)   18 **diseases of the south** i.e.,
venereal diseases   19–20 **gravel . . . palsies** kidney stones, apoplectic
strokes, paralysis of the limbs   21 **imposthume** internal abscess
22 **lime-kilns** psoriasis (burning red patches covered with scales)
23 **riveled** wrinkled   23 **fee-simple of the tetter** chronic ringworm (?)
("fee-simple" implies unlimited possession)   24 **discoveries** (referring
generally to—in Thersites' opinion—such absurd monstrosities as Patroclus)   28 **ruinous butt** dilapidated cask   29 **indistinguishable** shapeless (here suggesting mongrel)   31 **sleave silk** soft silk floss
32 **sarcenet** (a fine silk taffeta)

pestered with such water-flies, diminutives of nature.   35

Patroclus. Out, gall!

Thersites. Finch egg!

Achilles. My sweet Patroclus, I am thwarted quite
From my great purpose in tomorrow's battle.
Here is a letter from Queen Hecuba,   40
A token from her daughter, my fair love,
Both taxing° me and gaging° me to keep
An oath that I have sworn. I will not break it.
Fall Greeks, fail fame, honor or go or° stay,
My major vow lies here; this I'll obey.   45
Come, come, Thersites, help to trim my tent;
This night in banqueting must all be spent.
Away, Patroclus!   *Exit* [*with Patroclus*].

Thersites. With too much blood and too little brain,
these two may run mad; but if with too much brain   50
and too little blood they do, I'll be a curer of madmen. Here's Agamemnon, an honest fellow enough,
and one that loves quails,° but he has not so much
brain as ear-wax; and the goodly transformation
of Jupiter° there, his brother, the bull, the primi-   55
tive statue and oblique memorial of cuckolds°—
a thrifty° shoeing-horn in a chain, hanging at his
brother's leg°—to what form but that he is should
wit larded with malice and malice forced° with wit
turn him to? To an ass, were nothing; he is both   60
ass and ox. To an ox, were nothing; he is both ox
and ass. To be a dog, a mule, a cat, a fitchew,°

---

42 **taxing** censuring   42 **gaging** engaging to a promise   44 **or go or**
either go or   53 **quails** prostitutes   54–55 **transformation of Jupiter**
(i.e., into a bull, in which shape he seduced Europa)   55–56 **the primitive statue . . . of cuckolds** (in having horns, the emblem or symbol of
cuckoldry, although since Europa was not married, the parallel to Paris'
rape of Helen is "oblique")   57 **thrifty** stingy   57–58 **hanging at his
brother's leg** (1) as Agamemnon's tool, appropriately enough a "horn,"
his pretext for war (2) as being entirely dependent on Agamemnon
59 **forced** stuffed, intermixed   62 **fitchew** polecat

a toad, a lizard, an owl, a puttock,° or a herring
without a roe, I would not care; but to be Menelaus!
65 I would conspire against destiny. Ask me not what
I would be, if I were not Thersites, for I care not
to be° the louse of a lazar,° so I were not Menelaus.
Hey-day, sprites and fires!

Enter Agamemnon, Ulysses, Nestor, [Hector, Ajax,
Troilus, Menelaus,] and Diomedes, with lights.

Agamemnon. We go wrong, we go wrong.

Ajax.   No, yonder 'tis;
There, where we see the lights.

70 *Hector.*   I trouble you.

Ajax. No, not a whit.

Ulysses.   Here comes himself to guide you.

Enter Achilles.

Achilles. Welcome, brave Hector; welcome, princes
all.

Agamemnon. So now, fair prince of Troy, I bid good
night.
Ajax commands the guard to tend on you.

75 *Hector.* Thanks and good night to the Greeks' general.

Menelaus. Good night, my lord.

Hector. Good night, sweet Lord Menelaus.

Thersites. Sweet draught!° "Sweet," quoth 'a! Sweet
sink, sweet sewer.

80 *Achilles.* Good night and welcome both at once, to
those
That go or tarry.

---

63 **puttock** kite, a small hawk feeding on carrion 66–67 **I care not to
be** I wouldn't mind being 67 **lazar** leper 78 **draught** privy, cesspool

Agamemnon. Good night.
                         Exeunt Agamemnon, Menelaus.

Achilles. Old Nestor tarries, and you too, Diomed,
  Keep Hector company an hour or two.

Diomedes. I cannot, lord; I have important business,   85
  The tide° whereof is now. Good night, great Hector.

Hector. Give me your hand.

Ulysses. [*Aside to Troilus*] Follow his torch; he goes
  to Calchas' tent.
  I'll keep you company.

Troilus. Sweet sir, you honor me.

Hector.   And so, good night.   90
      [*Exeunt Diomedes, then Ulysses and Troilus.*]

Achilles. Come, come, enter my tent.
         Exeunt [Achilles, Hector, Ajax, and Nestor].

Thersites. That same Diomed's a false-hearted rogue,
  a most unjust knave; I will no more trust him when
  he leers than I will a serpent when he hisses. He
  will spend his mouth and promise like Brabbler   95
  the hound;° but when he performs, astronomers
  foretell it. It is prodigious, there will come some
  change. The sun borrows of the moon when Diomed keeps his word. I will rather leave to see°
  Hector than not to dog him. They say he keeps a   100
  Troyan drab, and uses the traitor Calchas' tent.
  I'll after—nothing but lechery! All incontinent var-
  lets!   [*Exit.*]

---

86 **tide** time   95–96 **Brabbler the hound** (a hunting hound who would
"spend his mouth" in barking while not on the scent would be called
"babbler" or "brabbler" by his master)   99 **leave to see** miss seeing

[Scene 2. *The Greek camp.*]

Enter Diomed.

Diomedes. What, are you up here, ho? Speak.

Calchas. [*Within*] Who calls?

Diomedes. Diomed. Calchas, I think. Where's your daughter?

Calchas. [*Within*] She comes to you.

Enter Troilus and Ulysses; [after them Thersites.]

5 *Ulysses.* Stand where the torch may not discover us.

Enter Cressid.

Troilus. Cressid comes forth to him.

Diomedes.   How now, my charge!

Cressida. Now, my sweet guardian! Hark, a word with you.   [*Whispers.*]

Troilus. Yea, so familiar!

Ulysses. She will sing any man at first sight.

10 *Thersites.* And any man may sing her, if he can take her cliff;° she's noted.°

Diomedes. Will you remember?

Cressida. Remember? Yes.

5.2.11 **cliff** clef (signifying the musical key; with an obscene pun on "cleft")   11 **noted** reputed a loose woman (with a pun on musical notes)

Diomedes. Nay, but do, then;
    And let your mind be coupled with your words.   *15*

Troilus. What shall she remember?

Ulysses. List!

Cressida. Sweet honey Greek, tempt me no more to
    folly.

Thersites. Roguery!

Diomedes. Nay, then——

Cressida.   I'll tell you what——   *20*

Diomedes. Foh, foh! Come, tell a pin. You are for-
    sworn.

Cressida. In faith, I cannot. What would you have me
    do?

Thersites. A juggling trick—to be secretly° open.

Diomedes. What did you swear you would bestow on
    me?

Cressida. I prithee, do not hold me to mine oath;   *25*
    Bid me do anything but that, sweet Greek.

Diomedes. Good night.

Troilus. Hold, patience!

Ulysses. How now, Troyan?

Cressida. Diomed——   *30*

Diomedes. No, no, good night; I'll be your fool no
    more.

Troilus. Thy better must.

Cressida.   Hark, a word in your ear.

Troilus. O plague and madness!

Ulysses. You are moved, prince; let us depart, I pray,

23 **secretly** privately, sexually

35   Lest your displeasure should enlarge itself
          To wrathful terms. This place is dangerous;
          The time right deadly. I beseech you, go.

Troilus. Behold, I pray you!

Ulysses.   Nay, good my lord, go off;
          You flow to great distraction. Come, my lord.

Troilus. I prithee, stay.

40   *Ulysses.*   You have not patience; come.

Troilus. I pray you, stay! By hell, and all hell's tor-
          ments, I will not speak a word!

Diomedes.   And so, good night.

Cressida. Nay, but you part in anger.

Troilus.   Doth that grieve thee?
          O withered truth!

Ulysses.   How now, my lord!

Troilus.   By Jove,
          I will be patient.

45   *Cressida.*   Guardian! Why, Greek!

Diomedes. Foh, foh! Adieu; you palter.

Cressida. In faith, I do not. Come hither once again.

Ulysses. You shake, my lord, at something. Will you
          go?
          You will break out.

Troilus.   She strokes his cheek!

Ulysses.   Come, come.

50   *Troilus.* Nay, stay; by Jove, I will not speak a word.
          There is between my will and all offenses
          A guard of patience. Stay a little while.

Thersites. How the devil Luxury,° with his fat rump

53 **Luxury** lechery

    and potato° finger, tickles these together. Fry,
lechery, fry!   55

Diomedes. But will you, then?

Cressida. In faith, I will, la; never trust me else.

Diomedes. Give me some token for the surety of it.

Cressida. I'll fetch you one.   *Exit.*

Ulysses. You have sworn patience.

Troilus.   Fear me not, my lord;   60
I will not be myself, nor have cognition
Of what I feel. I am all patience.

        Enter Cressida.

Thersites. Now the pledge! Now, now, now!

Cressida. Here, Diomed, keep this sleeve.

Troilus. O beauty, where is thy faith?

Ulysses.   My lord——   65

Troilus. I will be patient; outwardly I will.

Cressida. You look upon that sleeve; behold it well.
He loved me—O false wench! Give't me again.

Diomedes. Whose was't?

Cressida.   It is no matter, now I have't again.
I will not meet with you tomorrow night.   70
I prithee, Diomed, visit me no more.

Thersites. Now she sharpens.° Well said, whetstone!

Diomedes. I shall have it.

Cressida.   What, this?

Diomedes.   Ay, that.

Cressida. O, all you gods! O pretty, pretty pledge!

---

54 **potato** (potatoes were thought to be aphrodisiac)   72 **sharpens** i.e.,
whets Diomedes' desire

75   Thy master now lies thinking on his bed
      Of thee and me, and sighs, and takes my glove,
      And gives memorial° dainty kisses to it,
      As I kiss thee. Nay, do not snatch it from me;
      He that takes that doth take my heart withal.

80 *Diomedes.* I had your heart before; this follows it.

    Troilus. I did swear patience.

    Cressida. You shall not have it, Diomed; faith, you
          shall not;
      I'll give you something else.

    Diomedes. I will have this. Whose was it?

    Cressida.   It is no matter.

85 *Diomedes.* Come, tell me whose it was.

    Cressida. 'Twas one's that loved me better than you
          will.
      But, now you have it, take it.

    Diomedes.   Whose was it?

    Cressida. By all Diana's waiting-women° yond,
      And by herself, I will not tell you whose.

90 *Diomedes.* Tomorrow will I wear it on my helm,
      And grieve his spirit that dares not challenge it.

    Troilus. Wert thou the devil, and wor'st it on thy horn,
      It should be challenged.

    Cressida. Well, well, 'tis done, 'tis past. And yet it is
          not;
      I will not keep my word.

95 *Diomedes.*   Why then, farewell;
      Thou never shalt mock Diomed again.

    Cressida. You shall not go. One cannot speak a word
      But it straight starts you.°

77 **memorial** in remembrance   88 **Diana's waiting-women** i.e., the
stars clustered about the moon   98 **straight starts you** immediately
makes you start angrily away

Diomedes.   I do not like this fooling.

Thersites. Nor I, by Pluto; but that that likes° not you
  Pleases me best.   *100*

Diomedes. What, shall I come? The hour?

Cressida.   Ay, come—
  O Jove!—
  Do come—I shall be plagued.°

Diomedes.   Farewell till then.

Cressida. Good night. I prithee, come.
                                Exit [*Diomedes*].
  Troilus, farewell. One eye yet looks on thee,
  But with my heart the other eye doth see.   *105*
  Ah, poor our sex!° This fault in us I find,
  The error° of our eye directs our mind.
  What error leads must err. O, then conclude,
  Minds swayed by eyes are full of turpitude.   *Exit.*

Thersites. A proof of strength° she could not publish
    more,°   *110*
  Unless she said, "My mind is now turned whore."

Ulysses. All's done, my lord.

Troilus.   It is.

Ulysses.   Why stay we, then?

Troilus. To make a recordation to my soul
  Of every syllable that here was spoke.
  But if I tell how these two did coact,   *115*
  Shall I not lie in publishing a truth?
  Sith yet there is a credence in my heart,
  An esperance° so obstinately strong,
  That doth invert th' attest° of eyes and ears,
  As if those organs had deceptious° functions,   *120*
  Created only to calumniate.

99 **likes** pleases   102 **plagued** punished   106 **poor our sex** our poor
sex   107 **error** wandering (here, physically and morally)   110 **proof
of strength** strong proof   110 **publish more** confess more clearly   118
esperance hope   119 **attest** testimony   120 **deceptious** deceiving

Was Cressid here?

Ulysses.   I cannot conjure,° Troyan.

Troilus. She was not, sure.

Ulysses.   Most sure she was.

Troilus. Why, my negation° hath no taste of madness.

125 *Ulysses.* Nor mine, my lord. Cressid was here but now.

Troilus. Let it not be believed for° womanhood!
    Think we had mothers; do not give advantage
    To stubborn critics, apt, without a theme,
    For depravation,° to square the general sex
130   By Cressid's rule.° Rather think this not Cressid.

Ulysses. What hath she done, prince, that can soil our
    mothers?

Troilus. Nothing at all, unless that this were she.

Thersites. Will 'a swagger himself out on's own eyes?°

Troilus. This she? No, this is Diomed's Cressida.
135   If beauty have a soul, this is not she;
    If souls guide vows, if vows be sanctimonies,
    If sanctimony be the gods' delight,
    If there be rule in unity itself,°
    This was not she. O madness of discourse,°
140   That cause sets up with and against itself:
    Bifold authority,° where reason can revolt

---

122 **conjure** raise spirits   124 **negation** denial   126 **for** for the sake
of   128–29 **apt ... For depravation** ready and eager to claim the
depravity of women, but lacking examples   129–30 **square the ...
Cressid's rule** take the measure of womankind by Cressida's standard
133 **Will 'a ... on's own eyes?** i.e., will he bluff himself out of trusting
his own sight?   138 **If there ... unity itself** i.e., if it is a true principle
that one cannot be two (that Cressida may not be divided into two persons)   139 **discourse** reasonable sequence of thought   140–41 **That
cause ... Bifold authority** that case of principle wherein divided
authority both supports and confutes the question

Without perdition, and loss assume all reason
Without revolt.° This is, and is not, Cressid.
Within my soul there doth conduce° a fight
Of this strange nature that a thing inseparate°   *145*
Divides more wider than the sky and earth;
And yet the spacious breadth of this division
Admits no orifex° for a point as subtle°
As Ariachne's broken woof° to enter.
Instance,° O instance, strong as Pluto's gates;   *150*
Cressid is mine, tied with the bonds of heaven.
Instance, O instance, strong as heaven itself;
The bonds of heaven are slipped, dissolved, and
        loosed,
And with another knot, five-finger-tied,°
The fractions of her faith, orts° of her love,   *155*
The fragments, scraps, the bits, and greasy relics
Of her o'ereaten° faith, are given to Diomed.

Ulysses. May worthy Troilus be half attached°
With that which here his passion doth express?

Troilus. Ay, Greek! And that shall be divulgèd well   *160*
In characters as red as Mars his heart
Inflamed with Venus. Never did young man fancy
With so eternal and so fixed a soul.
Hark, Greek. Much as I do Cressid love,
So much by weight hate I her Diomed;   *165*
That sleeve is mine that he'll bear on his helm;
Were it a casque° composed by Vulcan's skill,
My sword should bite it. Not the dreadful spout
Which shipmen do the hurricano call,

141–43 **where reason . . . Without revolt** where reason can rebel without subsequent chaos, and loss of understanding assume the appearance
of reason without reason itself objecting   144 **conduce** go on   145 **thing
inseparate** that which is indivisible; i.e., Cressida   148 **orifex** opening
148 **subtle** finely sharp   149 **Ariachne's broken woof** (Ariachne was
a Lydian woman who challenged Athene to a weaving contest, but the
goddess, angered, tore her work to shreds and changed her to a spider)
150 **Instance** example, proof (here, in the sense of "for instance")
154 **five-finger-tied** (1) so tied because Cressida's hand is now
Diomedes' (?) (2) i.e., impossible to untie (?)   155 **orts** scraps, pieces
(as of food)   157 **o'ereaten** eaten through, picked over (as a dog will
eat the best pieces first, the last scraps left over)   158 **half attached** i.e.,
half so much affected (as it appears)   167 **casque** helmet

170   Constringed° in mass by the almighty sun,
      Shall dizzy with more clamor Neptune's ear
      In his descent than shall my prompted° sword
      Falling on Diomed.

Thersites. He'll tickle it for his concupy.°

175 *Troilus.* O Cressid! O false Cressid! False, false, false!
      Let all untruths stand by thy stainèd name,
      And they'll seem glorious.

Ulysses.   O, contain yourself;
      Your passion draws ears hither.

                    Enter Aeneas.

Aeneas. I have been seeking you this hour, my lord.
180   Hector, by this, is arming him° in Troy;
      Ajax, your guard, stays to conduct you home.

Troilus. Have with you,° prince. My courteous lord,
         adieu.
      Farewell, revolted fair; and Diomed,
      Stand fast, and wear a castle on thy head!

185 *Ulysses.* I'll bring you to the gates.

Troilus. Accept distracted thanks.
                    Exeunt Troilus, Aeneas, and Ulysses.

Thersites. Would I could meet that rogue Diomed. I
      would croak like a raven; I would bode,° I would
      bode. Patroclus will give me anything for the in-
190   telligence of this whore. The parrot will not do
      more for an almond than he for a commodious
      drab.° Lechery, lechery; still wars and lechery;
      nothing else holds fashion. A burning devil° take
      them!   *Exit.*

---

170 **Constringed** drawn together   172 **prompted** i.e., urged on, as
having its own motive   174 **He'll tickle it for his concupy** he'll be well
tickled for his concupiscence ("it" refers contemptuously to Diomedes)
180 **him** himself   182 **Have with you** let's go along   188 **bode** por-
tend disaster   191–92 **commodious drab** serviceable whore   193
burning devil venereal disease

[Scene 3. *Troy; Priam's palace.*]

Enter Hector and Andromache.

Andromache. When was my lord so much ungently
    tempered,
  To stop his ears against admonishment?
  Unarm, unarm, and do not fight today.

Hector. You train° me to offend° you; get you in.
  By all the everlasting gods, I'll go.   *5*

Andromache. My dreams will, sure, prove ominous
    to the day.°

Hector. No more, I say.

Enter Cassandra.

Cassandra.   Where is my brother Hector?

Andromache. Here, sister; armed and bloody in intent.
  Consort with me in loud and dear petition;
  Pursue we him on knees, for I have dreamed   *10*
  Of bloody turbulence, and this whole night
  Hath nothing been but shapes and forms of
    slaughter.

Cassandra. O, 'tis true.

Hector.   Ho, bid my trumpet sound.

Cassandra. No notes of sally, for the heavens, sweet
  brother.

Hector. Be gone, I say; the gods have heard me swear.   *15*

5.3.4 **train** tempt 4 **offend** injure, insult 6 **ominous to the day**
omens applicable to this day

Cassandra. The gods are deaf to hot and peevish°
        vows.
    They are polluted offerings, more abhorred
    Than spotted° livers in the sacrifice.

Andromache. O, be persuaded! Do not count it holy
20   To hurt by being just. It is as lawful,
    For° we would give much, to use violent thefts,
    And rob in the behalf of charity.

Cassandra. It is the purpose that makes strong the
        vow;
    But vows to every purpose must not hold.°
    Unarm, sweet Hector.

25 *Hector.*   Hold you still, I say.
    Mine honor keeps the weather° of my fate.
    Life every man holds dear; but the dear° man
    Holds honor far more precious-dear than life.

                Enter Troilus.

    How now, young man; mean'st thou to fight today?

30 *Andromache.* Cassandra, call my father to persuade.
                        Exit Cassandra.

Hector. No, faith, young Troilus; doff thy harness,
        youth.
    I am today i' the vein of chivalry.
    Let grow thy sinews till their knots be strong,
    And tempt not yet the brushes° of the war.
35   Unarm thee; go, and doubt thou not, brave boy,
    I'll stand today for thee and me and Troy.

Troilus. Brother, you have a vice of mercy in you,
    Which better fits a lion than a man.

___

16 **peevish** brash, perverse   18 **spotted** i.e., spoiled   21 **For** because
24 **But vows ... not hold** i.e., vows sworn indiscriminately or to
unlawful purpose should not bind the swearer   26 **keeps the weather**
i.e., maintains the position of advantage   27 **dear** valuable, worthy
34 **brushes** encounters

Hector. What vice is that? Good Troilus, chide me for
    it.

Troilus. When many times the captive Grecian falls,   40
    Even in the fan and wind of your fair sword,
    You bid them rise and live.

Hector. O, 'tis fair play.

Troilus.   Fool's play, by heaven, Hector.

Hector. How now? How now?

Troilus.   For the love of all the gods,
    Let's leave the hermit pity with our mother,   45
    And when we have our armors buckled on,
    The venomed vengeance ride upon our swords,
    Spur them to ruthful° work, rein them from ruth.°

Hector. Fie, savage, fie!

Troilus.   Hector, then 'tis wars.°

Hector. Troilus, I would not have you fight today.   50

Troilus. Who should withhold me?
    Not fate, obedience, nor the hand of Mars
    Beck'ning with fiery truncheon° my retire;
    Not Priamus and Hecuba on knees,
    Their eyes o'ergallèd° with recourse° of tears;   55
    Nor you, my brother, with your true sword drawn,
    Opposed to hinder me, should stop my way,
    But by my ruin.

            Enter Priam and Cassandra.

Cassandra. Lay hold upon him, Priam, hold him fast;
    He is thy crutch. Now if thou lose thy stay,°   60
    Thou on him leaning, and all Troy on thee,
    Fall all together.

---

48 **ruthful** i.e., to be pitied, woeful   48 **ruth** pity   49 **then 'tis wars**
that's what war is   53 **truncheon** (a kind of baton used by the referee
of a combat to signal the end of the fight)   55 **o'ergallèd** inflamed
55 **recourse** repeated coursing down, constant flowing   60 **stay** support

Priam.   Come, Hector, come; go back.
     Thy wife hath dreamt, thy mother hath had visions,
     Cassandra doth foresee, and I myself
65   Am like a prophet suddenly enrapt
     To tell thee that this day is ominous.
     Therefore, come back.

Hector.   Aeneas is afield;
     And I do stand engaged to many Greeks,
     Even in the faith of valor,° to appear
     This morning to them.

70 *Priam.*   Ay, but thou shalt not go.

Hector. I must not break my faith.
     You know me dutiful; therefore, dear sir,
     Let me not shame respect,° but give me leave
     To take that course by your consent and voice,
75   Which you do here forbid me, royal Priam.

Cassandra. O Priam, yield not to him!

Andromache.   Do not, dear father.

Hector. Andromache, I am offended with you.
     Upon the love you bear me, get you in.
                              Exit Andromache.

Troilus. This foolish, dreaming, superstitious girl
     Makes all these bodements.°

80 *Cassandra.*   O farewell, dear Hector!
     Look, how thou diest; look, how thy eye turns pale;
     Look, how thy wounds do bleed at many vents!
     Hark, how Troy roars, how Hecuba cries out,
     How poor Andromache shrills her dolors forth!
85   Behold, distraction, frenzy, and amazement,
     Like witless antics,° one another meet,
     And all cry Hector! Hector's dead! O Hector!

Troilus. Away! Away!

69 **the faith of valor** a brave man's promise   73 **shame respect** i.e.,
disgrace the respect due to a parent   80 **bodements** evil omens
86 **antics** madmen

Cassandra. Farewell. Yet, soft; Hector, I take my
 leave.
  Thou dost thyself and all our Troy deceive. *Exit.* 90

Hector. You are amazed, my liege, at her exclaim.
  Go in and cheer the town. We'll forth and fight;
  Do deeds worth praise and tell you them at night.

Priam. Farewell. The gods with safety stand about
  thee.   [*Exeunt Priam and Hector.*] *Alarum.*

Troilus. They are at it, hark. Proud Diomed, believe, 95
  I come to lose my arm, or win my sleeve.

                Enter Pandar.

Pandarus. Do you hear, my lord? Do you hear?

Troilus. What now?

Pandarus. Here's a letter come from yond poor girl.

Troilus. Let me read. 100

Pandarus. A whoreson tisick,° a whoreson rascally
  tisick so troubles me, and the foolish fortune of
  this girl; and what one thing, what another, that I
  shall leave you one o'the'se days; and I have a
  rheum in mine eyes too, and such an ache in my 105
  bones that, unless a man were cursed, I cannot tell
  what to think on't. What says she there?

Troilus. Words, words, mere words, no matter from
    the heart;
  Th' effect doth operate another way.
                [*Tearing the letter.*]
  Go, wind to wind, there turn and change together. 110
  My love with words and errors° still she feeds,
  But edifies another with her deeds. *Exeunt.*

---

101 **tisick** cough   111 **errors** meanderings, i.e., underhanded tricks (?)

[Scene 4. *The battlefield.*]

[Alarum.] Enter Thersites. Excursions.

Thersites. Now they are clapperclawing one another;
I'll go look on. That dissembling abominable varlet,
Diomed, has got that same scurvy doting foolish
young knave's sleeve of Troy there in his helm.
5 I would fain see them meet, that that same young
Troyan ass, that loves the whore there, might send
that Greekish whoremasterly villain with the sleeve
back to the dissembling luxurious drab, of a sleeve-
less° errand. O'the t'other side, the policy of those
10 crafty swearing° rascals—that stale old mouse-
eaten dry cheese, Nestor, and that same dog-fox,
Ulysses—is not proved worth a blackberry. They
set me up, in policy, that mongrel cur, Ajax,
against that dog of as bad a kind, Achilles; and
15 now is the cur Ajax prouder than the cur Achilles,
and will not arm today. Whereupon the Grecians
begin to proclaim barbarism,° and policy grows
into an ill opinion.

Enter Diomedes and Troilus.

Soft, here comes sleeve, and t'other.

20 *Troilus.* Fly not; for shouldst thou take the river Styx,
I would swim after.

Diomedes.   Thou dost miscall retire.

5.4.8–9 **sleeveless** futile, fruitless   10 **crafty swearing** craftily swearing, i.e., crafty to the extent of perjury   17 **proclaim barbarism** i.e.,
recognize the authority of chaos (to replace policy)

I do not fly, but advantageous care
Withdrew me from the odds of multitude.°
Have at thee!

Thersites. Hold thy whore, Grecian! Now for thy
whore,   25
Troyan! Now the sleeve, now the sleeve!
        [*Exeunt Troilus and Diomedes, fighting.*]

                Enter Hector.

Hector. What art thou, Greek? Art thou for Hector's
    match?
  Art thou of blood and honor?

Thersites. No, no, I am a rascal, a scurvy railing
    knave, a very filthy rogue.   30

Hector. I do believe thee; live.   [*Exit.*]

Thersites. God-a-mercy, that thou wilt believe me; but
    a plague break thy neck—for frighting me. What's
    become of the wenching rogues? I think they have
    swallowed one another. I would laugh at that mir-   35
    acle—yet, in a sort, lechery eats itself. I'll seek
    them.   *Exit.*

        [*Scene 5. The battlefield.*]

                Enter Diomed and Servant.

Diomedes. Go, go, my servant, take thou Troilus'
    horse;
  Present the fair steed to my Lady Cressid.
  Fellow, commend my service to her beauty;

22–23 **but advantageous . . . of multitude** care for my own advantage
led me to avoid facing absurdly heavy odds

Tell her I have chastised the amorous Troyan,
And am her knight by proof.

5 *Servant.*   I go, my lord.   [*Exit.*]

Enter Agamemnon.

Agamemnon. Renew, renew! The fierce Polydamas
 Hath beat down Menon; bastard Margarelon
 Hath Doreus prisoner,
 And stands colossus-wise, waving his beam,°
10 Upon the pashèd corses° of the kings
 Epistrophus and Cedius; Polyxenes is slain,
 Amphimachus and Thoas deadly hurt,
 Patroclus ta'en or slain, and Palamedes
 Sore hurt and bruised. The dreadful Sagittary°
15 Appals our numbers. Haste we, Diomed,
 To reinforcement, or we perish all.

Enter Nestor.

Nestor. Go, bear Patroclus' body to Achilles,
 And bid the snail-paced Ajax arm for shame.
 There is a thousand Hectors in the field;
20 Now here he fights on Galathe his horse,
 And there lacks work; anon he's there afoot,
 And there they fly or die, like scalèd sculls°
 Before the belching whale; then is he yonder,
 And there the strawy Greeks, ripe for his edge,°
25 Fall down before him, like a mower's swath.
 Here, there, and everywhere, he leaves and takes,
 Dexterity so obeying appetite
 That what he will he does, and does so much
 That proof° is called impossibility.

5.5.9 **beam** spear   10 **pashèd corses** battered corpses   14 **Sagittary**
(a centaur [half man, half horse], who was a splendid archer and aided the
Trojans)   22 **scalèd sculls** scaly schools of fish   24 **strawy ... edge**
i.e., Greeks who are like straw, ripe for the edge of the scythe   29 **proof**
visible fact

Enter Ulysses.

Ulysses. O, courage, courage, princes! Great Achilles   30
  Is arming, weeping, cursing, vowing vengeance!
  Patroclus' wounds have roused his drowsy blood,
  Together with his mangled Myrmidons,
  That noseless, handless, hacked and chipped, come
    to him,
  Crying on Hector. Ajax hath lost a friend,   35
  And foams at mouth, and he is armed and at it,
  Roaring for Troilus, who hath done today
  Mad and fantastic execution,
  Engaging and redeeming of himself
  With such a careless force and forceless° care   40
  As if that luck, in very spite of cunning,
  Bade him win all.

Enter Ajax.

Ajax. Troilus, thou coward Troilus!   *Exit.*

Diomedes.   Ay, there, there.

Nestor. So, so, we draw together.   *Exit.*

Enter Achilles.

Achilles.   Where is this Hector?
  Come, come, thou boy-queller,° show thy face;   45
  Know what it is to meet Achilles angry.
  Hector, where's Hector? I will none but Hector.
                            Exit.

40 forceless casual, reckless   **45 boy-queller** boy-killer

[Scene 6. *The battlefield*.]

Enter Ajax.

Ajax. Troilus, thou coward Troilus, show thy head!

Enter Diomedes.

Diomedes. Troilus, I say, where's Troilus?

Ajax. What wouldst thou?

Diomedes. I would correct him.

Ajax. Were I the general, thou shouldst have my office
5   Ere that correction.° Troilus, I say! What, Troilus!

Enter Troilus.

Troilus. O traitor Diomed! Turn thy false face, thou
   traitor,
And pay thy life thou owest me for my horse.°

Diomedes. Ha, art thou there?

Ajax. I'll fight with him alone. Stand, Diomed.

10 *Diomedes.* He is my prize; I will not look upon.°

Troilus. Come, both you cogging° Greeks; have at
   you both!   [*Exeunt, fighting.*]

[Enter Hector.]

Hector. Yea, Troilus? O, well fought, my youngest
   brother!

5.6.5 **correction** i.e., privilege to correct   7 **horse** (with a pun on whore?)   10 **look upon** stand by   11 **cogging** deceitful

Enter Achilles.

Achilles. Now do I see thee, ha! Have at thee,
    Hector!   [*They fight; Achilles tires.*]

Hector. Pause, if thou wilt.

Achilles. I do disdain thy courtesy, proud Troyan;   *15*
    Be happy that my arms are out of use.
    My rest and negligence befriends thee now,
    But thou anon shalt hear of me again;
    Till when, go seek thy fortune.   *Exit.*

Hector.   Fare thee well;
    I would have been much more a fresher man,   *20*
    Had I expected thee.

Enter Troilus.

        How now, my brother!

Troilus. Ajax hath ta'en° Aeneas! Shall it be?
    No, by the flame of yonder glorious heaven,
    He shall not carry him;° I'll be ta'en too,
    Or bring him off. Fate, hear me what I say!   *25*
    I reck not though thou end my life today.   *Exit.*

Enter one in armor.

Hector. Stand, stand, thou Greek; thou art a goodly
    mark.
    No? Wilt thou not? I like thy armor well;
    I'll frush° it and unlock the rivets all,
    But I'll be master of it. Wilt thou not, beast, abide?   *30*
    Why then, fly on, I'll hunt thee for thy hide.
                        Exit [*in pursuit*].

---

22 **ta'en** taken captive   24 **carry him** prevail over him   29 **frush** smash

[Scene 7. *The battlefield.*]

Enter Achilles with Myrmidons.

Achilles. Come here about me, you my Myrmidons;
  Mark what I say. Attend me where I wheel.
  Strike not a stroke, but keep yourselves in breath.
  And when I have the bloody Hector found,
5 Empale him° with your weapons round about;
  In fellest° manner execute° your arms.
  Follow me, sirs, and my proceedings eye;
  It is decreed Hector the great must die.
                       Exit [*with Myrmidons*].

Enter Thersites, Menelaus, Paris [*the last two fighting*].

Thersites. The cuckold and the cuckold-maker are at
10 it. Now, bull! Now, dog! 'Loo,° Paris, 'loo! Now,
  my double-horned Spartan! 'Loo, Paris, 'loo! The
  bull has the game;° 'ware horns, ho!
               Exeunt Paris and Menelaus.

Enter Bastard [*Margarelon*].

Bastard. Turn, slave, and fight.

Thersites. What art thou?

15 *Bastard.* A bastard son of Priam's.

Thersites. I am a bastard too; I love bastards. I am bastard begot, bastard instructed, bastard in mind, bas-

---

5.7.5 **Empale him** hem him in 6 **fellest** cruelest 6 **execute** use
10 **Now, bull! Now, dog! 'Loo** (Thersites compares the combat of
Menelaus and Paris to the baiting of a bull by a dog, as it was done in
such arenas as the Paris Garden) 12 **has the game** wins

tard in valor, in everything illegitimate. One bear will
not bite another, and wherefore should one bastard? Take heed, the quarrel's most ominous to us.   20
If the son of a whore fight for a whore, he tempts
judgment. Farewell, bastard.

Bastard. The devil take thee, coward!   *Exeunt.*

[Scene 8. *The battlefield.*]

Enter Hector.

Hector. Most putrefièd core, so fair without,
Thy goodly armor thus hath cost thy life.
Now is my day's work done; I'll take my breath.
Rest, sword; thou hast thy fill of blood and death.
                    [*Puts off his helmet, and
                    hangs his shield behind him.*]

Enter Achilles and Myrmidons.

Achilles. Look, Hector, how the sun begins to set,   5
How ugly night comes breathing at his heels.
Even with the vail° and dark'ning of the sun,
To close the day up, Hector's life is done.

Hector. I am unarmed; forgo this vantage, Greek.

Achilles. Strike, fellows, strike. This is the man I seek.   10
                    [*Hector falls.*]
So, Ilion, fall thou next! Come, Troy, sink down!
Here lies thy heart, thy sinews, and thy bone.
On, Myrmidons, and cry you all amain,
"Achilles hath the mighty Hector slain!"   *Retreat.*
Hark, a retire upon our Grecian part.   15

5.8.7 **vail** sinking, going down

One Greek. The Troyans' trumpets sound the like, my
    lord.

Achilles. The dragon wing of night o'erspreads the
    earth.
  And, sticklerlike,° the armies separates.
  My half-supped sword, that frankly° would have
    fed,
20 Pleased with this dainty bait, thus goes to bed.
                      [Sheathes his sword.]
  Come, tie his body to my horse's tail;
  Along the field I will the Troyan trail.   *Exeunt.*

[Scene 9. *The battlefield.*]

*Enter Agamemnon, Ajax, Menelaus, Nestor, Diomed,
  and the rest, marching. [Sound retreat. Shout.]*

Agamemnon. Hark, hark, what shout is that?

Nestor.   Peace, drums!

Soldiers. (Within)   Achilles!
  Achilles! Hector's slain! Achilles!

Diomedes. The bruit° is, Hector's slain, and by
  Achilles.

Ajax. If it be so, yet bragless let it be;
5 Great Hector was as good a man as he.

Agamemnon. March patiently along. Let one be sent
  To pray Achilles see us at our tent.
  If in his death the gods have us befriended,
  Great Troy is ours, and our sharp wars are ended.
                            Exeunt.

---

18 **sticklerlike** like an umpire separating combatants, and ordering the
field   19 **frankly** freely, abundantly   5.9.3 **bruit** rumor

[*Scene 10. The battlefield.*]

Enter Aeneas, Paris, Antenor, Deiphobus.

Aeneas. Stand, ho! Yet are we masters of the field.
  Never go home; here starve we out the night.

Enter Troilus.

Troilus. Hector is slain.

All.   Hector! The gods forbid!

Troilus. He's dead and at the murderer's horse's tail,
  In beastly sort, dragged through the shameful field.   5
  Frown on, you heavens, effect your rage with speed;
  Sit, gods, upon your thrones, and smile° at Troy.
  I say, at once let your brief plagues be mercy,°
  And linger not our sure destructions on.

Aeneas. My lord, you do discomfort all the host.   10

Troilus. You understand me not that tell me so.
  I do not speak of flight, of fear, of death,
  But dare all imminence that gods and men
  Address their dangers in.° Hector is gone.
  Who shall tell Priam so, or Hecuba?   15
  Let him that will a screech owl° aye be called
  Go in to Troy, and say there Hector's dead.
  There is a word will Priam turn to stone,
  Make wells and Niobes° of the maids and wives,

5.10.7 **smile** i.e., in derision   8 **let ... mercy** be merciful in letting the plagues you send destroy us quickly   13–14 **But dare ... dangers in** but instead dare whatever imminent dangers gods and men may be preparing   16 **screech owl** (a bearer of ill omen)   19 **Niobes** (Niobe wept for her slain children until she was turned into a column of stone, from which tears continued to flow)

20   Cold statues of the youth, and in a word
  Scare Troy out of itself. But march away.
  Hector is dead; there is no more to say.
  Stay yet. You vile abominable tents,
  Thus proudly pitched upon our Phrygian plains,
25 Let Titan° rise as early as he dare,
  I'll through and through you! And, thou great-sized
   coward,°
  No space of earth shall sunder our two hates.
  I'll haunt thee like a wicked conscience still,
  That moldeth goblins swift as frenzy's thoughts.
30 Strike a free march to Troy. With comfort go;
  Hope of revenge shall hide our inward woe.

     Enter Pandarus.

Pandarus. But hear you, hear you!

Troilus. Hence, broker, lackey! Ignominy and shame
  Pursue thy life, and live aye with thy name.
       Exeunt all but Pandarus.
35 *Pandarus.* A goodly medicine for my aching bones!
  O world, world! Thus is the poor agent despised.
  O traders and bawds, how earnestly are you
  set awork, and how ill requited! Why should our
  endeavor be so loved, and the performance
40 so loathed? What verse for it? What instance for
  it? Let me see.
   Full merrily the humble-bee doth sing,
   Till he hath lost his honey and his sting;
   And being once subdued in armèd tail,
45   Sweet honey and sweet notes together fail.
  Good traders in the flesh, set this in your painted
   cloths:°
  "As many as be here of Pandar's hall,
  Your eyes, half out, weep out at Pandar's fall;
  Or if you cannot weep, yet give some groans,

---

25 **Titan** (Helios, the sun, one of the Titans) 26 **coward** i.e., Achilles
46 **painted cloths** painted cloth hangings, used in brothels, sometimes
bearing mottoes

Though not for me, yet for your aching bones." 50
Brethren and sisters of the hold-door trade,°
Some two months hence my will shall here be
   made.
It should be now, but that my fear is this,
Some gallèd goose of Winchester° would hiss.
Till then I'll sweat° and seek about for eases, 55
And at that time bequeath you my diseases.

                          [Exit.]

51 **hold-door trade** prostitution 54 **gallèd goose of Winchester** angry prostitute (the Bishop of Winchester had once held jurisdiction over the area of London called Southwark, where many brothels stood; a prostitute—and sometimes a venereal disease—was called a "Winchester goose") 55 **sweat** (a treatment for gout or rheumatism, as well as for venereal disease)

Textual Note

It is now generally believed that the 1609 quarto of *Troilus and Cressida* was printed from a transcript made from Shakespeare's original draft of the play. It omits about forty-five lines, the Prologue, and many stage directions that appear in the Folio, but on the whole contains a text that stands closer to Shakespeare's original than does that of the Folio. Since the compositors of the Folio apparently worked not only from the Quarto but from Shakespeare's autograph manuscript, it is surprising that they did not produce the better text; their readings are mainly inferior to those of the Quarto.

The relative values of the two texts (both of them, in different ways, stemming from Shakespeare's manuscript, and both of them, therefore, authoritative) depend on the nature of the copy used by the compositors, and the care and intelligence with which they worked. It is possible that the Quarto represents the play as it was shortened for performance, but more likely that the transcriber of the original manuscript was confused by Shakespeare's own second thoughts and deletions and failed to record some revisions and added speeches. On the other hand, although the compositors of the Folio probably had for reference and collation not only the Quarto but the original manuscript itself, their goal was speed and not always accuracy. While they added many lines omitted in the Quarto, they also introduced many mistaken readings; one compositor in particular evidently suited himself in interpreting difficult words and phrases, and made hash of most of them. Other portions of the Folio text were printed with greater care, however, and since the manuscript at hand may have been used in the playhouse, these portions include more complete stage directions and speech heads than appear in the Quarto. The Folio, therefore, supplies the fuller text; it should be used occasionally to emend the Quarto, but the earlier edition remains the better text. Its readings are frequently superior to those of the Folio, although, naturally, where the Folio prints speeches entirely omitted in the Quarto, these must be considered authoritative. Similarly, those readings in the Folio which introduce corrections on the basis of copy which was either Shakespeare's or very close to his should be followed.

The present edition is based on the Quarto but adds passages from the Folio. (These additions are recorded in the list of departures printed below.) Act and scene divisions (none are given for this play in Quarto or Folio) have been added, along with simple indications of locale. Abbreviations have been amplified, spelling and punctuation have been modernized, and "and" is printed "an" when it means "if." The position of a few stage directions has been slightly altered when necessary. Other departures from the Quarto are listed below, the adopted reading first in italics, and then the original reading in roman. The adopted reading is most often from the Folio; when it is not, it is followed by (ed) to indicate that it is an editor's conjecture rather than an authoritative reading.

Dedicatory address 37 *state* (ed) states

Prologue (Q omits) 12 *barks* (ed; F has "Barke") 19 Sperr (ed; F has "Stirre")

1.1.78 *she were not* she were 80 *what care I* what I

1.2.17 *they* the 35 s.d. *Enter Pandarus* (Q omits) 187 *Ilium* Ilion 212 *man's heart* man heart 249 s.d. *Enter Common Soldiers* (Q omits) 294 s.d. *Exit Pandarus* (Q omits)

1.3.1 s.d. *Sennet* (Q omits) 13 *every* euer 31 *thy* the 36 *patient* ancient 54 *Returns* (ed) Retires 61 *thy* the 70–74 *Agamemnon. Speak . . . oracle* (Q omits) 75 *basis* ßases 110 *meets* melts 159 *unsquared* vnsquare 195 *and discredit* our discredit 212 s.d. *Tucket* (Q omits) 214 s.d. *Enter Aeneas* (Q omits) 247 *affair* affaires 250 *whisper him* whisper with him 252 *the attentive* that attentiue 256 *loud* alowd 263 *rusty* restie 267 *That seeks* And feeds 276 *compass* couple 294 *one* no 298 *will tell* tell 302 *youth* men 305 *first* sir 309 s.d. *Exeunt. Manent Ulysses and Nestor* (Q omits) 315 *This 'tis* (Q omits) 334 *his honor* those honours 354–56 *which . . . the limbs* (F emended from "in his" to "his"; Q omits) 390 *tarre* arre

2.1.11 s.d. *Strikes him* (Q omits) 14 *vinewed'st* (F: whinid'st) vnsalted 18 *oration* oration without booke 18 *a prayer* praier 42–43 *Ajax . . . Do, do* (Q assigns to Thersites as one speech) 47 *Thou scurvy-valiant* you scuruy valiant 57 s.d. *Enter Achilles and Patroclus* (Q omits) 58 *do you* do yee 74 *I* It 77 *I'll* I 104 *if he knock out* and knocke at 109 *your grandsires had nails on their toes* (F emended from "their" to "your") their grandsiers had nailes 120 *brach* (ed) brooch 127 *fifth* first 141 s.d. *Exit* (Q omits)

2.2.14–15 *surety, Surety* surely Surely 27 *father* fathers 33 *at reasons* of reasons 47 *Let's* Sets 64 *shores* shore 75 *truce* ttuce 86 *he* be 96 s.d. *with her hair about her ears* (Q omits) 104 *eld* (ed; F has "old") elders 210 *strike* shrike

2.3.23 s.d. *Enter Patroclus* (Q omits) 27 *wouldst* couldst 33 *art.* art not 49 *thyself* Thersites 57-62 *Patroclus. You . . . a fool* (Q omits) 65 *commanded of Agamemnon* commanded 69 *Creator* Prouer 71 *Patroclus* Come Patroclus 72 s.d. *Exit* (Q omits) 76–77 *Now . . . all* (Q omits) 81 *shent* (ed; F has "sent") sate 82 *appertainments* appertainings 91 *A word, my lord* (Q omits) 104 s.d. *Enter Patroclus* (Q omits) 132 *pettish lunes* (F emended from "lines" to "lunes") course, and time 132 *as if* and if 134 *carriage of this action* streame of his commencement 143 *enter you* entertaine 143 s.d. *Exit Ulysses* (Q omits)⁻ 160 *I hate* I do hate 193 *stale* (ed) staule 195 *titled* liked 205 *pash* push 214 *let his humor's* tell his humorous 222 *'A would . . . shares* (Q gives to Ajax) 224 *He's . . . warm* (ed; Q and F give to Ajax) 225 *praises* praiers 244 *beyond, beyond all erudition* beyond all thy erudition 250 *bourne* boord 251 *Thy* This 256 *cull* call

3.1. s.d. *Music . . . Servant* Enter Pandarus 24 *friend* (Q omits) 38 *that thou* thou 93 *your poor disposer's* your disposers 108 *lord* lad 115 *In . . . so* (Q omits) 118 *shaft confounds* shafts confound 150 *these* this 158 *thee* her

3.2.1 s.d. *and Troilus'* Troylus 3 *he stays* stayes 3 s.d. *Enter Troilus* (Q omits) 8 *Like* like to 10 *those* these 16 s.d. *Exit Pandarus* (Q omits) 28 s.d. *Enter Pandarus* (Q omits) 34 s.d. *Exit Pandarus* (Q omits) 38 *unawares* vnwares 68 *fears* (ed) teares 82 *This is* This 94 *merit crown it. No perfection* merit louer part no affection 101 s.d. *Enter Pandarus* (Q omits) 134 *Cunning* (ed) Comming 161 *aye* age 181 *Yet after* After 186 *and* or 194 *as wolf* or Wolfe 201 *pains* paine

3.3. s.d. *Flourish* (Q omits) 4 *come* (ed) loue 102 *giver* giuers 128 *abject* obiect 140 *on* one 141 *shrinking* shriking 155 *one* on 158 *hedge* turne 160 *hindmost* him, most 161–63 *Or . . . on* (F emended from "neere" to "rear"; Q omits) 164 *past* passe 177 *give* (ed) goe 183 *Than* That 197 *every grain of Pluto's gold* euery thing 198 *th' uncomprehensive deeps* the vncomprehensiue depth 224 *a dewdrop* dew drop 251 *he* a 267 *ambassador to him* Ambassador 275 *most valorous* valorous 279 *Grecian army* armie 279–80 *Agamemnon, et cetera* Agamemnon 294 *God b' wi' you* (ed) God buy you

4.1.4 *you* your   16 *But* Lul'd   36 *it was* twas   40 *do think* beleeue   50 s.d. *Exit Aeneas* (Q omits)   52 *the soul* soule   56 *soilure* soyle   76 *you* they

4.2.19 s.d. *Within* (Q omits)   22 s.d. *Enter Pandarus* (F places after line 20; Q omits)   51 *'Tis* Its   57 s.d. *Enter Troilus* (Q omits)   63 *to us; and for him forthwith* to him, and forth-with   72 *nature* neighbor Pandar   107 *I will* Ile   112 s.d. *Exeunt* (Q omits)

4.4.54 *the root* my throate   64 *there's* there is   76 *They're . . . nature* (Q omits)   79 *person* portion   139 s.d. *Sound trumpet* (Q omits)   144–48 *Deiphobus. Let us . . . chivalry* (F, with 144 assigned to Diomedes; Q omits)

4.5.94 *Ulysses. They . . . already* (Q omits)   95 *Agamemnon* Vlisses   98 *in deeds* deeds   131 *Of our rank feud* (Q omits)   132 *drop* day   164–69 *But that's . . . integrity* (Q omits)   177 *that I affect th' untraded oath* thy affect, the vntraded earth   187 *thy* th'   192 *shraped* (ed) shruped   205 *As they . . . courtesy* (Q omits)   254 *stithied* stichied   291 *she loved* my Lord

5.1.12 *these* this   14 *boy* box   19 *catarrhs* (Q omits)   23 *and the like* (Q omits)   48 s.d. *Exit* (Q omits)   55 *brother* be   57–58 *hanging at his brother's leg* at his bare legge   59 *forced* faced   61 *he is* her's   61–62 *dog, a mule* day, a Moyle   62 *fitchew* Fichooke   65 *ask me not* aske me   71 s.d. *Enter Achilles* (Q omits)   73 *good* God   79 *sewer* (ed) sure   80 *both at once* both

5.2.4 s.d. *Enter . . . Ulysses* (Q omits)   13 *Cressida* Cal   38 *Nay* Now   39 *distraction* distruction   46 *Adieu* (Q omits)   54 *these together* together   56 *But will* Will   57 *la* (ed) lo   66 *Troilus. I . . . will* (Q omits)   67 *Cressida* Troy   78 *Nay . . . me* (Q, F assign to Diomedes)   82 *Cressida* (Q omits)   88 *By* And by   103 s.d. *Exit* (Q omits)   115 *coact* Court   120 *had deceptious* were deceptions   131 *soil* spoile   154 *fine* finde   164 *Much as* as much

5.3.14 *Cassandra* Cres   20–22 *To hurt . . . charity* (F emended from "would count" to "would," and from "as" to "use"; Q omits)   23–25 *It is . . . sweet Hector* (Q assigns to Andromache)   29 *mean'st* meanest   58 *But by my ruin* (Q omits)   85 *distraction* destruction   90 *Exit* (Q omits)

5.4.4 *young knave's* knaues   9 *errand* (F has "errant") arrant   9 *O' th'* Ath   17 *begin* (ed) began   18 s.d. *Enter Diomedes and Troilus* (Q omits)   27 *art thou* art

5.5.22 *scalèd* scaling   41 *luck* lust

5.7.11 *double-horned* (ed) double-hen'd   12 s.d. *Exeunt* (ed) Exit   23 *Exeunt* Exit

5.8.16 *One Greek* (F has "Gree.") One

5.9.1 *what shout is that* what is this

5.10.2 *Never . . . night* (Q assigns to Troilus, and places his entrance before the line)   21–22 *But march away. Hector is dead* (Q omits)   23 *Vile* proud   32–34 *Pandarus. But hear you! . . . aye with thy name* (in F these lines appear as well after 5.3.112, concluding that scene)   33 *Ignominy and* ignominy   37 *traders* (ed) traitors   50 *your aching* my aking   51 *hold-door* hold-ore

A Note on the Sources of
Troilus and Cressida

There is no single source for *Troilus and Cressida,* but there are several works with which we can be certain Shakespeare was familiar, and which he probably used in composing the play. Modern editions of these are listed at the end of this note. Homer's poem, of course, stands behind the story of the war, and Shakespeare's Greek, while less than his small Latin, might have been sufficient to cope with it. He also used the first parts of Chapman's translation of the *Iliad,* published in 1598 (*Seaven Bookes of the Iliades* and *Achilles Shield*); Chapman's later work on Homer appeared too late for Shakespeare's use in this play. Certain details of characterization and action, however, indicate that he either consulted Homer directly or used one of the full Latin or French translations of the sixteenth century; some of these details, such as the characterization of Ulysses and the abuse of Hector's body, could not have resulted from hearsay or pseudo-Homeric versions. Other aspects of the camp scenes, both Greek and Trojan, stem from Lydgate's *Sege of Troye* (c. 1412–1420) or Caxton's *Recuyell of the Historyes of Troye* (1475). Both of these are derived ultimately from early pseudo-Homeric narratives, their more immediate source being the *Historia Troiana* (1287) of Guido delle Colonne; Guido had also provided one of the secondary sources for Chaucer's *Troilus and Criseyde*. Shakespeare also knew Arthur Golding's translation of Ovid's *Metamorphoses,* some parts of which touch upon the story of the Trojan war.

Shakespeare's major source for the love story was Chaucer's great narrative poem, *Troilus and Criseyde* (1382–1385), although one must qualify immediately the nature of his reliance upon it. The bones of the story, as Shakespeare knew it, and even some details of the action

are from Chaucer, but it would be most misleading to
assume that Shakespeare's treatment of the tale resembles
Chaucer's. The qualities of the story that attracted Shakespeare, and to which he added much more specific action
concerning the characters in the camp scenes, were not
those emphasized—nor perhaps even recognized—by his
most important predecessor in English literature. Chaucer's
treatment of the story emphasizes the charm of the lovers
and, while it lasts, the delight of their union. Pandarus is
a warmhearted, benevolent courtier, himself a servant of
love, though unsuccessful in his own amours. His humor
is invariably genial, and although some of his jests are
broad, they are never obscene. His main desire is the happiness of Troilus and Criseyde, and he is shocked into melancholy silence when he hears the news of Criseyde's
betrayal. The heroine herself is a young woman of considerable dignity, imagination, and charm, with none of the
coquetry or worldliness of Shakespeare's girl. She yields to
Troilus only after long persuasion, and, befriended by
Hector himself, enjoys a good reputation throughout the
city. Chaucer's Troilus, like Shakespeare's, is a faithful and
sensitive lover; but the affair is conducted in a vastly different manner in the two narratives. Pandarus, in Shakespeare's play, is glibly obscene, coarsely sentimental, and,
frequently, hardly more than a leering *voyeur,* anxious for
the lovers' happiness, but deriving from it what appears to
be sexual pleasure for himself. In Chaucer's poem, the
powers of love ennoble those who serve it, and the union of
Troilus and Criseyde is set forth as an event of great beauty
and cheer.

In Chaucer, the significance of Criseyde's fall is set
against that of the great city itself, and both become part of
a larger and more general sadness. Criseyde is shown to be
confused and weak, but her lonely position in the Greek
camp is also poignantly described. She becomes an instrument in the fortunes of both Troilus and Diomede, and
some emphasis is thereby withdrawn from her faithless act
itself. Her treachery is lamentable, but it is somehow over-
shadowed by the tragedy of Troy and the fate of mankind
in general. Far from acknowledging in Criseyde an implicit
harlotry, Chaucer sets forth, simply and with deep sadness,

the tale of her loss. He is as moved by it as Pandarus, and seems to learn, with Troilus, that solace, if it can be found at all, is to be found in something more permanent than the life of this world. It should not be assumed that Chaucer's psychology was less subtle than Shakespeare's; it is derived in this poem, in fact, from the elaborate pattern of behavior defined in the code of courtly love—a code that could effect great beauty and delicacy of human feeling. Although Shakespeare's times—and ours—would describe such behavior pejoratively, as based in an adulterous relationship, no condemnation is implicit in Chaucer's work. It should be noted that his Criseyde is a widow when she first sees Troilus. His characters are capable of great strength and constancy, but Chaucer shows that the capricious movement of Fortune's wheel can crush what is beautiful and cause what is apparently constant to pass. His narrative is tragic in its treatment of the lovers' fall, comic to the extent that its characters are prone to folly and delusion.

By the time Shakespeare decided to write *Troilus and Cressida,* the story of the lovers had been retold many times, and the character of Cressida had been debased to that of a harlot. Chiefly responsible for this metamorphosis was Henryson's *The Testament of Cresseid,* which after 1532, when it was printed as Chaucer's in an edition of his works, was thought to be authentically Chaucerian. Henryson's poem is a sequel to the earlier narrative, beginning after Diomed, tiring of her, dismisses Cresseid. The girl rails against the gods in whom she had placed her trust, particularly Venus and Cupid, and in anger they transform her into a leper; she laments and goes upon her way, and finally dies—but not before Prince Troilus, upon his horse, passes her in the road and, not recognizing her transformed face, gives her alms. Henryson's tale treats the character of Cresseid sympathetically and with great human insight, although she is condemned for her faithlessness and especially for her great pride. Nevertheless, the Elizabethans read the piece entirely in the light of Cresseid's treachery, and it was not long before she became synonymous with all the evil qualities that the character in Shakespeare's play is willing to acknowledge if she prove false: "Yea, let them

say, to stick the heart of falsehood,/'As false as Créssid' "
(3.2.196–97).

There had been other dramatic renderings of the story
before Shakespeare's, but all are lost; there is little doubt,
however, that Cressida appeared in these versions as a
strumpet. A surviving stage direction from the lost play by
Chettle and Dekker (1599) reads, "Enter Cressida, with
Beggars"—probably the company of lepers among whom,
in Henryson's poem, she dies. References to Cressida as a
whore abound in Elizabethan literature, and we may be
sure that, just as the word for a base procurer stems from
her uncle's name, her own became an equally common
epithet.

The significance of this transformation should not be
underestimated, although we may regret the violence it
appears to do Chaucer and even Henryson. Shakespeare, in
fact, may have been attracted to the plot, as I have suggested
in the Introduction, because of its apparently unqualified
statement of inconstancy. In this sense, his use of Homer
(and Chapman's Homer), Lydgate, and Caxton, is much
closer to our normal understanding of the word "source"
than is his reliance upon Chaucer. Although most of the
details of the story are transformed, those relating to the
camp and council scenes stand much closer to the originals
than does his treatment of the love story.

Modern editions of major sources:

H. Bergen, ed. Lydgate's *Troy Book. Early English Text
Society,* No. 97 (1906); Nos. 103, 106 (1908); No. 126
(1935).

Allardyce Nicoll, ed. *Chapman's Homer* (Bollingen
Series XLI). 2 vols. New York: Pantheon Books, Inc., 1956.

F. N. Robinson, ed. *Troilus and Criseyde,* in *The Complete Works of Geoffrey Chaucer.* Boston: Houghton Mifflin
Company; London: Oxford University Press, 1933. 2nd
ed., 1957.

R. K. Root, ed. *The Book of Troilus and Criseyde by*

Geoffrey Chaucer. Princeton, N. J.: Princeton University Press, 1945.

H. O. Sommer, ed. Caxton's *The Recuyell of the Histo-ryes of Troye*. 2 vols. London: 1894.

Commentaries

D. A. TRAVERSI

Troilus and Cressida

The close relationship between the values of love and war, which is one of the most marked features of *Troilus and Cressida,* corresponds to a conception of dramatic unity which, although its antecedents can be traced respectively to the sonnets and the historical plays, was, at the time of writing, new in his work. The novelty consists in uniting, in a manner mutually illuminating, a personal theme and its public, "social" extension. Instead of a political conflict objectively studied and commented on by a character (such as Falstaff) who stands, in a sense, outside it, we are presented with a personal issue—the story of two lovers of opposed parties—set in the context of the Trojan war. The situation of the lovers is variously connected with the cleavage between the warring parties to which they respectively belong; and the connection thus dramatically established is further strengthened by the pervasive presence of imagery which suggests disruptive tendencies barely contained within a common way of feeling. The result, in terms

From *An Approach to Shakespeare* by D. A. Traversi (2nd ed. rev. New York: Doubleday & Company, Inc. [Anchor Books], 1956). Reprinted by permission of the author.

of poetic drama, is less a finished and coherent creation than a statement of emotional ambiguity, the reflection of an experience deprived of order and seeking clarification through its own expression.

The nature of this ambiguity, and more particularly its relation to the preoccupation with time, which we have already considered in the sonnets, is perhaps best studied in the passage in which Troilus takes leave of Cressida:

> *Cressida.* And is it true that I must go from Troy? . . .
> Is it possible?
> *Troilus.* And suddenly; where injury of chance
> Puts back leave-taking, justles roughly by
> All time of pause, rudely beguiles our lips
> Of all rejoindure, forcibly prevents
> Our lock'd embrasures, strangles our dear vows
> Even in the birth of our own laboring breath;
> We two, that with so many thousand sighs
> Did buy each other, must poorly sell ourselves
> With the rude brevity and discharge of one.
> Injurious time now with a robber's haste
> Crams his rich thievery up, he knows not how;
> As many farewells as be stars in heaven,
> With distinct breath and consign'd kisses to them,
> He fumbles up into a loose adieu,
> And scants us with a single famish'd kiss,
> Distasted with the salt of broken tears.   (4.4.30–48)

The verbal intricacy of this speech is highly characteristic of the play and helps to throw light upon the peculiar nature of its inspiration. The experience it reflects is, verbally at least, tremendously rich, endlessly elaborate, but the ordering of it is not equal to the complexity. The adverse action of time upon the parting lovers is represented by an astonishing number of verbs—"puts back," "justles roughly by," "rudely beguiles," "forcibly prevents," "strangles"—but the emotion does not *develop,* does not acquire added coherence in the course of its expression. It remains a long and acutely sensed effort to express a single moment of conflicting feeling. It belongs, in short, to a period in Shakespeare's development in which the keenness of his apprehension of certain elements of experience (already for the most part indicated in the sonnets) was not accompanied by a corresponding sense of order and significance. We shall see that order and significance gradually growing out of the increasing mastery of his art.

Nonetheless, though unsatisfactory, the experience behind *Troilus* is highly individual. In each of the verbs of parting which we have just collected there is an element, sharply and vividly realized, of harsh and hostile physical contact. This labored feeling is balanced by the poignant thinness of the positive love imagery which so inadequately accompanies it. Troilus, whose awareness of separation is so acute, so tangibly conceived, can only express his passion in images as intense as they are airy and essentially bodiless. Love is indeed "rich" in his estimation, fit to be mentioned with the "stars in heaven"; but it can only be expressed in "sighs" and "laboring *breath*," in the hurried breathlessness of "distinct *breath* and consign'd kisses," and in the intensely palated but transitory delicacy of "Distasted with the salt of broken tears." Opposed to this "airy," pathetic passion, the full brunt of the senses is felt in every phrase that stresses parting. "Rudely," "roughly," "forcibly," time and hostile circumstance undermine the tragic brevity of love, so that the "lock'd embrasures" which should normally convey the intensity of physical union are felt to be only an effort to snatch a moment's identity in the face of events which are forcibly drawing the lovers apart. The parting imposed by external circumstances, indeed, is subsidiary to a certain weakness inherent in passion itself. The ideal, which is perfect union, is desired intensely, but is as light as "breath" or "air"; and the bodies through whose coming together alone this intensity can be enjoyed are always, while they are united, "laboring" against a tendency to separate. Their "labor," irrevocably frustrated, issues in nothing tangible or permanent. Throughout *Troilus* the elements in love-making for separation are too strong for those which desire union, and "injurious time" is the process by which separation is born out of desired consummation.

Troilus and Cressida, then, insofar as it deals with the central pair of lovers, projects a metaphysical situation into the evocation of a personal relationship. The play is, in this as in other respects, the product of a profound uncertainty about the value of experience. The personal consequence of this uncertainty, as it affects more particularly the love poetry of Troilus, is the corruption of romantic sentiment. This is apparent in his first account of Cressida:

> I tell thee I am mad
> In Cressid's love; thou answer'st "she is fair";
> Pour'st in the open ulcer of my heart
> Her eyes, her hair, her cheek, her gait, her voice,
> Handlest in thy discourse, O that her hand,
> In whose comparison all whites are ink
> Writing their own reproach, to whose soft seizure
> The cygnet's down is harsh, and spirit of sense
> Hard as the palm of ploughman. (1.1.53–61)

The underlying convention here is clearly Petrarchan, romantically abstracted from common reality. It makes itself felt in the assertion that Troilus is "mad" for love, in the strained use of "pour'st" and "handlest" to describe Pandarus's speech, in the comparison of Cressida's hand to the "cygnet's down," and in the introduction of "ink" to bring out by contrast its superlative whiteness. But the conventional imagery is transformed, as it were, from within in a manner so closely bound up with the convention that it acts as a corrupting agent, intimately related to the surface sentiment. By giving deep sensuous value to the Petrarchan images, it conveys simultaneously an impression of intense feeling and an underlying lack of content. "Handlest in thy discourse" is, as I have said, a farfetched, literary image; but it brings with it a notable keenness of touch which is developed in the contrast between harshness and the "soft seizure" of the cygnet's down and in the almost unnatural immediacy of "spirit of sense." Yet the conventional note remains, and with it the feeling that Troilus's passion, for all its surface intensity, has an inadequate foundation, is vitiated by the strained self-pity which allows him to refer to "the open ulcer of my heart," and by the weakness to which he confesses in the course of the same speech: "I am weaker than a woman's tear."

It is important to realize why this weakness, which Cressida shares with her lover, does not produce a tragedy of character, but of situation. The tragedy indeed consists less in the personal suffering of the lovers than in the overriding influence exercised by time upon all human relationships and feelings. In *Antony and Cleopatra,* at least while the lovers are united by their feeling for one another, personal emotion has become strong enough to override mutability; in *Troilus,* the supremacy of time is never really questioned, and so a consistent status as persons inevitably eludes the lovers. Their weakness reflects the uncertainty of mood in which the play was conceived and to which they owe the peculiar poignancy, more than sentimental and less than tragic, with which they meet their personal fortunes. Antony and Cleopatra, as lovers, are fully drawn human beings because their love, while it lasts and within its own clearly defined limitations, is valid and confers upon their emotions a full personal value. Conversely, the complete realization in evil of Regan and Goneril in *King Lear,* with the sensual ferocity that characterizes it, proves that when he wrote that play, Shakespeare felt himself able to distinguish between the various elements in his moral experience without falling into ambiguity and confusion. Antony and Cleopatra, Regan and Goneril have full reality as characters precisely because they proceed from a clear understanding in their creator of the value of human emotion as distinct from the evil possibilities contained in it. *Troilus and Cressida,* however, with its intuition of passion as vain and transitory, is compatible with no such individuality of presentation; for time, as it is understood in this play, destroys personal values and makes them invalid.

This limiting observation can be applied with equal force to the behavior of both lovers, and through the entire action. Cressida's falseness does not spring from a deep-seated perversity or even from a strong positive attraction for Diomed, but from the mere process of events, from a flaw inherent in the human situation. Her tragedy, such as it is, derives from awareness of her helplessness. We feel it in her pathetic appeal when Troilus prepares to leave her after the night they have spent together:

> Prithee, tarry;
> You men will never tarry,   (4.2.15–16)

and in the moment of self-knowledge in which she tells him:

> I have a kind of self resides with you,
> But an unkind self that itself will leave
> To be another's fool.   (3.2.149–51)

There is something in the expression of this uncertainty, half punning and conventional, which makes it difficult to conceive of Cressida as a fully realized being. At most she lives for us only in the mood of the moment, with barely a sign of that responsibility and consistency which is involved in the very conception of character. Any attempt to subject her inconsistency to a moral, of the kind which the medieval elaborators of this legend had in mind when they denounced her "faithlessness," is out of place because the spirit in which Shakespeare created her made it impossible for her to be shown as really responsible for her actions; and without responsibility there can be no moral evaluation. When she comments in the early part of the play on her refusal to reveal her feelings for Troilus:

> Yet hold I off. Women are angels, wooing;
> Things won are done; joy's soul lies in the doing,
> (1.2.298–99)

her aphoristic lines are not a revelation of wantonness, but simply an impression of the sense, which constitutes the only true tragedy of this play, of the impossibility, the meaninglessness of constancy in a world where time dominates human relationships and where attraction and separation seem necessary and connected aspects of a single situation.

This impossibility also dominates the poetry of Troilus himself and is there further developed from its original basis in romantic sentiment. Troilus's passion, even before it is faced with the necessity for separation, is strong only in anticipation. The intensity of its sensations is conveyed in a refinement of physical feeling, in an attempt to embody in terms of the senses an insubstantial and incorporeal emotion:

> I am giddy; expectation whirls me round.
> The imaginary relish is so sweet
> That it enchants my sense; what will it be,
> When that the watery palates taste indeed
> Love's thrice-repured nectar? death, I fear me,
> Swounding destruction, or some joy too fine,
> Too subtle-potent, tuned too sharp in sweetness,
> For the capacity of my ruder powers:
> I fear it much, and I do fear besides
> That I shall lose distinction in my joys . . . (3.2.17–26)

The sensations of this passage are intense enough, but only on the palate and through the senses; like the corresponding emotions of Cressida, they scarcely involve any full personality in the speaker. Troilus's emotions are concentrated on "expectation," on "the *imaginary* relish," and he feels that the "watery palates" will be too weak to sustain the actual consummation. The whole speech turns upon this contrast between the refined intensity of feeling which he seeks, self-consciously and with a touch of indulgence, in "Love's *thrice-repured* nectar," and the giddiness, the "swounding destruction," which would follow its impossible consummation. The experience of love, it is suggested, is so fine, so "subtle-potent," that it surpasses the "ruder powers" of the body and remains an incorporeal aspiration which the senses strive vainly to attain.

Yet, by a strange contradiction, it is precisely because fulfillment in love is sought by Troilus exclusively on the sensual level that it proves unattainable. We can see now why the poetry of this play makes such extensive use of the imagery of taste, why Cressida, for example, says, before she leaves Troy for the Greek camp:

> The grief is fine, full, perfect, that I taste. (4.4.3)

Taste is a sense at once luxurious, delicate, and transitory; also it can be connected, in gross opposition to Troilus's bodiless idealism, with digestion and the functioning of the body. For the weakness of Troilus's passion, as we have already suggested, implies that it is patent of corruption; and that corruption—it can now be added—is the logical consequence of an effort to extract from the refinement of the sensual a substitute for spiritual experience. Immediately before the speech just quoted there is a striking turn of phrase in his appeal to Pandarus:

> O, be thou my Charon,
> And give me swift transportance to those fields
> Where I may *wallow* in the lily-beds
> Proposed for the deserver.   (3.2.10–12)

The ideal aspirations of Troilus remain abstract, intangible; such intensity as they achieve derives from their subjection to time, from their awareness of their own transitory nature. But this impermanence makes them bodiless, so that the sensual instincts, unable to associate themselves fully with the insubstantial ideal of union in a mutual passion, express themselves both weakly and basely, "wallowing" in what would be, if it were more forceful, a corrupt satisfaction.

This special use of the contrasted implications of sensual experience is extended in the course of the play from the personal to the public action, and contributes thus to the unity of its conception. The refined imagery of taste given to the Trojans, and especially to Troilus, reflects a bodiless ideal which becomes, in the mouths of the scurrilous Thersites and the Greek cynics, a series of clogged, heavy references to the digestive processes. Thersites has "majestic jaws," and Achilles calls him "my cheese, my digestion," while Agamemnon tells Patroclus that Achilles's virtues

> like fair fruit in an unwholesome dish
> Are like to rot untasted.   (2.3.122–23)

In fact, the very sense which expresses the related intensity and lightness of Trojan passion becomes, in the Greeks, a symbol of inaction and distemper out of which issue the boils, "the botchy core," of Thersites's disgust.

In this way we pass from the individual to the public

action, from the love of Troilus and Cressida to the war between the Greeks and Troy. This connection between the private and the public theme is indeed the most original feature of the play. The two parties, like the two lovers, are divergent within a common type of feeling. The Trojans share the fragile intensity of Troilus. They are deeply concerned with the value of "honor" and with a view of love which aspires to be idealistic, while Hector shows the virtues of war which are so noticeably absent from the bulky Ajax and the graceless Achilles. Typical of them is the speech in which Troilus explains the case for continuing the war:

> But, worthy Hector,
> She is a theme of honor and renown;
> A spur to valiant and magnanimous deeds,
> Whose present courage may beat down our foes,
> And fame in time to come canonize us. (2.2.198–202)

Yet the lightness and grace of this idealism covers a certain artificiality. It reads, at this stage in Shakespeare's development, like a survival from earlier plays set against the contortions and involutions of so much of *Troilus*. The impression is neither accidental nor isolated. Hector's reasoning in the same scene shows clearly that the arguments advanced by Troilus are as flimsy in content as their expression is tenuous. For all this "honor," for which Troilus is ready to fight and, if need be, to die, is directed to the defense of Helen, whose worth has been destroyed by the manner in which she has been stolen from Menelaus. Even Paris can only plead that he

> would have the *soil* of her *fair* rape
> Wiped off in honorable keeping her,

and Troilus, conveying a slight but unmistakable twist to conventional imagery, declares that Paris

> . . . bought a Grecian queen,
> whose youth and *freshness*
> Wrinkles Apollo's and *makes stale* the morning.

The juxtaposition of "fair" and "soil," "freshness" and "stale," touches the basic weakness of Trojan idealism, and points to the way in which that idealism is organically connected in its expression with the sluggish inertia that prevails in the Greek camp.

The true nature of this Trojan weakness is perhaps most explicitly stated by Troilus when he sets forth, in an attempt at reasoned expression, his argument for the continuation of the war:

> I take today a wife, and my election
> Is led on in the conduct of my will;
> My will enkindled by mine eyes and ears,
> Two traded pilots 'twixt the dangerous shores
> Of will and judgment: how may I avoid,
> Although my will distaste what it elected,
> The wife I chose? There can be no evasion
> To blench from this, and to stand firm by honor. (61–68)

Troilus's terminology is indefinite and the expression of his argument, like so much of what passes for discussion in this play, far more complicated than its content. There seems at one point to be an opposition of "will," which we may associate here with sensual impulse, and "judgment," by which this impulse should normally be restrained and directed; the opposition, in short, of sensuality and moral control, which became a little later the central theme of *Measure for Measure*. In that play, however, the moral conflict is explicitly stated, and—what is more important—takes shape in a dramatic clash of clearly defined personalities; in *Troilus and Cressida* there is only an uncertainty, a sense of uneasiness, which the notable incoherence of the expression reflects. The conclusion reached by "judgment" is that affirmed by Hector—"value dwells not in particular will," but rather in a weighing of alternatives in the light of the principles of reason—but the whole trend of Troilus's reply is to annihilate, or at least confuse, the distinction between "will" and "judgment" themselves, to show that "judgment" is powerless and irrelevant once the sensual will has impelled man towards action. In other words, the basis of Troilus's "honor"

is simply sensual impulse, and its weakness lies largely in
his unwillingness to recognize this fact, and in the abstraction and lack of content which follow in the train of this
evasion.

Hector, indeed, is sufficiently outspoken on the subject of
Troilus's infatuation:

> Is your blood
> So madly hot that no discourse of reason,
> Nor fear of bad success in a bad cause
> Can qualify the same? (115–18)

The argument—though Troilus rejects it and Hector himself
fails to follow it to its conclusion—once more binds the personal love theme to that of the justification of public action.
Troilus—and in this he is typical of the Trojans—refuses
to admit the weakness of his conception of honor, which
is, however, implied in the very situation which brought
the war into being: for the reality of Helen, as Hector points
out, does not correspond to Troilus's embroidered and
Marlovian conception of her:

> Brother, she is not worth what she doth cost
> The holding (51–52)

But this same lack of solid foundation is apparent, as we
have seen, in the undertones of Troilus's own poetry, where
the unacknowledged sensual basis of his idealism refuses to
be entirely suppressed. Underlying the "poetical" quality of
Troilus's emotional flights, there is a distinct strain of
coarseness and inertia. It appears in the references, so typical
of this play, to the "soiled silks" and the "remainder viands"
which are thrown away "because we now are full." Most
typical of all, in the determination to hide its own weakness
which it implies, is the Trojan reaction to reason:

> Nay, if we talk of reason,
> Let's shut our gates, and sleep: manhood and honor
> Should have hare hearts, would they but *fat* their thoughts
> With this *crammed* reason: reason and respect
> Make *livers pale* and lustihood deject. (46–50)

This insistence upon mental inertia and the obstruction of physical processes, as applied to reason, stands in significant contrast to the lightness and artificiality of Troilus's idealistic outbursts, but they are organically related to them. The Trojan devotion to honor, Shakespeare would seem to infer, is devotion to an abstraction that has no sufficient basis in reason, that is, in fact, no more than an empty justification of impulse; but—it is equally important to realize—to abandon honor for its lack of rational foundation is to expose oneself to the danger of lethargy, to a rooted disinclination to act at all.[1] Once more we are faced with the split between motive and impulse, moral *value* and sensual substitutes, which dominates this play, without a real glimpse of resolution.

The analysis of this important scene suggests how the contrast between the Greek and Trojan parties, which most critics have noted, is modified by significant points of contact. The Trojans, for all their concern to defend honor against the Greeks, are strangely related to their enemies. This relationship, of course, is openly "symbolized" in the combat between Hector and Ajax (4.5), when Hector refuses to carry on the duel with his "cousin-german" and Ajax agrees to call a truce. But the contacts established through a common type of imagery are still more important for an understanding of the play. Where the Trojans reject reason in favor of ill-considered action, the Greeks accept it and are reduced to inaction. Agamemnon's very first speech, as the head and cornerstone of Greek unity, shows how inconclusive are the intellectual processes so painfully followed by the leaders who accompany him and how closely related they are to the views expressed by Troilus on "crammed reason":

> Princes,
> What grief hath set the jaundice on your cheeks?
> The ample proposition that hope makes
> In all designs begun on earth below
> Fails in the promised largeness; checks and disasters

[1] The relation of this to *Hamlet,* and in particular to such a soliloquy as "How all occasions do inform against me" (4.4) is worth careful consideration.

Grow in the veins of actions highest reared,
As knots, by the conflux of meeting sap,
Infect the sound pine and divert his grain
Tortive and errant from his course of growth.
Nor, princes, is it matter new to us
That we come short of our suppose so far
That after seven years' siege yet Troy walls stand;
Sith every action that hath gone before,
Whereof we have record, trial did draw
Bias and thwart, not answering the aim
And that unbodied figure of the thought
That gave it surmised shape.   (1.3.1–17)

Agamemnon's thought proceeds not from point to point
according to a definite logical sequence, but by a series of
indeterminate digressions which illustrate his incapacity to
come to a conclusion. His labored illustrations destroy the
coherence of an argument which they do nothing to further;
as so often in this play, there is no recognizable development
of thought to justify the complexity. The repeated doublings
of words—"checks and disasters," "tortive and errant,"
"bias and thwart"—all lay emphasis upon obstruction, upon
the speaker's struggle against obscure impediments which
hinder the Greeks from successful action; and the use of
unusual and unassimilated Latinized words, such as "conflux" and "tortive," produces a similar sense of resistance
and difficulty. More significantly still, these obstructions are
associated with disturbances and interruptions in organic
growth. The prospect of hope "fails in the promised large-
ness," does not grow to its anticipated stature. "Checks and
disasters" are intertwined with natural growth, and the very
rising of the sap in the "sound pine," which is so eminently
a natural process, produces infection and distortion in the
growth of the tree. Most important of all, because corresponding to the spirit expressed by Troilus, thought is
"unbodied" and its processes, separated from the actual
course of events, are equally cut off from the sensual immediacy which finds irresponsible expression in the comments
of Thersites. The keen nervous quality so noticeably lacking
in the theoretical observations of the Greek leaders breaks
out significantly in Thersites's sweeping affirmation of

anarchy and disorder; in a similar manner, Troilus's disembodied idealism covers a sensual impulse which he refuses to recognize.

It is only natural that this discrepancy in the Greeks between thought and action should be expressed in terms of physical disorder; and here the link with the Trojans becomes even more explicit. Thersites's boils and plague spots are related to Agamemnon's laborious thoughts on authority just as Troilus's contempt for "crammed reason" and his insistent sense of soilure and physical obstruction are connected with his abstract idealism. The vital point in Shakespeare's presentation of the Greeks is this association of continual ratiocination with a complete overthrow of "degree"; they are entirely unable to turn council into united action. The position in the Greek camp is briefly summed up by Thersites: "Agamemnon is a fool to offer to command Achilles, Achilles is a fool to be commanded of Agamemnon, Thersites is a fool to serve such a fool, and Patroclus is a fool positive" (2.3.64–67). While Agamemnon, Nestor, and Ulysses scheme and discuss, Ajax and Achilles "fust" out of action; the hand that executes is out of touch with the "*still and mental* parts" that contrive the conduct of the war. Perhaps the point is most clearly made by Ulysses in his account of Achilles's pride:

> imagined worth
> Holds in his blood such swoln and hot discourse
> That *'twixt his mental and his active parts*
> Kingdom'd Achilles in commotion rages
> And batters down himself. (175–78)

The conflict in Achilles between personal pride and duty to the Greek cause is stated here in terms of "blood," of sensual passion; the implications of "swoln and hot" suggesting feverish disorder due to extreme intemperance, are unmistakable. The adjective "kingdom'd," like so many of the words which characterize the poetry of this play, is not fully explicit, but it clearly refers the personal issue back to the general theme of "degree." The individual warrior, like the Greek polity at war, should be a unity founded upon "degree"; and "degree" in the individual is an ideal correspondence between thought and action, impulse and control, "blood" and "judgment."[2]

On both sides this balance is profoundly disturbed. The "cunning" of the Greek leaders is manifestly out of touch with practical considerations and expends itself in an activity completely disproportionate to the desired end: "it will not in circumvention deliver a fly from a spider, without drawing their massy irons and cutting the web" (2.3.16–18). On the Trojan side the infidelity of Cressida finally undermines Troilus's faith in "honor" as a basis for action and leaves him dimly aware of the incompatible and contrary elements which underlie what he had assumed to be the indivisible simplicity of passion:

> Within my soul there doth conduce a fight
> Of this strange nature, that a thing inseparate
> Divides more wider than the sky and earth;
> And yet the spacious breadth of this division
> Admits no orifex for a point as subtle
> As Ariadne's broken woof to enter.
> Instance, O instance! strong as Pluto's gates;
> Cressid is mine, tied with the bonds of heaven:
> Instance, O instance! strong as heaven itself,
> The bonds of heaven are slipp'd, dissolved and
>   loosed:
> And with another knot, five-finger-tied,
> The fragments of her faith, orts of her love,
> The fragments, scraps, the bits and greasy relics
> Of her o'er-eaten faith, are bound to Diomed.
>
> (5.2.144–57)

All the characteristics of the love poetry of Troilus can be recognized here—its tenuous and unnaturally refined

---

[2]Compare Hamlet:

> . . . blest are those
> Whose blood and judgment are so well commingled
> That they are not a pipe for fortune's finger
> To sound what stop she pleases.   (3.2)

expression, its subtlety in dealing with distinctions within an apparent unity, its sensuous thinness balanced by the imagery of disgust and repletion which connects it with the verse given to the Greeks and indicates the unifying factor in this play. For the ambiguous attitude towards experience which so deeply exercised Shakespeare in many of his sonnets is the determining factor in his presentation of both parties. Proceeding from his sense of the disharmony introduced by their subjection to the temporal process into the love of Troilus and Cressida, it extends to embrace the two parties in their fantastic and unreasonable conflict. The Trojans follow a false idealism, which deceives itself with talk of "honor," but is really based on "blood" and ends in a pathetic and helpless realization of its own insufficiency; the Greeks elaborate endlessly a "judgment" that is out of touch with the instinctive sources of action, until Agamemnon's chaotic reasoning finds its proper counterpart in the distorted bitterness of Thersites's diseased sensibility.

The fundamental impulse to this play, and the link which binds personal cleavage to political disorder, is now clear. Ulysses's argument on "degree" reduces itself finally to an intuition of self-consuming passion:

> Then everything includes itself in power,
> Power into will, will into *appetite;*
> And appetite, an universal wolf,
> So doubly seconded with will and power,
> Must make perforce an universal prey,
> And last eat up himself.   (1.3.119–24)

The speech is saved from the charge of abstraction by this relation of "degree" to the disorder introduced by passion or "appetite" into the human organism. This disorder, present on both sides in the conflict between Greeks and Trojans, is the real theme of the play. The Trojans seek to ignore the limitations of passion in a bodiless idealism; the Greeks, quite incapable of idealism, are weighed down by all that the Trojans try to forget. Both sides are bound together by the occasion of their quarrel; as Thersites says: "All the argument is a cuckold and a whore." Troilus, in one magnificent

phrase, sums up the crux from which the varied contradic-
tions of the play draw their interest:

> This is the monstruosity in love, lady, that the will
> is infinite and the execution confined, that the desire
> is boundless and the act a slave to limit. (3.2.82–85)

The infinity sought by the will is the idealistic love of
Troilus, which neglects the wearing action of time and the
related inability of passion to live up to ideals of love and
honor which can only be redeemed from abstraction by an
adequate spiritual integration; and the very boundlessness of
the desire, when it encounters the limits imposed by time
and the body to which, in the absence of such an integration,
it feels enslaved, turns to the clogged inertia of Achilles and
the endless self-scrutiny of the Greek camp.

S. L. BETHELL

From Shakespeare and the
Popular Dramatic Tradition

Troilus and Cressida is a consciously philosophical play.
Normally Shakespeare's philosophical notions are incar-
nated in character and action; and his poetic thought, always
concrete and image-filled, relates to character and action
directly, and only indirectly to whatever general truths may
be implied. The "Tomorrow, and tomorrow" speech (*Macbeth* 5.5.) expresses directly Macbeth's reaction to his
wife's death, and merely implies the atheism ("dusty
death," "Signifying nothing") which has resulted from his
gradual hardening in crime. In *Troilus and Cressida,* on the
other hand, the thought, only partially embodied in character and action, flows over into the dialogue, which, though
usually concrete enough and full of imagery, is frequently
developed almost independently of the situation to which it
refers. Ulysses' great speech on "degree" (*Troilus and
Cressida* 1.3.75) begins and ends with Troy, but is much
more concerned with generalities of political philosophy
than with the Trojan war: in *Troilus and Cressida* the story
is an excuse for thought rather than the embodiment of
thought. The metaphysical problems of the tragedies must,
from the first, have presented themselves to Shakespeare in
terms of concrete experience; but in *Troilus and Cressida*
he pursues philosophical abstractions with the impassioned
eagerness of Donne. Problems of time and value and their
mutual relations are thrust forward for the audience's
attention:

From *Shakespeare and the Popular Dramatic Tradition* by S. L. Bethell
(London: Staples Press, 1944; Durham, North Carolina: Duke University
Press, 1945). Reprinted by permission of Staples Press.

> Time hath, my lord, a wallet at his back,
> Wherein he puts alms for oblivion. (3.3.145)

As in Donne, philosophy is usually apprehended in terms of sense experience, but occasionally even the bare bones of abstract thinking appear, e.g., in Troilus' crucial but awkward query: "What is aught, but as 'tis valued?" (2.2.52).

In such a play it is no wonder to find characters with something of a "morality" flavor. As Thersites recalls the old Vice, so Ulysses conveys some suggestion of an abstract Worldly Wisdom. Most of the characters in *Troilus and Cressida* express themselves philosophically, but Ulysses has an especially large share of such speeches, including the famous "degree" speech and the speech on Time. With him even more than the others, what he says is infinitely more important than why he says it, and at times even his behavior is hard to interpret on naturalistic grounds. When Cressida arrives in the Grecian camp, Agamemnon receives her with a kiss:

> Our general doth salute you with a kiss, (4.5.19)

says Nestor. Ulysses comments with a pun:

> Yet is the kindness but particular;
> 'Twere better she were kiss'd in general. (20–21)

The others act upon this advice, and Cressida is kissed in turn by all the Greek leaders. When his own turn comes, however, there is a short wit-battle in which Ulysses insultingly rejects the kiss that Cressida is presumably willing to give:

Ulysses. May I, sweet lady, beg a kiss of you?

Cressida. You may.

Ulysses.   I do desire it.

Cressida.   Why, beg, then.

Ulysses. Why then for Venus' sake, give me a kiss,
    When Helen is a maid again, and his
    [i.e. Menelaus'].
Cressida. I am your debtor, claim it when 'tis due.

Ulysses. Never's my day, and then a kiss of you.

When Diomedes leads Cressida away, Ulysses bursts into denunciation:

> Fie, fie upon her!
> There's language in her eye, her cheek, her lip,
> Nay, her foot speaks; her wanton spirits look out
> At every joint and motive of her body.
> O, these encounterers, so glib of tongue,
> That give accosting welcome ere it comes,
> And wide unclasp the tables of their thoughts
> To every ticklish reader! set them down
> For sluttish spoils of opportunity
> And daughters of the game.   (54–63)

Speaking naturalistically, we should admire this moral rectitude more heartily, if Ulysses had not himself initiated the general kissing. Taken conventionally, however, the incident is central to the Troilus-Cressida theme. The handing over of Cressida to the Greeks is the handing over of Troilus' ideal love to the sullying of the world: we are to be prepared for his betrayal, and our knowledge of Cressida's character must be so established that no psychological doubt remain to befog the philosophical issue. Ulysses, at least during this incident (episodic intensification again!), represents an impersonal Wisdom, whose judgment we must accept. He devises a test for Cressida which sufficiently reveals her character and the character of those she has come among; and his own refusal to kiss her sets him apart from the others, in judicial aloofness, so that we are prepared to accept the verdict which he pronounces after Cressida is led away. The whole passage is in rhyme and full of wordplay: this not only emphasizes the tone of badinage and flirtation, but also serves to distance or frame the whole incident, which thus appears in a sort of vocal italics to draw attention to its symbolic function. To condemn Ulysses' conduct as ungentlemanly would be to attribute to the character a representational quality which the passage seems to disallow. There is a suggestion of deity about Ulysses: we must accept his moral judgments, but we must not search the morality of his own conduct, which is, as it were, an Olympian setting of the stage for human conflict. As the embodiment of wisdom, he is to be praised or blamed solely in reference to that one quality. It is only at times that this hint of allegory appears in the action and dialogue of Ulysses: Shakespeare's reversion to an older technique is probably unconscious; but it is none the less interesting on that account.

Troilus and Cressida, as probably the most intellectual of Shakespeare's plays, reveals an unusually high degree of conventionalism in the presentation of character; examples can be found of most of the conventions discussed in this chapter and the last. Thersites, whose relation to the Vice has already been mentioned, might perhaps best be classed as a "humor," his predominant characteristic being cynical and prurient wit. Lechery is his favorite theme:

> Nothing but lechery! all incontinent varlets! (5.1.102–03)

He does duty also as a scurrilous chorus upon the futility of war—a role comparable to that of Falstaff in the battle scenes of *Henry IV, Part 1*. His remark above occurs significantly at the end of a scene, and the next scene closes with a similar but even more emphatic outburst:

> Lechery, lechery; still, wars and lechery; nothing else holds fashion: a burning devil take them!   (5.2.192–94)

To close two successive scenes of the fifth act in this way is surely to commend the opinion of Thersites to our very serious attention. Ajax and Achilles are practically humors:

senseless vanity and strength in Ajax; selfish pride and strength in Achilles. Helen is also a humor: in the one scene in which she appears, her only characteristic is a weak and silly sex obsession:

> Let thy song be love: this love will undo us all. O Cupid, Cupid, Cupid!   (3.1.111–12)

Professor Wilson Knight is surely mistaken in considering her to be a worthy object of Trojan idealism.[1] This scene, which is almost central in position, is certainly central at any rate to one theme of the play: the theme of "fair without and foul within," which I shall later treat more fully. The Helen whose face had launched a thousand Marlovian ships is subjected to a remorseless Shakespearean "debunking"; in a few lines the real Helen is revealed, the inadequate object of so much misplaced idealism. Other characters in the play are more complex, though none is seen very clearly in the round. . . .

Action as well as character may be symbolic, even action which is not represented on the stage. Paris' request that Helen should "help unarm our Hector" (149) clinches the Helen scene and assures its central position. The outward show of chivalry is there; but we know Hector to be the worthiest of the Trojans, and Helen a worthless strumpet. That Hector should yield to fight in such a cause is the undoing of himself and of Troy: that Helen should play the role of his "fair lady"—a Helen who can be so much at home with Pandarus—is the height of Shakespearean irony. In the play's last act, action and character mingle in what is unique in Shakespeare—a direct allegorical presentation of his dramatic theme. Hector, despite the entreaties of Andromache, and the prophetic warnings of Cassandra, joins the battle, as his honor bids him. The usual battle confusion is presented in what modern editors unnecessarily divide into a series of short scenes. Near the end of Scene 6 there is a stage direction which reads, in our

---

[1]So at least he implies, in speaking of this scene: "the strains of music," he says, "herald the entry of Helen, queen of romance" (*The Wheel of Fire*, p. 67).

modern editions, *Enter one in sumptuous armor*. In the Quarto and Folios, it is simply *Enter one in armor*,[2] but Malone's addition of "sumptuous"[3] merely underlines Shakespeare's obvious intention, for Hector cries out to this anonymous figure:

> Stand, stand, thou Greek; thou art a goodly mark:
> No? Wilt thou not? I like thy armor well;
> I'll frush it and unlock the rivets all,
> But I'll be master of it: wilt thou not, beast, abide?
> Why, then fly on, I'll hunt thee for thy hide.
>
> (5.6.27–31)

At the beginning of Scene 8, we find Hector presumably standing over the mysterious person, whom he has now slain, and saying:

> Most putrefied core, so fair without,
> Thy goodly armor thus hath cost thy life.
> Now is my day's work done; I'll take good breath:
> Rest, sword; thou hast thy fill of blood and death.
>
> (5.8.1–4)

At this point "*Enter* Achilles *and* Myrmidons," and Hector meets his death unarmed at the hands of the cowardly hero and his pack. We hear from Troilus, two scenes later, that

> He's dead; and at the murderer's horse's tail,
> In beastly sort, dragg'd through the shameful field.
>
> (5.10.4–5)

Shakespeare took the incident of the "one in sumptuous armor" from Lydgate's *Troye Boke*,[4] but seems to have given it a wider significance. The crucial question here is, "Why 'putrefied core'?"[5] There is nothing in Lydgate to

---

[2,3]*Troilus and Cressida*, in *The Cambridge Shakespeare*, ed. William Aldis Wright (Macmillan, 1894), p. 159, note to 1.27.

[4]*Vide*, a note of Steevens, in Malone's edition of Shakespeare (pub. 1821), vol. viii, p. 437:

explain this remarkable apostrophe. What did Shakespeare intend by it? The "one in sumptuous armor" was surely not dead when he first entered, and he had had no time to putrefy after being killed. Or does it mean that he was old, or diseased, or infirm? In any event, Hector had won the armor which he coveted, so why this apparently embittered comment? I do not see any naturalistic explanation. What I suggest is that Shakespeare saw in the incident in Lydgate an allegory similar to the "whited sepulcher" of Holy Scripture: "a sumptuous armor" stands for the "outward show" which covers an inner corruption. Perhaps with the scriptural passage in mind, Shakespeare rendered his symbol complete by adding the "putrefied core," although the reference is incapable of natural explanation, and must be taken by the audience on an entirely different plane from the rest of the play. The "sumptuous armor" with its "putrefied core" thus becomes a symbol of all the play presents to us, an allegorical enactment of the theme of "fair without, and foul within," which is applicable almost everywhere in the Troy and Troilus stories as Shakespeare rewrites them. It applies to the war, with its false chivalry and inadequate aim; to Helen, to Cressida, and a good many more of the personages involved; and it applies, lastly, to the death of Hector, with which it is so closely linked in presentation. Hector was the

---

"This circumstance is taken from Lydgate's poem, p. 196:
'— Guido in his historic doth shew
By worthy Hector's fall, who coveting
To have the sumptuous armor of the king, etc.
So greedy was thereof, that when he had
The body up, and on his horse it bare,
To have the spoil thereof such haste he made
That he did hang his shield without all care
Behind him at his back, the easier
To pull the armor off at his desire,
And by that means his breast clean open lay,' etc.
This furnished Shakespeare with the hint for the following line:
'I am unarm'd; forego this vantage, Greek.' "
Malone obviously borrowed the epithet "sumptuous" from Steevens' quotation or its original.
⁵The word is "core," not "corse," and implies a metaphor from rotten fruit.

best of the Trojans, and better than the best of the
Greeks: he saw, most clearly of them all, the essential
evil of the war, waged to keep Helen from her lawful
husband:

> . . . 'tis mad idolatry
> To make the service greater than the god,
>
> (2.2.56–57)

he said. And yet he concluded for the continuation of
the war:

> For 'tis a cause that hath no mean dependance
> Upon our joint and several dignities.   (192–93)

Later, he ignored Andromache and Cassandra, in order to
fulfill the supposed duties of a false conception of honor.
Unworthy aims are bound to tarnish the most chivalrous
nature: and so Hector himself, a few moments before he is
brutally murdered, so far loses his chivalric courtesy as to
call out "beast" after the "one in sumptuous armor," and
then: "I'll hunt thee for thy hide"—the least worthy of
motives. His death and the shameful treatment of his corpse
are perhaps punishment in excess of his swerving, but they
point sharply to the previous degradation he had suffered.
Even in the *Troye Boke,* there is at least a suggestion that
Hector's death was in some sense a consequence of his
greed. Shakespeare elaborates the incident, places it at the
climax of his play, and removes all possibility of natural
explanation, so that he surely meant it to bear the extended
significance which I have suggested. Otherwise there seems
no point in his choice of this particular incident when so
many important happenings in the Troy story are necessarily
omitted, and absolutely no point in the further complication
of the "putrefied core."

Troilus and Cressida is thus a play which especially calls
for the exercise of multi-consciousness. In addition to the
usual dual consciousness of play world and real world, and
of past and present time, there is the dual consciousness of
story and philosophy, since the two are not wholly merged;

there is the dual consciousness of character as representative and as allegorical; and, further, there must be a dual consciousness of certain incidents in their naturalistic and their allegorical significances. . . .

REUBEN A. BROWER

From Poetic and Dramatic Structure in
Versions and Translations of Shakespeare

The typical "heresy" among critics of poetic drama two
generations back was to analyze the experience in terms of
dramatic "form"—plot, character, rising and falling action.
The typical heresy of the present generation has been to
reduce the well-made play to the well-wrought urn. *King
Lear* is no longer a bad play, but a supreme lyric poem
on order and disorder in nature. Both extremes of interpretation betray the same defect, the assumption that the play as
poem and the play as drama are separable entities. Although
every critic "knows better," acting better is another matter.
Whether we are formalists in the old sense or the new, what
we lack is not principles, but control of critical discourse,
mastery of a critical style for describing the experience of
drama, a style that will continually acknowledge the claims
of the poetic and the dramatic. This paper attempts to move
in the direction of creating such a style by exploring in a new
setting the connection between poetic and dramatic structures. The "new setting" offered is comparison of versions
and translations of Shakespeare's plays.

The aim of this study was first suggested by T. S. Eliot's
admirable remark in his essay on *Poetry and Drama:*
". . . when Shakespeare, in one of his mature plays, intro-
duces what might seem a purely poetic line or passage, it
never interrupts the action, or is out of character, but on the
contrary, in some mysterious way supports both action
and character." Another point of departure was Roman
Jakobson's paper, *Linguistics and Poetics*. In his analysis of

From *Poetics* (Polska Akademia Nauk, Instytut Badan Literackich, Warsaw, 1961). Reprinted by permission of the author and the editor.

Antony's funeral oration from *Julius Caesar,* Jakobson showed that by starting from the simplest uses of language, one could see that "The main dramatic force of Antony's exordium ... is achieved by Shakespeare's playing on grammatical categories and constructions." It should be noted here that I am approaching the problem of the poetic and the dramatic not as an expert in linguistics, but as a literary critic, not with the aim of making "censorious verdicts," but rather with the Arnoldian purpose of preparing for "the judgment which almost insensibly forms itself in a fair and clear mind, along with fresh knowledge." Like many English and American critics since the Richardsian revolution, I am concerned with interpreting works of imaginative literature, "imaginative" in the sense of offering experiences of a high degree of interconnectedness. (And we shall dine at journey's end with Coleridge and with Arnold.) Such works may be described as both "poetic" and "mimetic." "Poetic" structure is of the first importance: that is, language is being used to direct attention to the words as *heard* events and to produce "parallels" or "similarities." They are also "mimetic" in the sense that resources of language are being exploited in order to "mime," to represent men in action. In drama, obviously enough, all verbal resources, nonpoetic as well as poetic, are subdued to the mimetic function.

Translations offer most useful examples for exploring the connection between the two kinds of design because of the two necessary yet conflicting purposes of the translator. (1) He attempts to give the reader the same dramatic experience as that offered by the original (e.g., the experience of the voice, the role, the attitudes that equal *Hamlet*). (2) He attempts to produce this identity of effect through a different verbal medium, in another language. What happens when he undertakes this impossible task? What can we learn from his attempt about the interconnection of the poetic and the dramatic? (May I remind the reader that my aim is not to judge the translations, though judgments will now and then insensibly form themselves.). . .

Dryden's *Troilus and Cressida* is a more respectable example of Restoration "improvement" than Tate's *Lear,* and his transformations are also much more instructive. The blank verse is not despicable, and there is evidence that Dryden had a clear understanding of much that Shakespeare was doing. He is equally clear about the necessity of "correcting" Shakespeare's style, a necessity imposed by the state of the language, which he contrasts with that of Greek in the age of Aeschylus, when ". . . the Greek tongue was arriv'd to its full perfection. . . ." Consider the application of this doctrine in the reworking of Ulysses' great speech on "degree":

> *Ulysses*. Troy had been down ere this, and Hectors Sword
>   Wanted a Master but for our disorders:
>   The observance due to rule has been neglected;
>   Observe how many Grecians Tents stand void
>   Upon this plain; so many hollow factions:
>   For when the General is not like the Hive
>   To whom the Foragers should all repair,
>   What Hony can our empty Combs expect?
>   O when Supremacy of Kings is shaken,
>   What can succeed: How cou'd Communities
>   Or peacefull traffick from divided shores,
>   Prerogative of Age, Crowns, Scepters, Lawrells,
>   But by degree stand on their solid base!
>   Then everything resolves to brutal force
>   And headlong force is led by hoodwink'd will,
>   For wild Ambition, like a ravenous Woolf,
>   Spurd on by will and seconded by power,
>   Must make an universal prey of all,
>   And last devour it self.

The essential points in the Shakespearean argument are preserved, and key lines are kept or intelligently paraphrased. The case is clinched by the striking metaphor of the "ravenous Woolf"; but somehow the final line seems tame: we hardly feel that this beast will bite, let alone "devour itself." Comparison with Shakespeare's text shows why the metaphorical climax works so much better there than here. The whole speech—too long for quotation—has built up a highly particularized definition of "degree" as illustrated in different orders of society and in the cosmos, the disturbance of degree being expressed in violent metaphors of storm and

disease (with *related* imagery of feeding). The final paradox
has behind it a peculiar structure:

> Strength should be lord of imbecility,
> And the rude son should strike his father dead;
> Force should be right; or rather, right and wrong,
> Between whose endless jar justice resides,
> Should lose their names, and so should justice too,
> Then everything includes itself in power,
> Power into will, will into appetite;
> And appetite, an universal wolf,
> So doubly seconded with will and power,
> Must make perforce an universal prey,
> And last eat up himself.   (1.3.114–24)

Not only is "eat up himself" a cruder idiom; it is the sum-
ming up of a metaphorical and grammatical pattern. In sub-
stituting "ambition" for "appetite" Dryden shows that he had
not felt the way in which this image of self-cannibalism is
prepared for. We have a whole series of grammatical
"ingorgings" in which we hear one verbal mass, one name,
being eaten up, included, within another: right in force;
"right and wrong" in an "endless jar"; right, wrong, and justice "lose their names," absorbed in "everything"; "everything includes itself in power"; "power into will"; "will into
appetite" (and perhaps also will and power become seconds,
substitutes for appetite). Finally we hear the universal eater
consumed by the universal eaten (since appetite by eating
everything has become everything eaten). Appetite has been
verbally self-consumed a half dozen or more times before
the final paradox is released. Dryden's version is a perfect
example of poetic excitement diminished by the loss of a
peculiar grammatical figure. But the dramatic loss is equally
great. In the Shakespearean original we get a special sense
of a mind thinking and feeling its way through the process
of moral and social decay that is only *named* by the argument from degree. The fine intelligence projected by the
poetic progression, by the complexity of its grammatical
unfolding, largely disappears in the lines by Dryden. His
Ulysses is a pronouncer of clear and distinct platitudes,
much nearer to the public speakers of *Julius Caesar* than to

the tortured thinkers of this most metaphysical play. "Character" in this speech of Shakespeare is as much grammar as metaphor.

The reduction in style in this crucial passage of *Troilus and Cressida*—one that presents the key metaphor of "degree" in imagery that recurs throughout the play—has its effect much later in the main dramatic crisis, Troilus' discovery of Cressida's falsity:

[Troilus.] Was Cressid here?

Ulysses.   I cannot conjure, Trojan.

Troilus. She was not, sure.

Ulysses.   Most sure she was.

Troilus. Why, my negation hath no taste of madness.

Ulysses. Nor mine, my lord; Cressid was here but now.

Troilus. Let it not be believed for womanhood!
   Think we had mothers. Do not give advantage
   To stubborn critics, apt without a theme
   For depravation, to square the general sex
   By Cressid's rule; rather think this not Cressid.

Ulysses. What hath she done, prince, that can soil our mothers?

Troilus. Nothing at all, unless that this were she.

Thersites. Will 'a swagger himself out on's own eyes?

Troilus. This she? No; this is Diomed's Cressida.
   If beauty have a soul, this is not she;
   If souls guide vows, if vows be sanctimonies,
   If sanctimony be the gods' delight,
   If there be rule in unity itself,
   This is not she. O madness of discourse,
   That cause sets up with and against itself!
   Bifold authority! where reason can revolt
   Without perdition, and loss assume all reason
   Without revolt. This is, and is not, Cressid!
   Within my soul there doth conduce a fight
   Of this strange nature, that a thing inseparate
   Divides more wider than the sky and earth;

And yet the spacious breadth of this division
Admits no orifex for a point as subtle
As Ariachne's broken woof to enter.
Instance, O instance! strong as Pluto's gates:
Cressid is mine, tied with the bonds of heaven.
Instance, O instance! strong as heaven itself:
The bonds of heaven are slipped, dissolved and loosed,
And with another knot, five-finger-tied,
The fractions of her faith, orts of her love,
The fragments, scraps, the bits and greasy relics
Of her o'ereaten faith are given to Diomed.   (5.2.122–57)

The "revolt" of reason is expressed here not by sensuous imagery, but by mad "discourse" in which the same logical and grammatical routines repeat and repeat that "is" and "is not" are equal. Dryden's reduction shows that as in ritual, belief in nonsense depends largely on suggestive repetition:

Troilus. Was Cressida here?

Ulysses. I cannot conjure Trojan.

Troilus. She was not sure! she was not.
  Let it not be believ'd for womanhood:
  Think we had Mothers, do not give advantage
  To biting Satyr, apt without a theme,
  For defamation, to square all the sex
  By Cressid's rule, rather think this not Cressida.

Thersites. Will he swagger himself out on's own eyes!

Troilus. This she! no this was Diomedes Cressida.
  If beauty have a Soul, this is not she:
  I cannot speak for rage, that Ring was mine,
  By Heaven I gave it, in that point of time,
  When both our joys were fullest!—if he keeps it,
  Let dogs eat Troilus.

But the elimination of logical and grammatical hypnosis has a further effect. The great culminating metaphor,

The bonds of heaven are slipped, dissolved and loosed;

cannot be reached, the cosmic overtones disappear, and the connection of Troilus' personal chaos with the social and moral chaos described in Ulysses' speech and dramatized in the war scenes, utterly disappears. (It is not surprising that the accompanying imagery of foul feeding is also lost.) The bonds of metaphor are loosed, and with them the Shakespearean vision of the link between war and lechery is also broken. Not only do we lose a thematic design, but the large philosophic meaning of Troilus' act is lost, and it becomes a much smaller thing. The disturbance in the mind of Shakespeare's hero opens up into a vision of irrationality not only in the history of his love, but in the human mind and the cosmos. Again we find ourselves talking about losses in dramatic as well as philosophic meaning. Dryden's Troilus is less disturbed by the revolt of reason than by seeing his ring on Diomede's hand. Shakespeare's hero has been transformed from a Proustian dialectician with a heroic accent into an angry young man. In correcting grammar Dryden "corrected" a great deal else. Although we sometimes talk of plot and character as surviving in translation while poetry is lost, we must observe that if poetry is completely lost, plot and character tend to become unrecognizable. . . .

CAROL COOK

Unbodied Figures of Desire

In the scene in *Troilus and Cressida* which brings the lovers together, just prior to the consummation of their union, Troilus articulates a radical asymmetry at the heart of desire. This skewed relation between desire and its objects infects both the masculine enterprises which drive the play—his own quest for satisfaction in "Cressid's love," and the Greeks' and Trojans' competition for the "inestimable" prize of Helen:

> This is the monstruosity in love, lady, that the will is
> infinite and the execution confined; that the desire is
> boundless and the act a slave to limit.   (3.2.82–85)[1]

Troilus' description of the disproportion between aspiration and achievement has been anticipated earlier in Agamemnon's observation on his army's failure, after seven years, to topple Troy:

> The ample proposition that hope makes
> In all designs begun on earth below
> Fails in the promised largeness.   (1.3.3–5)

The passages, similar in their resignation to a certain impossibility in the nature of things, reinforce the close parallel between the war plot and the love plot. But their differences are also important. For Agamemnon, disappointment follows from "checks and disasters," obstacles and interruptions which "Grow in the veins of actions highest reared,"

From *Theatre Journal* 38 (March 1986), pp. 34–42.
[1]Quotations from the play are taken from this edition of *Troilus and Cressida*.

and would therefore seem interior to, inherent in, the action and designs they defeat; yet he displaces them onto an exterior agency—"the protractive trials of Great Jove" (3.1.20). Troilus, on the other hand, describes not a circumstantial defeat, but a "monstruosity," a paradox or outrageous enigma that doesn't "check" desire, but constitutes it. The monstrosity of love, I would suggest, is more than an issue which the play thematizes;[2] the play reveals a deeply problematic relation between desire and representation in which the play itself is entangled, a relation which is revealed particularly in the problematic status of women as objects of desire.

As a description of the operations of desire, Troilus' speech contains a notable absence: the drive has an aim—the execution of "the act"—but no object. This desire goes forth from its subject as a boundless energy and returns unspent in slavish acts. It repeatedly affirms the magnitude of the lover's subjective experience while negating the world of "acts" and effectively scotomizing the object, her with whom the lover must "coact." (Troilus bitterly uses this verb of Diomed and Cressida—5.2.115—uses it intransitively, as though to *co*act anything were degrading.) Furthermore, Troilus' reflection on the insufficiency of "the act" comes oddly just prior to a moment he has long anticipated in imagination, a moment he had described at the beginning of this scene as the lasting "indeed" of "Love's thrice-repurèd nectar," an experience perhaps "tuned too sharp in sweetness" to be sustained by the senses. Between that anticipated insufficiency of his own body, and his resignation to the insufficiency of "the act," both in the same scene, comes his first face to face encounter with Cressida.

[2]The failures of desire and aspiration in the play have been treated thematically by D. A. Traversi, *An Approach to Shakespeare* (Garden City, N.Y.: Doubleday and Co., Inc., 3rd Edition, 1969), pp. 324–40; Robert Ornstein, *The Moral Vision of Jacobean Tragedy* (Madison: University of Wisconsin Press, 1960), pp. 240–49; and Willard Farnham, "Troilus in Shapes of Infinite Desire," *Shakespeare Quarterly* 15:2 (1964), 257–64. Each of these critics discusses the problem as an ethical one (Troilus fails to establish "an adequate conception of value"—Traversi, p. 340) or as a comment on human limitation; in so doing, I would suggest they tend to reduce the "monstrosity" called to our attention by Troilus' language to rather commonplace thematic formulations which do not account for the peculiar relation of desire to its objects in the play.

In a discussion of Marlowe, Steven Greenblatt has written that the problematic elusiveness of objects of desire "is one of the major preoccupations of Renaissance thinkers from the most moderate to the most radical. . . ." As an example, Greenblatt cites in a note this passage from Giordano Bruno's *The Heroic Frenzies*:

> Whatever species is represented to the intellect and comprehended by the will, the intellect concludes there is another species above it, a greater and still greater one, and consequently it is always impelled toward new motion and abstraction in a certain fashion. For it ever realizes that everything it possesses is a limited thing which for that reason cannot be sufficient in itself . . . because the limited thing is not the universe and is not the absolute entity, but is contracted to . . . this form represented to the intellect. . . . As a result, from that beautiful which is comprehended, and therefore limited, and consequently beautiful by participation, the intellect progresses toward that which is truly beautiful without limit or circumspection whatsoever.[3]

Bruno resolves the monstrosity of desire by directing desire toward "the absolute entity," or God—a resolution not available (or certainly not explicitly) in the world of *Troilus and Cressida*. Bruno translates the restlessness of infinite desire into a desire of the infinite where, in Troilus' formulation, the possibility of an object commensurate with desire does not arise. Nonetheless Bruno's description of the restlessness itself seems very close to what we see in the play. For Bruno, the insufficiency of objects is discovered in their "limited" forms, in the fact of their being representable. The allure of what can be "represented to the intellect" is quickly exhausted, the intellect "impelled toward new motion and abstraction" in an attempt to escape the confines of representation.

The enigma of desire in *Troilus and Cressida* has much to do with an ambivalence toward representation. The desires and aspirations which drive the play—Troilus' passion, the enterprise of the Trojan War—are directed toward women,

[3]Stephen Greenblatt, *Renaissance Self-Fashioning* (Chicago: University of Chicago Press, 1981), pp. 218, 296.

toward Cressida and Helen. Yet the play consistently reveals the operations by which women— or, insofar as Helen is the legendary paragon of feminine allure, *woman*—are *produced* as objects. Masculine desire puts woman in the place of "that unbodied figure of the thought / That gave't surmisèd shape" (1.3.16–17). The woman's body becomes the means by which masculine desire represents itself to itself, but the insufficiency of the image provokes at moments violent impulses, a rage articulated in images of a fragmentation of the woman's body. While the play does insistently expose the element of narcissistic fantasy in this economy of desire, the monstrosity in love tends to appear as the monstrosity of women. The repetition of desire described by Bruno, which leads the desirer from object to object, is displaced onto Cressida in the scene of betrayal (though she seems able to experience desire only as its object), a displacement which assures Troilus of his authority as "truth's authentic author" (3.2.182). The only scene in which Helen appears, the center of the play in more ways than one (3.1), is fetid with a stupefying verbal repetition which seemingly emanates from her. Helen and Cressida can be enjoyed in fantasy as disbursed and fetishized signs, flickering images, unbodied figures of the thought, but as bodies they threaten a monstrous entrapment in finitude, repetition, representation.[4]

"Th'Imaginary Relish"

The play opens with the excruciating desire of Troilus, who experiences passion as that which tears him from within— "my heart, / As wedgèd with a sigh, would rive in twain . . ." (1.1.36–37). He is "mad in Cressid's love," beside himself, *not* himself as Pandarus tells Cressida in the next scene; his heart is an "open ulcer" and love a "knife" that "gashes." This first appearance of Troilus reveals some of the pecu-

---

[4]Though I do not discuss Cassandra in this essay—she doesn't figure significantly in the play as an object of desire—it may be relevant to consider her in this connection. A story which is not told in the play but borders on it tells how Cassandra comes by her gift and curse of prophecy: she is the object of Apollo's desire who, for her refusal to satisfy him, is doomed to the repetitious prophecy of Troy's destruction which no one heeds.

liarities which mark his love throughout the play. His desire is presented as radically fragmenting, threatening his reason, his identity, his very life. His enunciation of his desire also reveals its paradoxical relation to its object. His desire is intensely, excruciatingly physical and is directed at Cressida's body, but as it rends his body so it fragments hers. She figures in his speech as a Petrarchan *blazon* of parts and attributes—"Her eyes, her hair, her cheek, her gait, her voice" (56)—a body savored sequentially in imagination. At the same time, this body, which represents to Troilus the very essence of woman's beauty, becomes almost *pure* essence as his language gestures beyond the reaches of the visual imagination, a rarefied distillation of the physical. Troilus objects to Pandarus' "handling in his discourse"

> O, that her hand
> In whose comparison all whites are ink,
> Writing their own reproach; to whose soft seizure
> The cygnet's down is harsh, and spirit of sense
> Hard as the palm of plowman.   (57–61)

This ambivalent relation of desire to the body produces a dread which dominates Troilus' anticipation of union with Cressida. The prospect of the metaphorical "death" of sexual consummation carries some literal force in his imagination such that he perceives himself upon the threshold of extinction, stalking about Cressid's door "Like a strange soul upon the Stygian banks / Staying for waftage" (3.2. 8–9). As Pandarus goes to fetch Cressida, Troilus contemplates the effects of translating his "imaginary relish" into experience:

> I am giddy; expectation whirls me round,
> Th' imaginary relish is so sweet
> That it enchants my sense. What will it be
> When that the wat'ry palates taste indeed
> Love's thrice-repurèd nectar? Death, I fear me,
> Sounding destruction, or some joy too fine,
> Too subtle, potent, tuned too sharp in sweetness
> For the capacity of my ruder powers.
> I fear it much; and I do fear besides

That I shall lose distinction in my joys,
As doth a battle, when they charge on heaps
The enemy flying.   (17–28)

Troilus is intently engaged with the body here. He has longed to "wallow in the lily beds / Proposed for the deserver" (11–12), but now his enchanted "sense" appears to him possibly inadequate to the demands of "Love's thrice-repurèd nectar." He anticipates love as an intense and highly refined sensation received by the "sense," by the "palates," yet imagines it also as rarefied beyond the "capacity" of the body, of his "ruder powers," so that it threatens to overwhelm him completely, destroying all "distinction," all boundaries, all difference, and consuming him with a violence that registers in the incoherence of the image which describes it.[5] Significantly Cressida does not appear as a body here at all, but only as a disembodied experience which nearly defies representation. If the terrifying object of Troilus' desire is an experience beyond the capacity of his "ruder" bodily powers, how could that object *be* a body? Yet it is only in relation to Cressida's body, to her "eyes, her hair, her cheek," that Troilus' desire assumes any shape at all.

The question of Troilus' desire opens up the larger problem of the relation of desire to bodies in the play. Just as Troilus' desire for Cressida structures the love plot through its consummation in 3.2, so the desire of the Greeks for Helen (and the Trojans' desire to keep her) structures the containing action of the Trojan war. The play addresses itself explicitly to the operations of an economy of masculine desire and to the way it produces its objects. The eco-

[5] In " 'This Is and Is Not Cressid': The Characterization of Cressida," in *The (M)other Tongue*, ed. Shirley Nelson Garner, Claire Kehane, and Madelon Sprengnether (Ithaca: Cornell University Press, 1985), pp. 119–41, Janet Adelman treats at length the fantasy of maternal engulfment evident in the orality of Troilus' imagery. Adelman argues that Cressida is initially presented by the play as a fully realized character but comes to be subsumed by Troilus' ambivalent fantasy of union with the mother. In focusing on the problematic characterization of Cressida rather than on her character—recognizing that Cressida is not quite a character—Adelman illuminates some of the problems of representation in the play in a way that more psychologizing feminist readings of Cressida have not. Though I have not followed Adelman's own psychological treatment of Troilus' maternal fantasies, my understanding of the play's structure owes a debt to her incisive argument.

nomic nature of this system reveals itself not only through the insistent language of commerce in which desire is articulated in the play, but also in the use of women as objects of exchange mediating the relations among men. Troilus, while on the one hand imagining Cressida in terms which exceed any kind of coherent representation in the body, also conceives of her as a commodity: "Her bed is India; there she lies, a pearl," and of himself as "the merchant, and this sailing Pandar / Our doubtful hope, our convoy and our bark" (1.1.104, 107–08). In the course of the play, Troilus will obtain his "pearl" only to lose it to another transaction, as Cressida is "changed for Antenor."

Helen, of course, serves as the prototypical object of desire for whom "Every tithe soul, 'mongst many thousand dismes" had died. Like Cressida, Helen is referred to as "a pearl," a commodity within the circuit of exchange, stolen in recompense for "an old aunt whom the Greeks held captive" (2.2.77). The theft of Helen for Hesione suggests that the forcible "exchange" of women between Greeks and Trojans might have become an endless cycle of repetition; but Helen is given a peculiar status within this structure of violently competing desires which breaks the repetition. She functions at once as an object of exchange within this economy and also as the transcendent term governing the entire system. She is the pearl "Whose price hath launched above a thousand ships / And turned crowned kings to merchants" (82–83). Though her value is questioned by Hector, and treated as an obscene delusion by Thersites and Diomedes, none of them deserts the struggle for her—even Thersites remains engaged, if only in his voyeuristic fascination with "those that war for a placket" (2.3.20–21). The desire for Helen is the energy that drives the vast enterprise of the war, and to a large extent, therefore, the play. Helen functions as the source of all value because she herself is "inestimable" (2.2.88), not to be weighed "in a scale / Of common ounces" (27–28). The Trojans have nothing of comparable value for the Greeks to steal in return; the Greeks can only survive to retrieve what they have lost.

That Helen's value is produced by the economy which she also activates is repeatedly suggested by the play: it is in men's estimations that Helen is "inestimable." In the urgency of his desire for Cressida, Troilus impatiently berates the "fools on both sides" with the remark that "Helen must needs be fair, / When with your blood you daily paint her thus" (1.1.94–95). But though he recognizes Helen's value as a fiction created out of men's willingness to die asserting it, Troilus argues vigorously for keeping Helen. The war is "a quarrel / Which hath our several honors all engaged / To *make* it gracious" (2.2.123–25, my emphasis). He sees her value in the effects she produces: "She is a theme of honor and renown, / A spur to valiant and magnanimous deeds . . ." (199–200). Helen's worth is inestimable, absolute, unlimited, but has no basis outside of men's desire for such an object. She becomes the measure (in Troilus' view at least) of the Trojans' capacity to imagine, create, and desire the infinite.

Helen functions purely as a cipher in the world of *Troilus. and Cressida,* and it is only as such that she produces her powerful charge. Her absence from Menelaus' bed is the nothing or lack which generates both desire and violence, and which makes possible all value and identity. Her appropriation by the Trojans provides the occasion for the war, essentially a masculine ritual to establish difference: the difference between those who possess and those who lack Helen, the difference between Trojan and Greek, victor and vanquished.

Helen's mystique depends on her equivocal position, simultaneously outside of representation, of what can be "estimated," weighed in "a scale / Of common ounces," and within it, as what can be seen. She is "love's invisible soul," yet enjoyment of her is primarily visual. It is specifically as a sexual object, as a woman "whose youth and freshness / Wrinkles Apollo's and makes pale the morning," that she is prized. In arguing for keeping Helen, Troilus chooses a telling analogy to illustrate the problem of "election" and honor:

> I take today a wife, and my election
> Is led on in the conduct of my will—
> My will enkindled by mine eyes and ears,
> Two traded pilots 'twixt the dangerous shores
> Of will and judgment. How may I avoid,

> Although my will distaste what it elected,
> The wife I chose?   (61–67)

The analogy, with its insistence on the erratically stimulated "will," suggests that the "election" to steal Helen was similarly a matter of "enkindled" senses. Paris insists that he is not alone in enjoying "The pleasure such a beauty brings with it" (147).

Helen thus becomes the site of a contradiction similar to that which governs Troilus' conception of Cressida. The impossibility of representing what so provokes desire lies partly in the problematic relation of desire to the body. Helen is inestimable in her physical beauty, yet the discourse of desire obsessively reaches beyond literal corporeality. The most corporeal references to Helen describe her not as an object of desire, but as an object of loathing, disgust, and horror. As the empty marker of value in the economy of masculine desire, she is also the black hole which draws all things to it. She is thus conflated at certain moments with the devouring lust and violence which engulf the play, with "the hot digestion of this cormorant war" (6) which "consumes" all "honor, loss of time, travail, expense / Wounds, friends, and what else dear . . ." (4–5). Diomedes describes the "hell of pain and world of charge" Helen has cost:

> For every false drop in her bawdy veins
> A Grecian's life hath sunk; for every scruple
> Of her contaminated carrion weight
> A Troyan hath been slain.   (4.1.69–72)

Conceived as a body, as "a flat, tamèd piece" (62), Helen can be weighed in the common scale, "estimated" to the last scruple.

The rhetoric of *Troilus and Cressida,* both verbal and theatrical, effects a demystification of the object at its center. This Helen is not Marlowe's "face that launched a thousand ships, / And burnt the topless towers of Ilium," but "a pearl, / Whose price hath launched above a thousand ships, / And turned crowned kings to merchants"; the deflating allusion prevents our participation in Troilus' enthrallment with what he describes. Though Helen is a subject of discussion from the beginning, she is withheld from the audience until Act 3, Scene 1, nearly the middle of the play. When she does appear, she appears precisely as an empty center, a vacuous "Nell" who draws those around her into flirtatious imbecility. This scene—Helen's only appearance in the play—breathes a stale air of insipidity and boredom, its language reduced to fatuous repetition in the ingratiating babble Pandarus speaks to Helen ("Sweet queen, sweet queen, that's a sweet queen, i'faith . . . What says my sweet queen, my very, very sweet queen?") and in her own bathetic effusions: "Let thy song be love. This love will undo us all. O Cupid, Cupid, Cupid!" (3.1.72–73, 81–82, 111–12).

Through the war for Helen's possession, the play represents the powerful effects she produces as the object of masculine desire. But it also represents her as the vacancy at its center. As long as she is withheld from the stage, the *idea* of Helen ("the mortal Venus, the heartblood of beauty, love's invisible soul") serves, notwithstanding its attendant ironies, to rationalize the play of drives.[6] Her presentation on the stage, however, confronts the spectator with the disparity between the idea and its embodiment in the flesh. This scene has often been treated as a moment of satiric unmasking. S. L. Bethell, for example, sees in it "the theme of 'fair without and foul within,' . . . a remorseless Shakespearean 'debunking' " in which "the real Helen is revealed, the inadequate object of so much misplaced idealism."[7] Such an argument implicitly treats the disparity as an ethical problem, a matter of duplicity, as Bethell's tone of moral censure suggests (he characterizes Helen as "a worthless strumpet"). His "without/within" metaphor and the emphasis on revelation suggest the exposure of an imposture: the "real Helen" (worthless strumpet that she is) is not the *real* Helen.

---

[6]Pandarus' confusion over whether these "attributes" belong to Helen or to Cressida (3.1.35–37) suggests the interchangeability of women as signifiers for the idealized object of desire.

[7]S. L. Bethell, *Shakespeare and the Popular Dramatic Tradition* (London: Staples Press, 1944), rpt. in this edition of *Troilus and Cressida*, p. 173.

Could any object be "adequate" to the desires which aggregate around Helen and Cressida? The play reaches toward a more fundamental questioning of the relation between desire and its objects than discussions of the women's "inadequacy" have been able to address. In explicitly portraying the production of objects of desire through "estimation," fantasy, "th'imaginary relish," the play locates desire not in the realm of satiable need, but in the register of the symbolic. Lacan's distinction between *need* (the internal tension which achieves satisfaction in its appropriate object, as for example, the infant's hunger is satisfied with its mother's milk), *demand* (the attempt to articulate and address the need), and *desire,* which resides in the gap between need and demand, between the biological and its symbolic formulation, points to the inherently "excentric and insatiable"[8] nature of desire which is the monstrosity in love:

> [D]esire is situated in dependence on demand—which, by being articulated in signifiers, leaves a metonymic remainder that runs under it, an element that is not indeterminate, which is a condition both absolute and unapprehensible, an element necessarily lacking, unsatisfied, impossible, misconstrued (méconnu), an element that is called desire.[9]

Desire is the drive's mediation through signs, fantasy, "hallucinations," and is maintained in the subject's relation not to bodies—objects—but to signs.[10] The very impossibility of satisfaction through objects, however, makes possible another kind of satisfaction through fantasy: the pleasure of omnipotence in relation to the object. In the absence of an other who might introduce upon the subject's pleasure with other demands, other desires, the subject fantasizes without obstacle. What presents itself as obstacle to the subject's

---

[8]Alan Sheridan, "Translator's Note," in Lacan, *Four Fundamental Concepts of Psychoanalysis* (New York: W. W. Norton & Company, 1978), p. 278.

[9]Lacan, *Four Fundamental Concepts,* p. 154.

[10]Freud describes wish fulfillment as a recathexis of a "mnemic image" or hallucination of an original "experience of satisfaction" which was biological but is available thereafter only through the mediation of signs. See *The Interpretation of Dreams*, trans. James Strachey (New York: Avon Books, 1965), pp. 604–5.

access to the object removes any obstacle to the subject's gratification in fantasy. Instead of being that in which desire is satisfied, the object, subsumed as fantasy, becomes that in which desire is kindled, its signs serving a fetishistic function.[11] In the absence of Cressida's body, Troilus savors in imagination "her eyes, her hair, her cheek. . . ." The conventions of courtly love, represented in *Troilus and Cressida* by the chivalric Trojans, establish the conditions for this fetishization of woman. As Cressida knows, "Men prize the thing ungained more than it is" (1.2.301).

"Some obstacle is necessary," writes Freud, "to swell the tide of libido to its height; at all periods of history, wherever natural barriers in the way of satisfaction have not sufficed, mankind has erected conventional ones in order to be able to enjoy love."[12] The lover worships from afar: the inaccessibility of the lady guarantees his enjoyment of her as fantasy object, his enjoyment of his desire, of himself as desirer. Troilus, in his longing, invokes a mythic prototype of his desire and a topographical image of his relation to Cressida:

> Tell me, Apollo, for thy Daphne's love,
> What Cressid is, what Pandar, and what we.
> Her bed is India; there she lies, a pearl.
> Between our Ilium and where she resides
> Let it be called the wild and wand'ring flood,
> Ourself the merchant, and this sailing Pandar
> Our doubtful hope, our convoy, and our bark.
>
> (1.1.102–08)

The "wild and wand'ring flood" suggests both the obstacle barring access to Cressida and the swollen tide of Troilus' passion, a desire that is its own obstacle, an obstacle that swells what it restrains; and it intersects a symbolic land-

[11]Sheridan, p. 279, suggests this: "Desire (fundamentally in the singular) is a perpetual effect of symbolic articulation. It is not an appetite: it is essentially excentric and insatiable. That is why Lacan coordinates it not with the object that would seem to satisfy it, but with the object that causes it (one is reminded of fetishism)."

[12]Sigmund Freud, "The Most Prevalent Form of Degradation in Erotic Life" (1912), in *Sexuality and the Psychology of Love*, ed. Philip Rieff (New York: Collier Books, 1963), p. 67.

scape mapped out in the language of mercantile venture. Cressida is the rare commodity for which Troilus negotiates, a pearl, a self-enclosed, luminous, petrified sphere. Is Daphne, the petrified woman, the ideal object—forever unavailable as woman, forever available as sign? . . .

CLAIRE M. TYLEE

From The Text of Cressida and Every Ticklish Reader: *Troilus and Cressida,* The Greek Camp Scene

It is perhaps because *Troilus and Cressida* raises the question of women's sexual identity that it was scarcely performed for three hundred years. I am going to discuss ways in which Shakespeare's Cressida has been construed by recent critics, producers, and actresses, and how these interpretations might affect the understanding of the play by an audience in the 1980s. Until the 1970s most interpretations manifested precisely that coercive dominance of a particular set of cultural values which is the theme of the play. This was especially marked with respect to what G. Wilson Knight called 'the pivot incident of the play': Cressida's arrival at the Greek army camp. My discussion will centre on this scene, to show how it is a key to the significance of one of the main questions posed by the play: whether a person's nature or identity is determined by the valuation set on that person by others. This question forms part of the general platonic scepticism which the play develops with regard to the possibility of anything's having absolute value or identity in a world subject to the digestive effects of time and human judgement. Within the world of the play Cressida is unable to maintain a sense of her own integrity. Similarly, in the course of changes in Western society, the character of Cressida in the text of the play has been subject to changing readings and widely divergent performances. This has inevitably affected the comprehension of the whole play.

From Claire M. Tylee, "The Text of Cressida and Every Ticklish Reader: *Troilus and Cressida,* The Greek Camp Scene," *Shakespeare Survey* 41 (1989): 63–76. Cambridge University Press. The footnotes have been renumbered.

Two actresses who have played Cressida recently have left us their responses to the coercive effect of male interpretations of their role.[1] Juliet Stevenson felt herself threatened by Howard Davies's interpretation of Cressida's relationship with Pandarus and Troilus for the RSC production in 1985. Davies wanted to create a sense of an intimacy between the three of them like the mutual affection in *Jules et Jim*. This went counter to Juliet Stevenson's understanding of the nervous defensiveness that Cressida displays against Pandarus at the beginning, and of her apprehension about Troilus' promises of constancy (which seems justified in the event by what Stevenson took for his betrayal of Cressida to Diomedes). Howard Davies's idea about this happy threesome echoes what Anton Lesser said in Fenwick's account of Jonathan Miller's 1981 production for BBC Television, in which Lesser had also played Troilus: 'It's an amazing triumvirate, Pandarus and Troilus and Cressida—what we discovered together was the mutual dependence that they had, which led to the emotional trauma when one of them is ejected and the triple relationship breaks up.' This does not cohere with what Suzanne Burden says about her understanding of Cressida in the same article: 'Taught by Pandarus, she's just about learned the ropes and she's quite aware that to him she's a puppet, a plaything he enjoys, but as soon as he's through playing that game he'll forget her . . . I felt she was a victim of states and men and rulers.' Miller himself sounds much more sympathetic to Cressida than Pandarus or Ulysses do, at first, but then he reveals himself as another ticklish reader: 'What we see is not the inevitable blossoming of a corrupt and sexually titillating girl, but the disintegration of a girl whose innocence is too inexperienced to handle the shock and the overwhelming stimulus of these rough attractive Greek warriors she comes across.' Under his direction Suzanne Burden played Cressida as sexually excited by being kissed, as thoroughly enjoying the game and her own power of arousal. She herself said:

[1]Juliet Stevenson, "Foolish Dreaming Superstitious Girls—Female Perspectives in the Plays (and in the Rehearsal Room)," an unpublished talk given at Royal Shakespeare Theatre Summer School, Stratford, 1985 and Suzanne Burden, in an interview for Henry Fenwick, "The Production," *The BBC Television Shakespeare* Troilus and Cressida (London, 1981).

I used to get terribly upset in the first days of rehearsal when people would say, 'She's nothing but a tart and a sexual tease.' Instinctively I would feel quite angry but I couldn't explain why she wasn't. I saw her as a witty, intelligent young woman . . . just discovering herself . . . She's been brought up in a sophisticated man's world and she's enormously unprotected . . . She doesn't know what's happening and she's terrified, and her survival instincts come into play. She thinks, 'There's got to be a way out of this and if I have to use my sex I will'.

Juliet Stevenson managed to develop on the stage the idea of Cressida's vulnerability. She believed that, being hustled away from Troilus on the first morning after losing her virginity to him, Cressida is emotionally raw and experiences the kissing-game as a brutal sexual assault from which she defends herself by her only weapon: sarcasm. Stevenson's interpretation was partially successful for at least one other critic in the audience besides Robert Wilcher. Roger Warren saw that Stevenson's playing of a 'mercurial Cressida' in Act 1 was to use 'a brazen manner [as] a cover to protect herself from becoming a love-object like Helen'. But, after 'the generals subjected her to brutally violent kisses that amounted to assault', at first appalled, she then begins 'to play their game' and becomes a love-object like Helen after all: 'Ulysses made the parallel with Helen specific'.[2] It seems to me that Cressida was lost from the first moment she tried to take Troilus' sport seriously, but she is still demanding fair play at that moment of confrontation with Ulysses, a stalemate that is ended only by Diomedes' intervention. In the last analysis, women do not even have the power to play hard to get; they can be assaulted both physically and mentally, which is what Ulysses does make clear. Yet it is not until she is called out of her father's tent by her 'guardian' that Cressida finally succumbs to being a toy in a boys' game, treating Troilus' token for what it is worth. Stevenson acted the flirtation scene with Diomedes as if Cressida had been emotionally cauterized.

[2] Roger Warren, "Shakespeare in Britain, 1985," *Shakespeare Quarterly* 37 (Spring 1985), p. 117.

Juliet Stevenson's Stratford talk was ironically entitled: 'Foolish Dreaming Superstitious Girls' with the clear implication that some women, Cassandra-like, may have a true vision of the play which men might consider mad. Yet, as we can see from the example of Alice Walker and Joyce Carol Oates, most women's ability to see is as much conditioned as men's by the dominant values and conceptions of their culture.[3] The text cannot determine how either women or men read it, although editors, producers, and actors may incline our understanding towards their particular reading, since they control the medium by which we come to the text. Joyce Carol Oates, writing in 1967, was even more vehement than Victorian male critics had been in her denunciation of Cressida as 'villainous'. The one Victorian critic to speak up for Cressida was G. B. Shaw, who was vilified for the stand he took against war fever during the 1914–18 War. One of the first recorded English productions was mounted by the pacifist William Poel as that fever was gathering momentum in 1912; it was not a success, and the play only gained appreciative audiences from among the war-weary in 1920. Despite the wide regard for Jan Kott's views, the critical revision of Cressida did not gather strength until the 1970s.

The general move towards exonerating Cressida for inauthenticity (although there was still no agreement as to whether Ulysses was 'clear-sighted' or not) took place on both sides of the Atlantic. In a paper published in 1972, the time of the war in Vietnam, the American critic Audrey Yoder spoke of *Troilus and Cressida* as 'our play', because 'we know what this society and its war has done to our best youth'. Quoting with approval from Kott with regard to Cressida's 'rude awakening', Yoder said that 'among the Greeks [Cressida] is bound to be exposed and degraded . . . the Greek generals are taking what Cressida, essentially a captive, has no real power to refuse. She plays their game with wit and spirit, for that is her best defence . . . it is self-

---

[3] For other morally unfavourable judgements of Cressida by women see: Ellis-Fermor, *The Frontiers of Drama;* Winifred Nowottny, " 'Opinion' and 'Value' in *Troilus and Cressida,*" *Essays in Criticism* 4 (1954), 282–96; Mary Ellen Rickey, " 'Twixt the Dangerous Shores': *Troilus and Cressida* Again," *Shakespeare Quarterly* 15 (1964), 3–13.

righteous for her world to judge Cressida. After all, she is simply practicing the way of that world.'[4] In a further sympathetic reading of Cressida published in 1975, not long after Watergate, Voth and Evans challenged the 'constant' critical judgement that Cressida is 'a mere prostitute, a cold and calculating woman': 'Insofar as her actions are determined by the real world of the play, a world which makes human attempts at ideals nothing more than attempts to give "fair" covering to sordidness and corruption, Cressida is not responsible, except for 'the "folly" of ignoring her knowledge of this world'.[5] By this date the women's movement in America was creating a new perspective on literature and expressly feminist criticism of Shakespeare was gaining official recognition.[6] However, in 1977 Carolyn Asp developed a view of Cressida which she had first indicated in 1971, contesting the general critical opinion that Cressida was 'either shallow or calculating, or both'. Asp claimed that the text will not allow us [sic] 'to dismiss her as Ulysses describes her, merely "a daughter of the game" '; rather, she shares 'the weakness of those who cannot see value in themselves independently of perceivers'. Conforming to Ulysses' insistence that 'it is public opinion that reveals the inner self', Cressida 'attempts to establish her value by the only way her culture allows. She uses her physical beauty to attract the praise of men.'[7] This interpretation not only ignores the sex and cultural power of 'the perceivers'; it slides over the particular vulnerability of women which is the 'weakness' Cressida shares. The first politically feminist interpretation of Cressida's character appeared in 1980: Gayle Greene's 'Shakespeare's Cressida: "A kind of self" '. Commencing by stating that 'human nature is not "natural", but is, rather, shaped by social forces', Greene follows Raymond Southall's characterization of Cressida's

[4] Richard Yoder, "Sons and Daughters of the Game," *Shakespeare Survey* 25 (1972), pp. 122–23.

[5] Grant L. Voth and Oliver H. Evans, "Cressida and the World of the Play," *Shakespeare Studies* 8 (1975), p. 237.

[6] Preface to Carol Ruth Swift Lenz et al., eds, *The Woman's Part* (Urbana, 1980).

[7] Carolyn Asp. "In Defence of Cressida," *Studies in Philology* 74 (1977) pp. 406–10 and also see " 'Th' Expense of Spirit in a Waste of Shame,' " *Shakespeare Quarterly* 22 (1971), 345–57.

society as 'a world informed with the "spirit of capitalism . . . busily reducing life to the demands of the belly" '. Cressida, treated as a cake or pearl, 'reminds us of the effects of capitalism on women'. Cressida is 'a cynical coquette' who treats 'love as combat' because she understands the principles of her society, 'though she is helpless to act on what she knows'.[8] It would have been interesting if Greene had made the connection between the greedy spirit of capitalism implicit in the play's language and the envious rivalry of militarism in the action of the play, to show how Shakespeare traces the source of war in the depreciation of women and 'feminine' values.

The general revaluation of Cressida in England seems to have commenced in 1975 with an article by John Bayley which suggested that 'When Ulysses calls her a daughter of the game we may feel obscurely that he is wrong.' Recognizing that 'Social exigencies compel [both Chaucer's and Shakespeare's Cressidas] to act in ways which society then condemns', he nevertheless considers that the play's action 'exhibits but does not explain' Cressida's predicament.[9] In 1978 Ann Thompson could still find Cressida 'repellant'[10] and in 1980 Kenneth Palmer was still speaking of Cressida as inexplicably 'transformed as she enters the Greek camp', and repeating, without qualification, Ulysses' judgement of Cressida as a whore.[11] Kenneth Muir felt that 'it should not be held against Cressida' that she is sensuous, or 'treated as a sex-object', but he also repeats the idea of her as a whore and speaks of her 'uninhibited behaviour on her arrival in the Greek camp'.[12] The views of Muir and Palmer are likely to be influential since their editions will be used in schools and universities. However, in 1982 a group of papers read at a conference in Leeds tried to explain Cressida's predicament in terms of the ideology of her society. Ironically, in view of the imminent Falklands conflict, Valerie Smith concluded:

[8] Gayle Greene, "Shakespeare's Cressida," in Carolyn Ruth Swift Lenz et al., eds. (Urbana, 1980), p. 137.

[9] John Bayley, "Time and the Trojans," *Essays in Criticism* 25 (1975), 55–73, quotations from pp. 67, 68, and 69 respectively.

[10] Ann Thompson, *Shakespeare's Chaucer: A Study in Literary Origins* (Liverpool, 1978), p. 126.

[11] Kenneth Palmer, ed., *Troilus and Cressida* (London, 1982), p. 57.

[12] Kenneth Muir, ed., *Troilus and Cressida* (Oxford, 1982), pp. 36–37.

Part of the change in critical attitudes towards the play has been brought about by a change in public attitudes towards war. Two world wars have made people wary of the public-school heroism of Hector and Achilles, who talk about the Trojan campaign as though it were an extended Test Match. More particularly, where Cressida is concerned, the new current of feminist thinking has led to a revaluation of traditional attitudes towards women.[13]

Jonathan Dollimore discussed *Troilus and Cressida* in 1984 as part of a general re-appraisal of sixteenth- and seventeenth-century drama in terms of the contemporary debate about natural law and concluded that: 'The discontinuity in Cressida's identity stems not from her nature, but from her position in the patriarchal order.'[14]

Such political radicalism may not be widespread, but after the powerful influence of the Women's Movement, Juliet Stevenson's audience in 1985 might have been less inclined to view the play through Troilus' eyes as directed by Ulysses. Ros Asquith, reviewing that production for *The Observer* (30 June 1985), thought that 'almost every woman on the planet' could have the insight to see Cressida 'as a human being torn between love and survival, rather than as a flirtatious plaything'. Perhaps now more women would consider, apparently 'instinctively' like Suzanne Burden did, that Cressida may not behave as she does merely in order to tease, even if men find her tickling. Her attempts to gain the upper hand over Diomedes by playing hard-to-get are pitiful, but sympathy for 'her choice . . . between rapist or protector' as Asquith put it need not be sentimentalized. Burden points out that Cressida never tells Diomedes that she loves him. No, but she talks of giving her heart together with Troilus' love token, dangling it tantalizingly in a context that equates 'heart' with 'cunt'. If she has become emotionally 'hollow', that is because no real choice of emotional commitment has been left open to her. I think one difficulty for women in the audience now is that they may sympathize too much with Cressida, identifying too far with a feminist

[13] Valerie Smith, "The History of Cressida," in *Self and Society,* eds. J. A. Jowitt and R. K. Taylor (Leeds, 1982), p. 76.

[14] Jonathan Dollimore, *Radical Tragedy* (Brighton, 1984), p. 48.

wish for female integrity to be able to acknowledge what she is finally forced to become. If she is not precisely a whore, she is synthetic. Ros Asquith found that: 'Juliet Stevenson is . . . a startling and forceful Cressida.' Someone who is as much in two minds as Cressida states herself to be, and as 'subject to exploitative definitions of her by men' (which she is shown as powerless to control), can scarcely be forceful. In this play valuing is not detached appraisal; it is an active, dynamic process which affects what is valued. Pursued for her sexual allure, Cressida gradually learns to read her own self through the double-minded male discourse that dominates her by the end of the play; degraded, she becomes as it were a corrupt text.

Ros Asquith praised Howard Davies's production, describing it as 'visually seductive'. This statement pinpoints a problem inherent in most of this century's productions. If the text is now generally agreed to be concerned with the seductive process by which the pursuit of fair appearances corrupts reality itself, then producers and designers need to find a mode which will express this to the audience. Any mode chosen still has to overcome a pre-established adherence to the very values which the play exposes as inauthentic. Naturalism actually tends to reproduce the aggressively materialistic representations of women's sexuality which our culture enforces, along with the egoistic greediness which leads to rivalry and war. Making a production as glamorously 'realistic' as possible simply encourages the audience to read with its eyes only, superficially. Shakespeare's text tells us little about the theatrical conventions of his time, but certain scenes are pointedly non-naturalistic. Hector's encounter with the enticing corpse in armour is an example of such an emblematic scene.[15] My own feeling is that, despite the insight into the play to be gained from Juliet Stevenson's committed performance and Howard Davies's choice of a Victorian setting in 1985–6, modern audiences, both women and men, might benefit from the reintroduction of two non-naturalistic conventions of Shakespeare's time:

[15] Significantly, this scene had to be omitted from Davies's modern dress production, see Alan C. Dessen, "Price-tags and Trade-offs: Chivalry and the Shakespearean Hero in 1985," *Shakespeare Quarterly*, 37 (1986), 102–06, p. 104.

doubling and the use of male actors for female roles. The way in which readers are influenced by their own sexual expectations might be better brought home if the female parts were played not by glamorous, nubile young women, but by men. The point that women are constructed by cultural values would be made more effectively if the two wives, Andromache and Helen, were played by the same actor, and if one other actor played both Cassandra and Cressida. Audiences, of course, do not much enjoy being estranged in this way. Like other readers, they prefer to be tickled pink by vicarious excitement.

BARBARA E. BOWEN

Troilus and Cressida on the Stage

After being absent from the stage for almost three hundred years—the longest gap in the history of any Shakespeare play—*Troilus and Cressida* is now almost continuously in performance. Since 1945 it has received more than ninety separate productions, sixty-three of them in the years between 1960 and 1979 alone. The extraordinary reversal in the play's stage history coincides with a critical history no less remarkable: although many other plays have undergone reevaluation in what J. L. Styan calls "the Shakespeare revolution," none has been so radically reappraised as *Troilus*. Its sudden rehabilitation after centuries of obscurity has led many observers to conclude that the play is uncannily modern. In the twentieth century, the theory goes, with our sense of alienation and our consciousness of world war and nuclear holocaust, we are uniquely able to appreciate a play whose bitterness would have baffled earlier audiences. Many chroniclers would agree with Bernard Shaw, who remarked in 1898 that in *Troilus and Cressida* Shakespeare "is ready and willing to start at the twentieth century if the seventeenth would only let him." Attractive as Shaw's assessment is, however, I would like to resist his conclusion—and its implication that we have at last discovered the "true" *Troilus and Cressida*—long enough to explore another reading of the play's theatrical history.

One reason that *Troilus* seems "amazing and modern," to quote Jan Kott, is precisely that its theatrical history is so short. Critics and directors alike come to it as a play unseen on the illusionistic stages of the eighteenth and nineteenth centuries; *Troilus and Cressida* has almost no tradition of performance except in the twentieth century's nonnaturalistic mode. There is nothing in its history comparable to the two thousand pots of fern trucked weekly to a London theater to simulate the Forest of Arden, or to the moment in an 1820 *King Lear* when Edmund Kean was so delighted with the realism of the storm scene that he interrupted his own performance to applaud the trees. We see *Troilus* as modern partly because we have so little history of nonmodern readers seeing the play. By 1975, one critic felt the necessity of pointing out "the fallacy that *Troilus and Cressida* really *is* about Vietnam"; such warnings might not be necessary if the play came to us mediated by the kind of critical and theatrical tradition that informs our perception of *Hamlet,* say, or *King Lear*.

The lack of early performances of *Troilus* has made it especially tempting to think that we alone see the play as it is, that our performances are definitive. Yet even with this play, no performance escapes its own time and culture, none can claim to be universally true. In one sense, the rediscovery of *Troilus and Cressida* for the stage tells us more about history than it does about the play itself, so deeply is every production embedded in its culture. Even the idea of "the play itself" is called into question by a stage history, for each production is necessarily a reinvention of the play. Performance, even more obviously than criticism, *produces* the play it claims to reveal. And nowhere is this more true than in performances of Shakespeare, for his iconic status has made his plays the site for working out cultural issues that go far beyond the plays themselves. Shakespeare, as Margot Heinemann writes, "has become part of the way that literally millions of people, consciously or unconsciously, imagine and fantasize and think about the world." Thus we shall find that the history of *Troilus and Cressida*'s extraordinary career on the stage points to and participates in a much larger history of cultural politics.

From the start, the play's theatrical history has posed problems of interpretation. As Daniel Seltzer explains in his Introduction, the record of *Troilus*'s first performance is still a matter of dispute. Put briefly, the question is which of two contemporary sources to believe: the 1603 Stationer's Register entry that grants to James Roberts permission to print a "booke of Troilus and Cresseda as yt is acted by my lo[rd] Chamberlens Men," or the 1609 edition of the play that claims: "you have heere a new play, neuer stal'd with the Stage, neuer clapper-clawd with the palmes of the vulger." Both sources raise questions of their own (for instance, the 1609 edition is a corrected version of an edition that originally described the play "As it was acted by the Kings Maiesties seruants at the Globe"), but the central issue is how to reconcile the two. Most scholars now believe that James Roberts had no reason to lie in his entry in the Stationer's Register, a document that listed intentions to print, and that the play must have been performed at least once by Shakespeare's acting company, the Lord Chamberlain's Men, by 1603. This speculation tallies with the uncorrected 1609 Quarto edition of the play, for by 1609 Shakespeare's company had been renamed The King's Men and was acting at the Globe Theatre. Why Bonian and Walley, printers of the Quarto edition, felt they had to change their title page and add a disclaimer about performance remains a mystery.

The combination of the play's obscure early history and its linguistic difficulty has tempted many scholars to theorize that there was something unusual about its first performance: that *Troilus* was performed publicly by 1603 but was such a disaster that its later printers thought the performance would be better forgotten; or that Shakespeare's company had planned to perform the play but withdrew it while still in rehearsal; or, the most popular of the theories, that the play was performed privately, perhaps for the young lawyers at the Inns of Court, but was never acted at a public theater. The idea that this dense and allusive play was written for a private audience of highly educated young men has gained wide appeal, but there is no evidence for such a conclusion and no other similar instance in Shakespeare. In the end, what we are left with is just speculation; we have no sketches revealing styles of costume as for *Titus Andronicus,* no journal entries describing performances as for *Julius Caesar* and *Twelfth Night.* There is nothing to establish even the traces of an early theatrical tradition, and *Troilus and Cressida*'s first performance appears irrecoverable.

Nothing is heard of the play again until 1679. In itself the silence is not unusual, for Cromwell's Puritan government closed the public theaters from 1642 until 1660, fearful of their power to incite the populace to moral laxity and civil disorder. Although the closing left the theaters idle for less than twenty years, it was long enough to create a significant breach in a theatrical tradition that had stretched uninterrupted for more than five centuries. By the time the two London theaters (the only ones licensed under the new government) opened in the 1660s, the drama of Shakespeare and his contemporaries had acquired for Restoration audiences the quaintness of a remote historical period. Thus we can find poet and playwright John Dryden speaking one moment about "the incomparable Shakespeare," and the next saying this about adapting Shakespeare's works: "I undertook to remove that heap of rubbish under which many excellent thoughts lay wholly buried." That heap of rubbish was most of *Troilus and Cressida;* both quotations come from Dryden's preface to his 1679 rewriting of the play, entitled *Truth Found Too Late.* Fresh from the success of his *All For Love,* two years earlier, an adaptation of Shakespeare's *Antony and Cleopatra,* Dryden was probably drawn to *Troilus* because it shared a Classical setting with *Antony* and presented a political situation in which he found his own century reflected. Ironically, though, it is probably the political content that doomed *Truth Found Too Late,* for Dryden's play was too reminiscent of the Catholic threat to their own government to succeed with Restoration audiences. It was performed only a few times during its first run, a few times again in 1697, and dropped in revival after 1734. Canons of taste have changed, and the Romantic culture of originality has intervened between Dryden's century and ours in a way that makes it difficult to take his version of Shakespeare as a serious attempt to represent the play, but to his audience *Truth Found Too Late* was just as authentic an interpretation of Shakespeare as our modern-dress versions are to us. Like the twentieth-

century director who gives us a feminist Cressida or portrays the Trojans in the nude, Dryden was genuinely
attempting to represent the *Troilus and Cressida* he read,
complicated though his reading may be by an awareness of
coming *after* Shakespeare. That Dryden's version of the
play is so different from a version we would recognize
speaks forcefully about cultural change, but it might also
suggest that there are aspects of *Troilus* visible to Dryden
in the seventeenth century that are invisible to us in the
twentieth.

One thing immediately apparent to Dryden was that Cressida was too unsettling a female figure for the Restoration
stage. His most startling change in the text was the complete
revision of the fifth act: Cressida only pretends to be
attracted to Diomedes, thinking that her compliance will
allow her to return to Troy; Diomedes lies to Troilus about
Cressida's fidelity; Troilus believes him and will not be
convinced of Cressida's innocence until she commits suicide to "prove" it. "But, Oh, thou purest, whitest innocence,
/ (For such I know thee now, too late I know it!)" declares
Troilus: Cressida's chastity is the truth he finds too late.
Cressida dies having heard herself exonerated ("And I die
happy that he thinks me true"), and the play ends with a
battle in which Troilus kills Diomedes and is finally killed
himself by the Myrmidons. No Pandarus enters to deflate
this heroic scene; instead we get somber pronouncements
by the Greek generals, ending in these politically resonant
words by Ulysses:

> Then, since from homebred Factions ruine springs,
> Let subjects learn obedience to the Kings.

This is a long way from the chaotic and satirical ending
of Shakespeare's play. Although the play's original editors had classified it variously as a tragedy, a history, and
a comedy, Dryden began with the conviction that *Troilus*
was a tragedy, and almost all his changes stem from the
choice of genre. He saw his role as uncovering and puri-
fying the tragedy hidden in Shakespeare's heap of rubbish, writing in the Preface that "the tongue in general is

so much refin'd since Shakespeare's time, that many of his words, and more of his Phrases, are scarce intelligible." Calling *Troilus and Cressida* "the Tragedy I have undertaken to correct," he sets out to bring Shakespeare's play into line with the classicizing drama of Racine then paramount on the English stage. Trojans are made uniformly heroic, Greeks unfailingly villainous; the war plot is dwarfed in importance by the now clearly tragic love plot; scenes in the Greek and Trojan camps are grouped together according to the usual practice in the Restoration theater ("no leaping from Troy to the Grecian tents and thence back again in the same Act"); Helen, significantly, is omitted, and Thersites is made purely comic rather than satirical. It is almost as if *Troilus,* like *Antony and Cleopatra,* gives Dryden a chance to rival Shakespearean tragedy without attempting to rewrite the major tragedies directly; his vindication of Cressida's innocence sounds more like a scene from *Othello* than from *Troilus and Cressida,* and one scene he adds—a quarrel and reconciliation between Troilus and Hector—is closely modeled on *Julius Caesar.* Whatever complex goals lie behind Dryden's adaptation, the result is a clear, unified tragedy of love. Throughout *Troilus and Cressida*'s history on stage, we shall find few productions that give equal weight to the military and the romantic; if Dryden's play marks the beginning of a shift away from interest in the war plot, we may now be witnessing a resurgence of interest in the story of the lovers, after fifty years in which the war plot was clearly dominant. But *Troilus and Cressida* was to go through many incarnations before that shift occurred.

By the play's next appearence, or near-appearance, more than a century later, its focus was beginning to move away from the love plot, although its sense of genre was still deeply indebted to Dryden. In the late 1790s, the actor and manager John Philip Kemble prepared a version of *Troilus and Cressida* for performance, rearranging much of the text and casting all the parts, but decided at the last moment that the play could not be performed. *Troilus and Cressida* never came even this close again to being acted for another hundred years. Though Kemble's version got no further than the prompt book (which is still available in the Folger Library), it does suggest how the play had to be changed for a late eighteenth-century audience, and also reveals some of the pressures that kept *Troilus* off the stage for so long. Unlike *All For Love* or Nahum Tate's famous rewriting of *King Lear,* which held the stage until 1838, Dryden's *Truth Found Too Late* disappeared fairly quickly from the English repertory. Although the eighteenth century saw a huge revival of interest in Shakespeare (mostly in versions almost unrecognizable to us now), other "improvers" of Shakespeare's plays were probably wary of *Troilus* because of Dryden's relative lack of success with it. By the end of the century, too, conditions in the theater had changed to favor a star system in which the actor became almost more important than the play. *Troilus and Cressida*'s lack of a clear starring role made it an unlikely choice in such a theatrical climate, as did its treatment of the lovers at a time when sentimental drama was in ascendance.

Kemble, however, found something in the play interesting enough to warrant a rewriting, though he turned it into an epic drama of war whose lovers behave in true sentimental fashion. In one sense, his alterations are the opposite of Dryden's, for he magnified the war plot and diminished the importance of the lovers. Shakespeare's ending was restored—no suicide this time—but Kemble still found Cressida a problematic figure, and seems to have resolved his discomfort by making her a straightforward victim of Diomedes. The betrayal scene in his version of the play shows Cressida yielding to intense pressure from Diomedes, not teasing him as in some modern productions or secretly resisting him as in Dryden. Like Dryden's, Kemble's Cressida does not speak the "ward" (position of defense in swordplay) speech ("Upon my back, to defend my belly . . ." 1.2.272), but she does undergo the "kissing in general" by the Greeks (4.5.22ff.), a scene Dryden obviously found beneath the dignity of his tragic heroine. Together with Ulysses' speech on "degree" (1.3.85ff.) these two moments in Cressida's career allow for some of the most pointed contrasts among productions of the play; by 1985, in Howard Davies' production, we find the "ward" speech and the kissing scene among the central moments in the play, and the speech on "degree" reduced to a parody to be mocked by the other generals. For his production, Kemble makes Cressida the true sentimental heroine; she is infantilized first as a morally fragile girl and later as "the fallen woman." That Kemble was anxious about Cressida is suggested, too, by his treatment of Helen: as in Dryden, her role is completely cut; there is no place for Helen as Shakespeare portrays her in a world where women are never responsible for their moral choices. Interestingly, the discomfort with Cressida persists even in very recent productions. In 1965, Joseph Papp conceived of a victimized Cressida, but influenced by the feminist movement, he saw her as a victim not only of Diomedes, but also "of men, their wars, their desires, and their double standards." Papp became so engaged in defending Cressida that he reports in his notes on directing the play that his defense "created an unfortunate conflict between me and the actor playing the role of Troilus." The male director's difficulty with the figure of Cressida suggests another way of reading the history of this play and perhaps explains something about its long absence from the stage. At the same time, it raises questions about what a female director, presumably less threatened by Cressida's "betrayal" of a man or less rivalrous with Troilus, would make of the character. (Though there have been several notable women directors of Shakespeare, none, as far as I have been able to find, has attempted *Troilus*.) Could it be that Kemble withdrew the play from production because he still found Cressida too unruly a woman to bring to life on the stage? If she did not kill herself as Dryden's heroine obligingly did, would she remain too far outside the bounds of decorum for an audience at the end of the eighteenth century?

Whatever the reasons for Kemble's withdrawal of *Troilus* from the London stage, his gesture remained definitive until 1907. Charles Fry produced the play that year at the Great Queen Street Theatre, the first English performance of Shakespeare's text since 1603. Fry may have been emboldened by productions in Germany at the turn of the century (or perhaps by reading Shaw's comment about the play's modernity), for *Troilus and Cressida* had been performed in Munich in 1898 and in Berlin in the following year and in 1904. The first modern production of the play was in Munich's Theater am Gärtenplatz in April 1898 (there is one reference to an earlier German production, but it hasn't been substantiated), and shows the influence of nineteenth-century German scholarship. It attempted to re-create the original performance of the play at the Globe, framing a text cut in length by two-thirds with a representation of Elizabethan street life. In the interest of historical authenticity it cast men in the women's parts, and also took the revolutionary step of stripping the stage of scenery and writing scene changes on a blackboard. For the most part, the production was not well received, though it achieved success with its daring interpretation of Thersites, who was transformed from what one reviewer calls "a common scold into a censor of the world." The idea of Thersites as social critic is to appear as a major feature of the modern *Troilus,* though not for several years after the Munich production.

Fry's 1907 performance was received with equal coolness, *The Times* pronouncing that "the main result was the conviction that it is impossible to arrange the play for the stage." As if in defiance of this review, the next London production refused to change the play; instead it reimagined the stage. Undoubtedly the most important production in the play's history until that time is William Poel's *Troilus and Cressida* of 1912. Tyrone Guthrie, who was himself to become one of the play's major interpreters, wrote of Poel, "I believe that he, if anybody, ought to be regarded as the founder of modern Shakespearean production." Poel's innovation was to return to the non-illusionistic stage of the Renaissance. In this he was anticipated by the scholarly German productions of the previous century, and though he may not have known it, a participant in the larger movement in the theater that led to the interrogation of illusion in Pirandello, Cocteau, Brecht, and Beckett. Influenced by advances in historical scholarship—the 1596 de Witt drawing of the Swan Theatre was published in 1888; the papers of the Elizabethan theater manager Philip Henslowe began to appear in 1904 — Poel concluded that "Shakespeare invented his dramatic construction to suit his own particular stage," and insisted that Shakespeare's plays could be understood only if performed under the conditions for which they were written. Though Poel's faith in his ability to replicate the Elizabethan theater may now strike us as historically naive, his innovations remain enormously influential. He took actors out of Victorian costumes and dressed them as Elizabethans; he speeded up the delivery of the verse line; and he eliminated almost all scenery, allowing Shakespeare's scenes to be performed for the first time in two hundred years in their original order, free of the transpositions necessitated by the cumbersome scenery of the eighteenth and nineteenth centuries.

Troilus and Cressida, with its swift alternation of scenes, was especially well suited to Poel's new methods. His entire performance took place without scenery, in front of a single backdrop of black and purple draperies designed in what one shocked reviewer called "the most modern of modernist ways." Though the Greeks and Trojans were given real historical specificity as Elizabethans, the production reflected the antimilitarism of some of Poel's generation in the tense years leading up to the First World War. Not surprisingly, the twentieth-century history of this play is bound up with the twentieth-century history of war. Most of the major productions have coincided with war years, and more often with years that felt the threat rather than the actual presence of war: Poel's in 1912; MacOwan's in 1938; Guthrie's in 1956, a year of Cold War, Korea, and Suez; Papp's in 1965 and Barton's in 1968, both of which alluded to Vietnam. The relation between history and performance is complex, but it may be that producing *Troilus,* at least as the play is currently imagined, is a way for directors to express antimilitarism within the safe confines of Shakespearean theater. At the same time, productions of *Troilus* promise critical and commercial success in periods when the public is generally receptive to a criticism of war.

Poel may have had the play's antimilitarism in mind when he recalled in a speech given just before his production opened that *Troilus and Cressida* was one of the two Shakespearean plays that he had been told as a student he must never read (the other was *Measure for Measure*), because they were not "proper." Now, he asserted, *Troilus* seemed to him "the most ethical thing Shakespeare ever wrote." Gone was the infantilized Cressida of Kemble's version—Poel stipulated that Shakespeare "had in mind a woman who is not a girl"—and in her place was what one reviewer called "a real woman." Poel's Cressida was a fashionable Elizabethan, given naturalistic stage business and allowed to act bored as Troilus protested his love. He gave the part to Edith Evans, a young workingwoman who was not even a professional actress, but who went on from her role as Cressida to enjoy one of the most brilliant careers on the modern English stage. Poel himself took the part of Pandarus, a choice that implies another move away from earlier concepts of the play. Dryden had given his best actor, Thomas Betterton, the part of Troilus; Kemble had cast himself as Ulysses; and now Poel takes on Pandarus. Charles Fry made an even more unorthodox choice in 1907 when he cast himself as Thersites. The focal point of the play, at least as measured by the assignment of parts, has definitely shifted; before the end of this history we shall see it shift clearly toward Thersites, and now it appears to be shifting again, toward Cressida.

Although many critics resisted Poel's innovations and disliked his *Troilus,* his production of the play was obviously electrifying for other actors and directors. Poel's influence is felt in almost all of the English productions of the play for the next fifty years. Nugent Monck, who had been the stage manager of Poel's company, went on to form his own amateur company in Norwich and pursued the idea of an authentic Elizabethan theater even more vigorously than Poel. He produced a *Troilus* in 1928 in his tiny, intimate Maddermarket Theatre, and arranged for one scene to follow the next with a rapidity that changed the shape of the play. Monck's pioneering technique of having actors from one scene exiting as the speaking of the next scene began—

by now almost a cliché of Shakespearean production—suggests how much the vision of the play had changed since Dryden, who congratulated himself on limiting the scene changes to six.

More influential, though, than Monck's delicate and scholarly *Troilus* was a series of productions of the play by the Cambridge Marlowe Society, beginning in 1922. An academic company formed to produce Elizabethan and Jacobean plays neglected by the commercial theater, the Society included in its members William Poel's nephew, and was well versed in Poel's methods. *Troilus and Cressida* was a natural choice for the group, and they attempted in their performance to come as close as possible to the Elizabethan theatrical style. Women's parts were played by men, scene changes were rapid, and the text was scrupulously followed. Most striking in their interpretation of the play was that they explored its comic possibilities, reducing Helen and Cressida to completely farcical characters. Even in the 1920s, then, the play's female figures were still provoking evasions from directors; unwilling to tamper with the text as Dryden and Kemble had done, director Frank Birch seems to have found another way of controlling the play's problematic women.

Birch's production is seminal in the history of *Troilus and Cressida* not so much because of the way it imagined the play as because it introduced *Troilus* to the generation of performers who were to become its most important English interpreters. George Rylands, who played Diomedes in Birch's production, went on to produce the play himself no fewer than four times: in 1940, 1948, 1954—the first television version—and 1956. Anthony Quayle, who played Hector in another Birch production, also felt drawn to directing the play, and put it on at Stratford-upon-Avon in 1948. John Barton, who co-directed the 1956 production with Rylands and obviously inherited Rylands' fascination with the play, has mounted three major productions with the Royal Shakespeare Company, the most recent in 1976. Even Tyrone Guthrie's *Troilus* in some sense originates with the Marlowe Society, for Guthrie worked with Rylands at the Cambridge Festival Theatre in the thirties. Although the Marlowe Society productions did not reach a large audience, their influence has been tremendous. We may still be feeling the effects, at least in the major English productions of *Troilus,* of an acting tradition that began in an academic society. The attention to textual accuracy, for instance, in even the most daring RSC productions, is a direct legacy of Rylands' and Barton's scholarly background. And more important, the effect of the original Cambridge audience—highly educated, upper-class, and male—may still be shaping productions in ways we have yet to realize. Certainly the Marlowe Society succeeded in generating interest in *Troilus,* and in defining it as an intellectual play, at least until Michael MacOwan dared to perform it at a commercial theater in modern dress in 1938.

In an age where we have to be reminded that *Troilus and Cressida* is not a play about Vietnam, the shock of modern dress is hard to recapture, but to London audiences its first appearance in performances of Shakespeare was a cause for derision. The return to contemporary costuming, though not espoused by Poel, was part of the movement toward immediacy in the theater he inspired; with it came a relaxation in the style of the verse-speaking that made Shakespeare's plays accessible to a wider audience. MacOwan's is the first English production of the play to be a commercial success; it took *Troilus* definitely out of the study and into the theater. Part of the reason for his success is that he deliberately invoked the specter of the Munich Conference, held in September of that year. Greeks and Trojans were dressed in contemporary military uniforms, and sets and props alluded to a European war. The love plot was reduced to little more than a distraction, one critic reporting that Troilus had become by his final love scene "something of a bore." Thersites, first played as a social critic in the 1898 production, now received full treatment as a choric figure. MacOwan's brilliant and much-copied idea was to express Thersites' detachment as well as his voyeurism by making him a war correspondent for a left-wing newspaper. Sporting a bedraggled raincoat and a red tie (his leftist leanings), MacOwan's satirical Thersites set the tone for the entire production and helped to establish *Troilus and Cressida* as the bitter exposé of war many recognize today.

MacOwan's production laid the foundation for what must be one of the two or three most important stagings of the play: Tyrone Guthrie's 1956 *Troilus* at the Old Vic in London. The year of Suez and Hungary, 1956 is almost predictably a major year for productions of *Troilus and Cressida,* as well as a turning point in the history of modern English drama. A few months after Guthrie's bitterly comic version of *Troilus* startled London audiences, John Osborne rocked the theater establishment with the rage and sensuality of his *Look Back in Anger.* Meanwhile the BBC had decided to commission a television production of *Troilus,* John Barton was codirecting the play in Cambridge, and Jan de Meester was staging a controversial version, complete with futuristic interplanetary warfare, in Belgium. There had been several English productions of *Troilus and Cressida* between MacOwan's and Guthrie's, but most had tried to restore an aura of romanticism to the play. Both productions at Stratford in the forties and early fifties, for instance, transposed Pandarus' scathing epilogue so that they ended on a heroic gesture, while Luchino Visconti's 1949 production in Florence transformed the whole of the Boboli Gardens into a sumptuous outdoor set for Troy.

Guthrie, however, located himself clearly in the tradition of Poel and MacOwan and saw the play as a sharp indictment of war. He commented in his Program Notes: "Shakespeare, we believe, was concerned to show that the causes of war, so far as the causes of any event can be determined, were utterly confused and unreasonable." Despite his sense of the bleakness of the play, Guthrie brought to his production the liberating use of the stage and the interest in drama as ritual that made him one of this century's great directors of Shakespeare. With his design for an open stage at the Festival Theater in Ontario in 1953, he revolutionized Shakespearean production, breaking the grip in which the proscenium arch had held actors and audience for three hundred years. Like Brecht, who was a major influence on his work, Guthrie realized that the proscenium stage encouraged passivity; it created a drama in which the audience was invited to be empathetic, rather than analytical, in its stance toward the stage. Although Guthrie lacked Brecht's political analysis of the audience's role, he was equally forceful in his rejection of realism, envisaging the audience as "assisting" in the ritual act of performance. The traditional theater at the Old Vic he regarded as at best "a compromise," but he used it to produce a *Troilus* of real originality.

Guthrie set the production in 1913, on the eve of World War I, explaining that it was the last time that Europeans could think of war as a game. (Howard Davies seems to have had the same thing in mind when he set his 1985 production during the Crimean War, while Jack Landau placed the turning point in warfare at the American Civil War, the setting for his production in 1961.) To convey what he termed the "frivolity" of the Trojans, Guthrie made them Edwardians of the leisure class; Cressida appeared in riding costume and Pandarus with field glasses and a top hat of Ascot gray for the scene in which they view the Trojan warriors. The conception of Helen was particularly striking: won over to the Trojan way of life, she perched on a piano, sipping champagne and dangling a long cigarette as Pandarus played his love song for her. Under Guthrie's direction, Thersites definitely replaced Ulysses as the spokesman for the play: the "degree" speech was severely cut and Thersites gained even more prominence than in MacOwan's version. Again in the war correspondent's role, Thersites now had the addition of a camera, which he was constantly setting up on stage as if to underline his voyeurism. Guthrie cut the text freely, removing the Prologue and much of the play's intellectual debate, particularly the discussion of value among the Trojans (2.2.), which has become a cornerstone of recent productions. Although reviewers recognized Guthrie's success in making war "look tremendously ceremonious and abysmally silly," they generally found the production too irreverent a treatment of Shakespeare and without the powerful sense of ceremony that had distinguished Guthrie's work in Ontario.

But the movement begun by MacOwan's and Guthrie's productions of *Troilus* has proven irresistible. Together, they made the play a standard in the repertory of Shakespearean theater, and established it as a satire against war. Although recent productions explore aspects of the play untouched by MacOwan or Guthrie, the satirical tone they set has continued practically unquestioned in performances till this day. After 1956, the role of the lovers in productions of *Troilus* became increasingly peripheral, and the threat posed by Cressida seemed to diminish; it is not until the 1980s, when the image of the unruly woman is at least superficially a positive one, that the love plot again takes priority. By the sixties, *Troilus* had become a play every director wanted to attempt, every Shakespeare festival to stage. With the war in Vietnam, the antiwar movement in the United States, and growing anti-imperialism in Europe, *Troilus and Cressida* gained new urgency as a play for the modern stage. Productions proliferated: Joseph Papp achieved considerable success with his outdoor production in 1965, stressing the play's antiheroism and casting James Earl Jones as a clownish Ajax; the Swedish director Alf Sjöberg produced an anti-imperialist version in 1967, playing the Trojans as a dark-skinned people beset by French and American colonists in parachute gear; at the height of the Civil Rights movement in 1963, Michael Langham produced "a genuine shudder throughout the audience" by dressing the Myrmidons to resemble Ku Klux Klansmen for their murder of Hector; Adrian Hall tried to suggest the bloody and repetitive nature of war in his 1971 production by costuming Greeks and Trojans in military uniforms of many different periods, and allowing Hector to be pelted with "blood-soaked" sponges until his body was reddened and the stage covered with splotches of gore; in Warsaw in 1978 Marek Grzesiński placed both Greeks and Trojans on a revolving set, suggesting that they were just two sides of the same world; Keith Hack suspended a carefree Helen on a swing throughout his 1977 production to suggest the absurdity of the war being fought below. By 1979 the identification of *Troilus* with contemporary politics had reached a level of near-absurdity; we find one reviewer criticizing a Swiss staging for portraying the destruction of Troy so "comfortably" while there was a war going on in Southeast Asia. The price we have paid for the explosion in popularity of *Troilus and Cressida* is a loss of the historical distance which might enable a more critical and finally more political appreciation of the play. Because of its adaptability to twentieth-century attitudes, *Troilus* raises one of the most vexed questions about performing Shakespeare for a modern audience: how to reach a wide public while avoiding the suggestion that the plays are "universal," that they transcend history.

John Barton, perhaps the premier director of *Troilus and Cressida* in the sixties and seventies, has raised this question in three separate productions. The evolution of the play in his hands encapsulates much of the play's history in the postwar period, as he takes it out of the Cambridge Marlowe Society and into increasingly controversial productions with the Royal Shakespeare Company. Barton's version with Peter Hall in 1960, during Hall's first year as director of the RSC, is most notable for its staging and its restoration of the complete text. Unlike Guthrie and others who had had success with *Troilus* in performance, Barton and Hall insisted on playing a nearly complete text, and restored some of the intellectual complexity missing from Guthrie's productions. Yet they were influenced by Guthrie's campaign for an open stage and built an apron projecting beyond the proscenium into the audience at Stratford. Max Adrian as Pandarus used the new stage to great effect, stepping beyond "the fourth wall" and making direct contact with the audience. Also from Guthrie they borrowed the idea of what has been called "a permanent and suggestive set, carefully unlocalized and non-pictorial": a sharply raked stage containing a large octagonal platform covered with sand. The central, brilliantly lit sandpit may allude also to Brecht, who staged his 1948 *Antigone* in a circle of white light. The effect of Barton and Hall's set was to concentrate the action of *Troilus,* and at the same time to literalize the spiritual aridity and shifting moral foundation that the directors saw in the play. Cressida domesticated the desertlike space in her love scene with Troilus, allowing the sand to slip languorously through her fingers as she talked about time.

The 1960 production took few interpretative liberties, though it followed the trend of emphasizing war over love, and succeeded in pleasing both audience and critics (despite a surprisingly weak performance as Thersites by Peter O'Toole). In 1968, however, Barton met with nothing short of outrage when he staged the play again, in a year of uprisings in France and Czechoslovakia, assassinations in the United States, and massive protests against the Vietnam War. He was explicit about the parallels; the Trojan War, he asserted, "is an image of a Vietnam situation, where both sides are inexorably committed." The set for the production was nearly the same as in 1960; what shocked the critics was Barton's treatment of eroticism. There was almost no erotic attraction between Troilus and Cressida; instead it was all between the Greeks and the Trojans. In a way that anticipated René Girard's treatment of this play, Barton emphasized the role of envy and sexual attraction in male warfare, portraying the Trojans as lean, oiled warriors in scanty costumes and the Myrmidons as nude throughout. Sexual and linguistic violence were linked, as Thersites appeared with a mouth-shaped codpiece from which he could release a bright red tongue/penis. Benedict Nightingale, one of the most sympathetic reviewers, explained Barton's concept this way: "War is sex and sex is war. Cressida destroys Troilus, and the Trojans meet the Greeks like lovers, almost naked, agog for the dark orgasmic flutter of killing or being killed." Others, however, were less sympathetic, even homophobic, in their responses, one pronouncing the production "no more and no less than a slightly ritualized performance of sodomy." In this *Troilus,* as could be expected, the interest was almost entirely in the war plot, with the roles of the lovers cut until they seemed of very minor importance. The most compelling love scene had now been given to Achilles and Patroclus; Alan Howard playing Achilles as a campy bisexual and Patroclus appearing in drag. If Barton, like almost all producers of this play before him, was struggling with the representation of Cressida, he solved the problem brilliantly by creating an intense focus on male eroticism. Although his Cressida appeared in the nude (the first in a long line of nude Cressidas), she remained outside the central conflict, and the sexuality of the lovers went largely unexplored.

Despite the censure this production received, Barton's staging began to seem the definitive English *Troilus,* and there were no major productions in England until he took up the play again in 1976. Though most critics considered the 1976 *Troilus* little more than a tired reworking of the 1968 production, it seems to me an important turn in the fortunes of the play, particularly in its treatment of women. Barton himself tried to explain some of his fascination with *Troilus* in an interview: "I think that it is one of [Shakespeare's] greatest plays precisely because of the way in which he invites in the course of a single play all the different kinds of response one can have in the theater, which are normally isolated from one another." What Barton responded to in 1976 was the play's portrayal of women in a world based on male desire. This production became the first major version of *Troilus* since before MacOwan to examine the love plot as seriously as the plot about war. Much in Barton's production was familiar from 1968: the seminude Trojans, the effeminate Achilles, the suppurating Thersites. But what was new was centered on the female characters, and suggested that Barton wanted to complicate his vision of homoeroticism as the basis of the Trojan conflict. Helen appeared bound to Paris by a golden chain, with which she was led about the stage; Cressida in the betrayal scene was given a courtesan's mask to wear on the back of her head, revealing it only as she turned to exit with Diomedes; and in the strangest gesture, Pandarus donned a death mask for his final scene and descended into a gravelike vault which revealed, when closed, Thersites clutching a life-sized female doll. Although many in the audience found those moments incoherent and distracting, it seems clear that Barton was

suggesting that Cressida's self-division—"I have a kind
of self resides with thee"—is inevitable in a world that
turns women into icons. Barton's final image, then, of
Thersites holding a doll becomes a bitter parody of Paris
and Helen, Troilus and Cressida, Cressida and Diomedes;
in fact, of the whole Trojan conflict over sexuality as
possession.

While Barton's production suggested the direction a
feminist production might take—as Papp's production had
done in a more naturalistic way in 1965—the first production of *Troilus* to be widely recognized as feminist (and
this tells us as much about the critics as it does about the
production) was not until 1985. Howard Davies' *Troilus*
of that year, at Stratford-upon-Avon, seemed so strikingly
to reimagine the play that one scholar remarked: "Henceforth we will never discuss this text in quite the same
way." Davies set the production in the Crimean War of the
1850s, a single set of a war-shattered mansion creating an
image of loss and belatedness. Trojans and Greeks were
differentiated by their uniforms and the props they carried
with them into the central room, the Greeks appearing
with a phonograph and a ticker tape machine, laughing
openly as Ulysses delivered his great speech. Thersites
was now a rebellious lower-ranking soldier whose difference in class from the officers allowed him to see the hol-
lowness of their chivalric code. And in what must be a
tribute to Guthrie, Davies placed Pandarus at a piano,
playing obsessively even during the battle scenes as his
civilization collapsed around him. The image of aristocratic ineffectuality in the face of social collapse proved
a haunting one for audiences in Margaret Thatcher's
Britain.

The greatest inventiveness in Davies' production, though,
lay in his discovery of a way to reanimate the love plot. If
Barton's 1968 production eroticized the political aspects
of the play, Davies' politicized the erotic. Reflecting
a growing collaboration between Shakespearean performance and the academy, Davies' *Troilus* clearly exhibited
the influence of feminist cultural criticism and analysis of
Shakespeare in the past fifteen years. His Cressida was a

nineteenth-century "New Woman," for whom the "ward" speech became a serious statement about sexual politics and a touchstone for the entire production. Juliet Stevenson played Cressida not as a coquette but as a woman deeply in love with Troilus; her vulnerability in the Trojan sexual economy was directly connected to the unself-consciousness of her love. This is a new Cressida, and one that several critics found at odds with the text. As late in the play as Act 4, Scene 4, immediately before her departure with Diomedes, Davies had Cressida still dressed in a nightgown and leaping into Troilus' 'rms when he enters for their parting scene. Obviously frightened, she listens as Troilus and Diomedes discuss her value, her face, according to reviewer Alan Dessen, registering the shock of Troilus' "lack of potency in her new life with the Greeks." Moments later she arrives in the Greek camp, still clad only in a nightgown, where the "kissing in general" scene has now become almost a gang rape. Though terrified, Cressida finally begins to play the Grecians' game; she replies to Ulysses' demand for a kiss by indicating to him to kneel—"Why beg, then"—and snapping her fingers for him to rise. In this context, Cressida's choice of Diomedes becomes an understandable reaction to the need for a guardian, and her "betrayal" of Troilus appears guiltless and inevitable. Militarism and sexism have begun to seem so deeply intertwined that one reviewer found Davies' production presenting them as "the twin roots of the patriarchy."

We are a long way here from Dryden and Kemble, or so it seems. In the end, though, Davies' production may be closer to theirs than it appears. Like Dryden with his chaste suicide and Kemble with his fallen woman, Davies has found a way to exonerate Cressida—and thus control the threat she poses—in the terms available in his culture. Is Davies' protofeminist forced into a pose of submission finally so different from Dryden's heroine who has no way to prove her chastity but to kill herself? Although Davies' *Troilus* may herald a new explosion in the popularity of this play for a generation influenced by feminism, it still leaves us having to think hard about how to stage the play without appropriating it as a twentieth-century work. We may still need to answer the question raised by Brecht, one of this century's great readers of Shakespeare: "We need to develop the historical sense ... into a real sensuous delight. When our theaters perform plays of other periods they like to annihilate distance, fill in the gap, gloss over the differences. But what becomes then of our delight in comparisons, in distance, in dissimilarity—which is at the same time a delight in what is close and proper to ourselves?"

Bibliographic Note. This study is indebted to several works on Shakespearean performance, beginning with H. N. Hillebrand's survey of productions in the New Variorum edition (1953). David Bevington gives an excellent account of the early and recent performance history of *Troilus* in his edition for the Arden Shakespeare, Third Series (1998).

The seminal work on the Inns of Court theory is Peter Alexander's article in *Library* 9 (1928–9). For Dryden's version of the play I have drawn on the edition of his works by Alan Roper (1984), on Hazelton Spencer's *Shakespeare Improved* (1927), and on conversation with Ed Schiffer. For Kemble's production, Jeanne T. Newlin's article in *The Triple Bond,* ed. Joseph G. Price (1975), is essential. William Poel's work is examined in Robert Speaight's biography (1954), as well as in J. L. Styan's *The Shakespeare Revolution* (1977), a book from which this study has profited throughout. Surveys of Shakespeare in performance that I have found helpful include Samuel L. Leiter's *Shakespeare Around the Globe* (1986), William Babula's *Shakespeare in Production* (1981), Richard David's *Shakespeare in the Theatre* (1978), Ralph Berry's *Changing Styles in Shakespeare* (1981), which has a fine chapter on *Troilus,* and the periodic reviews in *Shakespeare Quarterly* (since 1950) and *Shakespeare Survey* (annually since 1948). Joseph Papp discusses his production in the Festival edition of the play (1967); John Barton is interviewed in *Shakespeare Survey* 25 (1972). Simon Russell Beale discusses his performance of Thersites (Royal Shakespeare

Company, 1990) in *Players of Shakespeare 3* ed. Russell Jackson and Robert Smallwood (1993). There is a recent dissertation entirely on the stage history of *Troilus* (unavailable at present writing) by Margaret Westley (Toronto, 1985).

Postscript: *Troilus and Cressida,* 1990–2001

The popularity of *Troilus and Cressida* since the 1960s intensified in the final two decades of the twentieth century. For a play with virtually no performance history before 1900, its fortunes had radically changed by 1999, when London newspapers were writing of the proximity of three major productions. Between 1990 and 2001 experienced directors of Shakespeare were either finally getting to the play (Trevor Nunn) or revisiting it (Peter Hall), and younger directors were helping to make names for themselves (Sam Mendes and Michael Boyd) with a play that reflected a postmodern preoccupation with moral and social chaos.

Sam Mendes in 1990 directed a highly praised Royal Shakespeare Company production at its intimate thrust-stage Swan Theatre. The solid cast included more than a few rising film and theater stars. Mendes himself later won an Oscar for directing *American Beauty*; his cast included Ralph Fiennes as Troilus (Fiennes later was nominated for Oscars in *Schindler's List* and *The English Patient*), Amanda Root (Cressida), Ciaran Hinds (Achilles) and Simon Russell Beale (Thersites), all of whom soon assumed starring film and theater roles. The sets were minimal and without a specific historical setting; a set of wide ladders at the back of the stage was placed in front of a ten-foot-high faux Greek mask that was smooth and beautiful on one half and decayed on the other. There was an eclectic mix of costumes, epitomized by the Greek hierarchy wearing classical-style breastplates under modern cardigans or overcoats while Achilles strutted in a black net shirt, leather trousers, and occasionally a long black leather coat.

Throughout the production's relatively full text, the clarity of the speaking gave a fresh sense of drama to even the long-winded council scene speeches. Ulysses angrily rustled papers on the field tent desk to illustrate his considerable anger at Achilles' dismissing the Greek hierarchy's intelligence and "policy" as "bed-work, mapp'ry, closet war" (1.3.205). Aeneas was later greeted with outrage at his inability to recognize "the high and mighty Agamemnon," and the frustrated Agamemnon finally confirmed his identity by defiantly showing a nameplate of the sort that belongs on a desk of a modern executive. As one of the many examples in the play where personal value and identity are questioned, Mendes emphasized the indignation Aeneas was able to provoke with his failure to immediately discern status and authority.

Thersites was played with the usual degree of spite and disgust (he was first seen secretly spitting on Ajax's dinner), but there was an innovative sense of intelligence and even nobility in his speech and demeanor. He looked like a tramp, in a tattered flasher's raincoat and a skullcap that framed a gargoyle-like face, but he wore a necktie as a belt to hold up his trousers, and both tie and trousers were the uniform of an exclusive boarding school that intimated a more noble and educated past. He could speak with a sophisticated air of superiority as well as a depraved scurrility, moving within a speech from a mock aristocratic English accent to a bitingly cynical observation that had the audience laughing in agreement and revulsion at his "spiteful execrations." Beale's Thersites revealed more than just an ability to degrade; he relished the remarkable vocabulary of a character whose sense of superiority grew out of an insight into the lack of nobility in the supposedly heroic war. The production also emphasized Thersites' role as a licensed fool, or a "privileged man" as Achilles calls him (2.3.59). He ingratiated himself into Achilles' service with the use of a jester's stick and some comic routines: his railing took on the air of a vaudeville act (2.3) and he later performed an elaborate impersonation of Ajax (3.3.271).

The dapper figure of Pandarus (Norman Rodway) delivered the prologue and set the tone for Mendes' production. Pandarus and the production as a whole were able to maintain a high level of intelligence without losing the irony that undermines many of the characters' pretensions. This was not a Pandarus that the audience found immediately appalling as a voyeur, but one that began as endearing and playful in his seductions of Troilus for Cressida, Cressida for Troilus, and, as the Prologue, he was also able to perform a kind of seduction of the audience. He helped the first scenes with Troilus and Cressida begin the play with humor and even some romantic optimism, with a particularly successful and comically exaggerated enthusiasm as Pandarus and Cressida watched the soldiers return from battle (1.2). When the lovers came together, and especially after they spent their single night together, Rodway's Pandarus became a more disturbing mediator and intruder in the love relationship. His anger and passionate distress upon hearing of Cressida's exchange was disconcerting in its dismissal of Cressida's predicament. As she sought to find out where Troilus was, and later sobbed uncontrollably at the news of her imminent departure, Pandarus coldly ignored her questions and tears in his distress for the effect her departure would have on Troilus. By the end of the play, when Troilus rejects Pandarus on the battlefield, the well-dressed sprightly character from the beginning of the play had become a pale, coughing, and disheveled casualty of the war and his all too self-interested involvement in the love of Troilus and Cressida. It seemed particularly fitting that the character who had earlier been so solicitous to the audience as the Prologue (calling them "fair beholders") would turn on them and bequeath them his venereal diseases to end the play.

While Mendes added to Pandarus' choric status by having him both end the play with his epilogue and also begin it with the prologue, the tradition of increasing Thersites' choric presence was continued in more recent productions. RSC productions directed by Ian Judge (1996) and Michael Boyd (1999), and an Off Broadway New York production directed by Peter Hall (2001) all had Thersites deliver the prologue. Assigning the prologue to a character who elsewhere speaks to the audience and comments on the action and characters certainly seems an obvious choice for a modern director, but it might also overwhelm the play with satire and perhaps undermine some of the more serious and complex themes of the play. To see that "all the argument is a whore and a cuckold," as Thersites implores us, is certainly important, but it is also as limited as Troilus' naïve view that Helen "is a theme of honor and renown" (2.2.199). Perhaps Thersites works in the play to warn the audience that cynicism can be exaggerated to an extreme, and giving him the prologue may involve the audience too much in his point of view.

The choice to have Thersites open the play does, however, also give an opportunity for a production to introduce its vision of the play. Judge had a Thersites (Richard McCabe) who delivered the prologue as a stand-up comedian, opening the play with a sense that the audience would enjoy watching the debunking of heroic characters. Even the long-winded council scenes and the love scenes were found to contain a good deal of comic potential in Judge's production. Boyd's Thersites (Lloyd Hutchinson) presented a slide show of war images during the prologue, introducing some of the eclectic war settings (World War I, Ireland, the Balkans) that would characterize the production. Once again, Boyd's Thersites carried a camera as a kind of war correspondent, snapping photos of important political moments such as the embrace of Hector and Ajax after their abbreviated duel. This role of chronicler, enhanced by Thersites introducing the play as the Prologue, led up to his role as a newscaster in the trenches and as a kind of master of ceremonies for the final battle.

Even more elaborate was the opening of Peter Hall's production. Thersites (Andrew Weems) began the production by coming onstage to view several skeletons that occupied the stage's central sand pit. From a dusty bag he pulled out bones that made up other skeletons and distributed a helmet and various pieces of armor around the stage. He also retrieved from his bag a modern edition of the play, took a long drag on his cigarette, and began a sarcastic reading, from the modern edition, of the 1609 Quarto's epistle to the reader. Throughout these preliminary actions the house lights remained on, and only after Thersites finished his reading did the audience move into darkness and Thersites began performing the prologue in a different, more serious voice, at least in the beginning. This opening was theatrically self aware in a number of ways, making the props, the stage, and the play text an obvious mixture of discovered and created visions of ancient, Elizabethan and (post)-modern times. Thersites' direct relationship with the production and the audience was reinforced at the end of the play, where Thersites made an extratextual appearance to observe Pandarus' final speech, and gave a signal to turn out the stage lights and end the production.

Recent players of Pandarus have not been as subtle as Norman Rodway was in Mendes' production. Both Mark Wing Davy (at the Delacorte Theatre in Central Park, New York, 1995) and Ian Judge had Pandarus dressed as a geisha, and more than a few reviewers of both productions thought he had escaped from a production of *The Mikado*. The virtual cross-dressing of Pandarus gave him an immediate sense of debauchery and lasciviousness, allowing the lovers' mediator to intimate an unsettling attraction for both his niece and Troilus. Judge's production multiplied the homoerotic desire for Troilus (played by Joseph Fiennes, who, like his brother, followed his playing of Troilus with a successful film career, most notably as the title character in *Shakespeare in Love*). In the already complex scene of observation and desire where Thersites watches Ulysses and Troilus watches Cressida and Diomedes (5.2), Judge had Ulysses restrain Troilus in a particularly physical, almost molesting way. Regardless of textual justification, the interpretation fit the production: male bodies were often on display in little more than G-strings, and Achilles opened his long coat to "flash" Hector with his line "Behold thy fill" in answer to Hector's desire to "let me look on thee" (4.5. 234–5).

Judge, Boyd, and Nunn all presented Cressida in a way that allowed for her sexuality to be seen in light of a more modern understanding of her position in a patriarchal society. Judge's Cressida (Victoria Hamilton) went through a range of emotions when she was kissed by the Greeks. She was disgusted and a bit shocked by the dirty old men imposing kisses on her (Agamemnon and Nestor), but she enjoyed the attention and kiss of a hero of Achilles' stature (leaping up to straddle his waist as he passionately kissed her). She gained confidence as Patroclus and Menelaus argued over her, but her playful banter with Menelaus and

Ulysses backfired. Judge decided to follow the Folio place-
ment of her exit from the scene, which kept her onstage until
after Ulysses' damning speech, where he "reads" her as a
slut (54–63). While Cressida's sexuality may be empow-
ering (as when she plans to play hard to get with Troilus) or
enjoyable (in her kissing Troilus or even Achilles), she was
unprepared for how men would interpret her sexuality.
During Ulysses' speech she stared at the audience in a way
that suggested she was learning that using men's desires for
her empowerment was coming at the cost of being demo-
nized as a whore.

Boyd's Cressida (Jayne Ashbourne) was similarly caught
in a situation in the Greek camp that quickly changed mood.
Her kissing was staged as an elaborate and ever quickening
tango. What began as an enjoyable dance became a disturbing situation resembling the start of a gang rape where
she was thrown from one Greek to another, quicker and
quicker, until she was caught in a menacing circle of Greeks.
Once again, the production provided another moment where
Cressida was initially enjoying the attention to her sexuality
only to be eventually overpowered by male aggression.

Nunn's Cressida (Sophie Okonedo) was portrayed even
more clearly as a victim, and the director highlighted and
exaggerated her isolation throughout the play with some
inventive rearrangement of scenes. The prologue was staged
with most of the cast onstage, in a swirling mass that eventually divided into black actors playing Trojans on one side
and white actors playing Greeks on the other. After an armed
warrior delivered the prologue and a quick battle followed,
the stage was emptied for Cressida to enter, alone, before
Pandarus came through the audience to join her and begin
the dialogue with their watching the soldiers return from
battle (1.1 and the beginning of 1.2 were staged later). Nunn
also rearranged the text to bring Cressida onstage at the end
of the play, with Pandarus, so that Troilus rejected both
characters. After Pandarus delivered his final speech, he
tried to bring Cressida offstage with him, but she broke free
and remained onstage, alone and confused, as the final
image of the play. What Nunn's arrangement highlights was
the interpretation, and indeed the modern desire, to understand Cressida going through an enormous ordeal in the

course of the play. What was once considered by critics and directors as simple faithlessness in Cressida has become more commonly viewed as the inevitable destruction of truth and love in the face of circumstances and a culture where women are treated and traded as objects in a world controlled by manipulating men.

While this brief survey discusses major productions in New York and Stratford-upon-Avon, there were other important professional versions staged in Berlin, Munich, Washington, D.C., Oxford, and elsewhere. The complexity of the play seems particularly appropriate for spurring a wide variety of performance choices that differently balance and interpret the war and love plots. While attitudes about war, sexuality, and indeed theater will continue to spark new interpretations, we can also look forward to a production at the reconstructed Globe Theatre in London, where some interesting insights into the original staging of the play may be revealed.

Suggested References

The number of possible references is vast and grows alarmingly. (The *Shakespeare Quarterly* devotes one issue each year to a list of the previous year's work, and *Shakespeare Survey*—an annual publication—includes a substantial review of biographical, critical, and textual studies, as well as a survey of performances.) The vast bibliography is best approached through James Harner, *The World Shakespeare Bibliography on CD-Rom: 1900–Present*. The first release, in 1996, included more than 12,000 annotated items from 1990–93, plus references to several thousand book reviews, productions, films, and audio recordings. The plan is to update the publication annually, moving forward one year and backward three years. Thus, the second issue (1997), with 24,700 entries, and another 35,000 or so references to reviews, newspaper pieces, and so on, covered 1987–94.

Though no works are indispensable, those listed below have been found especially helpful. The arrangement is as follows:

1. Shakespeare's Times
2. Shakespeare's Life
3. Shakespeare's Theater
4. Shakespeare on Stage and Screen
5. Miscellaneous Reference Works
6. Shakespeare's Plays: General Studies
7. The Comedies
8. The Romances
9. The Tragedies
10. The Histories
11. *Troilus and Cressida*

The titles in the first five sections and in the eleventh section are accompanied by brief explanatory annotations.

1. Shakespeare's Times

Andrews, John F., ed. *William Shakespeare: His World, His Work, His Influence,* 3 vols. (1985). Sixty articles, dealing not only with such subjects as "The State," "The Church," "Law," "Science, Magic, and Folklore," but also with the plays and poems themselves and Shakespeare's influence (e.g., translations, films, reputation).

Byrne, Muriel St. Clare. *Elizabethan Life in Town and Country* (8th ed., 1970). Chapters on manners, beliefs, education, etc., with illustrations.

Dollimore, John, and Alan Sinfield, eds. *Political Shakespeare: New Essays in Cultural Materialism* (1985). Essays on such topics as the subordination of women and colonialism, presented in connection with some of Shakespeare's plays.

Greenblatt, Stephen. *Representing the English Renaissance* (1988). New Historicist essays, especially on connections between political and aesthetic matters, statecraft and stagecraft.

Joseph, B. L. *Shakespeare's Eden: the Commonwealth of England 1558–1629* (1971). An account of the social, political, economic, and cultural life of England.

Kernan, Alvin. *Shakespeare, the King's Playwright: Theater in the Stuart Court 1603–1613* (1995). The social setting and the politics of the court of James I, in relation to *Hamlet, Measure for Measure, Macbeth, King Lear, Antony and Cleopatra, Coriolanus,* and *The Tempest.*

Montrose, Louis. *The Purpose of Playing: Shakespeare and the Cultural Politics of the Elizabethan Theatre* (1996). A poststructuralist view, discussing the professional theater "within the ideological and material frameworks of Elizabethan culture and society," with an extended analysis of *A Midsummer Night's Dream.*

Mullaney, Steven. *The Place of the Stage: License, Play, and Power in Renaissance England* (1988). New Historicist analysis, arguing that popular drama became a cultural institution "only by . . . taking up a place on the margins of society."

Schoenbaum, S. *Shakespeare: The Globe and the World*

(1979). A readable, abundantly illustrated introductory book on the world of the Elizabethans.

Shakespeare's England, 2 vols. (1916). A large collection of scholarly essays on a wide variety of topics, e.g., astrology, costume, gardening, horsemanship, with special attention to Shakespeare's references to these topics.

2. Shakespeare's Life

Andrews, John F., ed. *William Shakespeare: His World, His Work, His Influence,* 3 vols. (1985). See the description above.

Bentley, Gerald E. *Shakespeare: A Biographical Handbook* (1961). The facts about Shakespeare, with virtually no conjecture intermingled.

Chambers, E. K. *William Shakespeare: A Study of Facts and Problems,* 2 vols. (1930). The fullest collection of data.

Fraser, Russell. *Young Shakespeare* (1988). A highly readable account that simultaneously considers Shakespeare's life and Shakespeare's art.

–––. *Shakespeare: The Later Years* (1992).

Schoenbaum, S. *Shakespeare's Lives* (1970). A review of the evidence and an examination of many biographies, including those of Baconians and other heretics.

–––. *William Shakespeare: A Compact Documentary Life* (1977). An abbreviated version, in a smaller format, of the next title. The compact version reproduces some fifty documents in reduced form. A readable presentation of all that the documents tell us about Shakespeare.

–––. *William Shakespeare: A Documentary Life* (1975). A large-format book setting forth the biography with facsimiles of more than two hundred documents, and with transcriptions and commentaries.

3. Shakespeare's Theater

Astington, John H., ed. *The Development of Shakespeare's Theater* (1992). Eight specialized essays on theatrical companies, playing spaces, and performance.

Beckerman, Bernard. *Shakespeare at the Globe, 1599–1609* (1962). On the playhouse and on Elizabethan dramaturgy, acting, and staging.

Bentley, Gerald E. *The Profession of Dramatist in Shakespeare's Time* (1971). An account of the dramatist's status in the Elizabethan period.

———. *The Profession of Player in Shakespeare's Time, 1590–1642* (1984). An account of the status of members of London companies (sharers, hired men, apprentices, managers) and a discussion of conditions when they toured.

Berry, Herbert. *Shakespeare's Playhouses* (1987). Usefully emphasizes how little we know about the construction of Elizabethan theaters.

Brown, John Russell. *Shakespeare's Plays in Performance* (1966). A speculative and practical analysis relevant to all of the plays, but with emphasis on *The Merchant of Venice*, *Richard II*, *Hamlet*, *Romeo and Juliet*, and *Twelfth Night*.

———. *William Shakespeare: Writing for Performance* (1996). A discussion aimed at helping readers to develop theatrically conscious habits of reading.

Chambers, E. K. *The Elizabethan Stage*, 4 vols. (1945). A major reference work on theaters, theatrical companies, and staging at court.

Cook, Ann Jennalie. *The Privileged Playgoers of Shakespeare's London, 1576–1642* (1981). Sees Shakespeare's audience as wealthier, more middle-class, and more intellectual than Harbage (below) does.

Dessen, Alan C. *Elizabethan Drama and the Viewer's Eye* (1977). On how certain scenes may have looked to spectators in an Elizabethan theater.

Gurr, Andrew. *Playgoing in Shakespeare's London* (1987). Something of a middle ground between Cook (above) and Harbage (below).

———. *The Shakespearean Stage, 1579–1642* (2nd ed., 1980). On the acting companies, the actors, the playhouses, the stages, and the audiences.

Harbage, Alfred. *Shakespeare's Audience* (1941). A study of the size and nature of the theatrical public, emphasizing the representativeness of its working class and middle-class audience.

Hodges, C. Walter. *The Globe Restored* (1968). A conjectural restoration, with lucid drawings.

Hosley, Richard. "The Playhouses," in *The Revels History of Drama in English*, vol. 3, general editors Clifford Leech and T. W. Craik (1975). An essay of a hundred pages on the physical aspects of the playhouses.

Howard, Jane E. "Crossdressing, the Theatre, and Gender Struggle in Early Modern England," *Shakespeare Quarterly* 39 (1988): 418–40. Judicious comments on the effects of boys playing female roles.

Orrell, John. *The Human Stage: English Theatre Design, 1567–1640* (1988). Argues that the public, private, and court playhouses are less indebted to popular structures (e.g., innyards and bear-baiting pits) than to banqueting halls and to Renaissance conceptions of Roman amphitheaters.

Slater, Ann Pasternak. *Shakespeare the Director* (1982). An analysis of theatrical effects (e.g., kissing, kneeling) in stage directions and dialogue.

Styan, J. L. *Shakespeare's Stagecraft* (1967). An introduction to Shakespeare's visual and aural stagecraft, with chapters on such topics as acting conventions, stage groupings, and speech.

Thompson, Peter. *Shakespeare's Professional Career* (1992). An examination of patronage and related theatrical conditions.

———. *Shakespeare's Theatre* (1983). A discussion of how plays were staged in Shakespeare's time.

4. Shakespeare on Stage and Screen

Bate, Jonathan, and Russell Jackson, eds. *Shakespeare: An Illustrated Stage History* (1996). Highly readable essays on stage productions from the Renaissance to the present.

Berry, Ralph. *Changing Styles in Shakespeare* (1981). Discusses productions of six plays (*Coriolanus*, *Hamlet*, *Henry V*, *Measure for Measure*, *The Tempest*, and *Twelfth Night*) on the English stage, chiefly 1950–1980.

———. *On Directing Shakespeare: Interviews with Contemporary Directors* (1989). An enlarged edition of a book first published in 1977, this version includes the seven interviews from the early 1970s and adds five interviews conducted in 1988.

Brockbank, Philip, ed. *Players of Shakespeare: Essays in Shakespearean Performance* (1985). Comments by twelve actors, reporting their experiences with roles. See also the entry for Russell Jackson (below).

Bulman, J. C., and H. R. Coursen, eds. *Shakespeare on Television* (1988). An anthology of general and theoretical essays, essays on individual productions, and shorter reviews, with a bibliography and a videography listing cassettes that may be rented.

Coursen, H. P. *Watching Shakespeare on Television* (1993). Analyses not only of TV versions but also of films and videotapes of stage presentations that are shown on television.

Davies, Anthony, and Stanley Wells, eds. *Shakespeare and the Moving Image: The Plays on Film and Television* (1994). General essays (e.g., on the comedies) as well as essays devoted entirely to *Hamlet*, *King Lear*, and *Macbeth*.

Dawson, Anthony B. *Watching Shakespeare: A Playgoer's Guide* (1988). About half of the plays are discussed, chiefly in terms of decisions that actors and directors make in putting the works onto the stage.

Dessen, Alan. *Elizabethan Stage Conventions and Modern Interpretations* (1984). On interpreting conventions such as the representation of light and darkness and stage violence (duels, battles).

Donaldson, Peter. *Shakespearean Films/Shakespearean Directors* (1990). Postmodernist analyses, drawing on Freudianism, Feminism, Deconstruction, and Queer Theory.

Jackson, Russell, and Robert Smallwood, eds. *Players of Shakespeare 2: Further Essays in Shakespearean Performance by Players with the Royal Shakespeare Company* (1988). Fourteen actors discuss their roles in productions between 1982 and 1987.

————. *Players of Shakespeare 3: Further Essays in Shakespearean Performance by Players with the Royal Shakespeare Company* (1993). Comments by thirteen performers.

Jorgens, Jack. *Shakespeare on Film* (1977). Fairly detailed studies of eighteen films, preceded by an introductory chapter addressing such issues as music, and whether to "open" the play by including scenes of landscape.

Kennedy, Dennis. *Looking at Shakespeare: A Visual History of Twentieth-Century Performance* (1993). Lucid descriptions (with 170 photographs) of European, British, and American performances.

Leiter, Samuel L. *Shakespeare Around the Globe: A Guide to Notable Postwar Revivals* (1986). For each play there are about two pages of introductory comments, then discussions (about five hundred words per production) of ten or so productions, and finally bibliographic references.

McMurty, Jo. *Shakespeare Films in the Classroom* (1994). Useful evaluations of the chief films most likely to be shown in undergraduate courses.

Rothwell, Kenneth, and Annabelle Henkin Melzer. *Shakespeare on Screen: An International Filmography and Videography* (1990). A reference guide to several hundred films and videos produced between 1899 and 1989, including spinoffs such as musicals and dance versions.

Sprague, Arthur Colby. *Shakespeare and the Actors* (1944). Detailed discussions of stage business (gestures, etc.) over the years.

Willis, Susan. *The BBC Shakespeare Plays: Making the Televised Canon* (1991). A history of the series, with interviews and production diaries for some plays.

5. Miscellaneous Reference Works

Abbott, E. A. *A Shakespearean Grammar* (new edition, 1877). An examination of differences between Elizabethan and modern grammar.

Allen, Michael J. B., and Kenneth Muir, eds. *Shakespeare's Plays in Quarto* (1981). One volume containing facsimiles of the plays issued in small format before they were collected in the First Folio of 1623.

Bevington, David. *Shakespeare* (1978). A short guide to hundreds of important writings on the subject.

Blake, Norman. *Shakespeare's Language: An Introduction* (1983). On vocabulary, parts of speech, and word order.

Bullough, Geoffrey. *Narrative and Dramatic Sources of Shakespeare*, 8 vols. (1957–75). A collection of many of the books Shakespeare drew on, with judicious comments.

Campbell, Oscar James, and Edward G. Quinn, eds. *The Reader's Encyclopedia of Shakespeare* (1966). Old, but still the most useful single reference work on Shakespeare.

Cercignani, Fausto. *Shakespeare's Works and Elizabethan Pronunciation* (1981). Considered the best work on the topic, but remains controversial.

Dent, R. W. *Shakespeare's Proverbial Language: An Index* (1981). An index of proverbs, with an introduction concerning a form Shakespeare frequently drew on.

Greg, W. W. *The Shakespeare First Folio* (1955). A detailed yet readable history of the first collection (1623) of Shakespeare's plays.

Harner, James. *The World Shakespeare Bibliography*. See headnote to Suggested References.

Hosley, Richard. *Shakespeare's Holinshed* (1968). Valuable presentation of one of Shakespeare's major sources.

Kökeritz, Helge. *Shakespeare's Names* (1959). A guide to pronouncing some 1,800 names appearing in Shakespeare.

———. *Shakespeare's Pronunciation* (1953). Contains much information about puns and rhymes, but see Cercignani (above).

Muir, Kenneth. *The Sources of Shakespeare's Plays* (1978). An account of Shakespeare's use of his reading. It covers all the plays, in chronological order.

Miriam Joseph, Sister. *Shakespeare's Use of the Arts of Language* (1947). A study of Shakespeare's use of rhetorical devices, reprinted in part as *Rhetoric in Shakespeare's Time* (1962).

The Norton Facsimile: The First Folio of Shakespeare's Plays (1968). A handsome and accurate facsimile of the first collection (1623) of Shakespeare's plays, with a valuable introduction by Charlton Hinman.

Onions, C. T. *A Shakespeare Glossary*, rev. and enlarged by R. D. Eagleson (1986). Definitions of words (or senses of words) now obsolete.

Partridge, Eric. *Shakespeare's Bawdy*, rev. ed. (1955). Relatively brief dictionary of bawdy words; useful, but see Williams, below.

Shakespeare Quarterly. See headnote to Suggested References.

Shakespeare Survey. See headnote to Suggested References.

Spevack, Marvin. *The Harvard Concordance to Shakespeare* (1973). An index to Shakespeare's words.

Vickers, Brian. *Appropriating Shakespeare: Contemporary Critical Quarrels* (1993). A survey—chiefly hostile—of recent schools of criticism.

Wells, Stanley, ed. *Shakespeare: A Bibliographical Guide* (new edition, 1990). Nineteen chapters (some devoted to single plays, others devoted to groups of related plays) on recent scholarship on the life and all of the works.

Williams, Gordon. *A Dictionary of Sexual Language and Imagery in Shakespearean and Stuart Literature*, 3 vols. (1994). Extended discussions of words and passages; much fuller than Partridge, cited above.

6. Shakespeare's Plays: General Studies

Bamber, Linda. *Comic Women, Tragic Men: A Study of Gender and Genre in Shakespeare* (1982).

Barnet, Sylvan. *A Short Guide to Shakespeare* (1974).

Callaghan, Dympna, Lorraine Helms, and Jyotsna Singh. *The Weyward Sisters: Shakespeare and Feminist Politics* (1994).

Clemen, Wolfgang H. *The Development of Shakespeare's Imagery* (1951).

Cook, Ann Jennalie. *Making a Match: Courtship in Shakespeare and His Society* (1991).

Dollimore, Jonathan, and Alan Sinfield. *Political Shakespeare: New Essays in Cultural Materialism* (1985).

Dusinberre, Juliet. *Shakespeare and the Nature of Women* (1975).

Granville-Barker, Harley. *Prefaces to Shakespeare*, 2 vols. (1946–47; volume 1 contains essays on *Hamlet, King Lear, Merchant of Venice, Antony and Cleopatra*, and *Cymbeline*; volume 2 contains essays on *Othello, Coriolanus, Julius Caesar, Romeo and Juliet, Love's Labor's Lost*).

———. *More Prefaces to Shakespeare* (1974; essays on *Twelfth Night, A Midsummer Night's Dream, The Winter's Tale, Macbeth*).

Harbage, Alfred. *William Shakespeare: A Reader's Guide* (1963).

Howard, Jean E. *Shakespeare's Art of Orchestration: Stage Technique and Audience Response* (1984).

Jones, Emrys. *Scenic Form in Shakespeare* (1971).

Lenz, Carolyn Ruth Swift, Gayle Greene, and Carol Thomas Neely, eds. *The Woman's Part: Feminist Criticism of Shakespeare* (1980).

Novy, Marianne. *Love's Argument: Gender Relations in Shakespeare* (1984).

Rose, Mark. *Shakespearean Design* (1972).

Scragg, Leah. *Discovering Shakespeare's Meaning* (1994).

———. *Shakespeare's "Mouldy Tales": Recurrent Plot Motifs in Shakespearean Drama* (1992).

Traub, Valerie. *Desire and Anxiety: Circulations of Sexuality in Shakespearean Drama* (1992).

Traversi, D. A. *An Approach to Shakespeare,* 2 vols. (3rd rev. ed, 1968–69).

Vickers, Brian. *The Artistry of Shakespeare's Prose* (1968).

Wells, Stanley. *Shakespeare: A Dramatic Life* (1994).

Wright, George T. *Shakespeare's Metrical Art* (1988).

7. The Comedies

Barber, C. L. *Shakespeare's Festive Comedy* (1959; discusses *Love's Labor's Lost, A Midsummer Night's Dream, The Merchant of Venice, As You Like It, Twelfth Night*).

Barton, Anne. *The Names of Comedy* (1990).

Berry, Ralph. *Shakespeare's Comedy: Explorations in Form* (1972).

Bradbury, Malcolm, and David Palmer, eds. *Shakespearean Comedy* (1972).

Bryant, J. A., Jr. *Shakespeare and the Uses of Comedy* (1986).

Carroll, William. *The Metamorphoses of Shakespearean Comedy* (1985).

Champion, Larry S. *The Evolution of Shakespeare's Comedy* (1970).

Evans, Bertrand. *Shakespeare's Comedies* (1960).

Frye, Northrop. *Shakespearean Comedy and Romance* (1965).

Leggatt, Alexander. *Shakespeare's Comedy of Love* (1974).

Miola, Robert S. *Shakespeare and Classical Comedy: The Influence of Plautus and Terence* (1994).

Nevo, Ruth. *Comic Transformations in Shakespeare* (1980).

Ornstein, Robert. *Shakespeare's Comedies: From Roman Farce to Romantic Mystery* (1986).

Richman, David. *Laughter, Pain, and Wonder: Shakespeare's Comedies and the Audience in the Theater* (1990).

Salingar, Leo. *Shakespeare and the Traditions of Comedy* (1974).

Slights, Camille Wells. *Shakespeare's Comic Commonwealths* (1993).

Waller, Gary, ed. *Shakespeare's Comedies* (1991).

Westlund, Joseph. *Shakespeare's Reparative Comedies: A Psychoanalytic View of the Middle Plays* (1984).

Williamson, Marilyn. *The Patriarchy of Shakespeare's Comedies* (1986).

8. The Romances (*Pericles, Cymbeline, The Winter's Tale, The Tempest, The Two Noble Kinsmen*)

Adams, Robert M. *Shakespeare: The Four Romances* (1989).

Felperin, Howard. *Shakespearean Romance* (1972).

Frye, Northrop. *A Natural Perspective: The Development of Shakespearean Comedy and Romance* (1965).

Mowat, Barbara. *The Dramaturgy of Shakespeare's Romances* (1976).

Warren, Roger. *Staging Shakespeare's Late Plays* (1990).

Young, David. *The Heart's Forest: A Study of Shakespeare's Pastoral Plays* (1972).

9. The Tragedies

Bradley, A. C. *Shakespearean Tragedy* (1904).

Brooke, Nicholas. *Shakespeare's Early Tragedies* (1968).

Champion, Larry. *Shakespeare's Tragic Perspective* (1976).

Drakakis, John, ed. *Shakespearean Tragedy* (1992).

Evans, Bertrand. *Shakespeare's Tragic Practice* (1979).

Everett, Barbara. *Young Hamlet: Essays on Shakespeare's Tragedies* (1989).

Foakes, R. A. *Hamlet versus Lear: Cultural Politics and Shakespeare's Art* (1993).

Frye, Northrop. *Fools of Time: Studies in Shakespearean Tragedy* (1967).

Harbage, Alfred, ed. *Shakespeare: The Tragedies* (1964).

Mack, Maynard. *Everybody's Shakespeare: Reflections Chiefly on the Tragedies* (1993).

McAlindon, T. *Shakespeare's Tragic Cosmos* (1991).

Miola, Robert S. *Shakespeare and Classical Tragedy: The Influence of Seneca* (1992).

———. *Shakespeare's Rome* (1983).

Nevo, Ruth. *Tragic Form in Shakespeare* (1972).

Rackin, Phyllis. *Shakespeare's Tragedies* (1978).

Rose, Mark, ed. *Shakespeare's Early Tragedies: A Collection of Critical Essays* (1995).

Rosen, William. *Shakespeare and the Craft of Tragedy* (1960).

Snyder, Susan. *The Comic Matrix of Shakespeare's Tragedies* (1979).

Wofford, Susanne. *Shakespeare's Late Tragedies: A Collection of Critical Essays* (1996).

Young, David. *The Action to the Word: Structure and Style in Shakespearean Tragedy* (1990).

———. *Shakespeare's Middle Tragedies: A Collection of Critical Essays* (1993).

10. The Histories

Blanpied, John W. *Time and the Artist in Shakespeare's English Histories* (1983).

Campbell, Lily B. *Shakespeare's "Histories": Mirrors of Elizabethan Policy* (1947).

Champion, Larry S. *Perspective in Shakespeare's English Histories* (1980).

Hodgdon, Barbara. *The End Crowns All: Closure and Contradiction in Shakespeare's History* (1991).

Holderness, Graham. *Shakespeare Recycled: The Making of Historical Drama* (1992).

———, ed. *Shakespeare's History Plays: "Richard II" to "Henry V"* (1992).

Leggatt, Alexander. *Shakespeare's Political Drama: The History Plays and the Roman Plays* (1988).

Ornstein, Robert. *A Kingdom for a Stage: The Achievement of Shakespeare's History Plays* (1972).

Rackin, Phyllis. *Stages of History: Shakespeare's English Chronicles* (1990).

Saccio, Peter. *Shakespeare's English Kings: History, Chronicle, and Drama* (1977).

Tillyard, E. M. W. *Shakespeare's History Plays* (1944).

Velz, John W., ed. *Shakespeare's English Histories: A Quest for Form and Genre* (1996).

11. *Troilus and Cressida*

For discussions with the stage history of the play, see the suggested references on pages 236–37.

Adelman, Janet. *Suffocating Mothers*. (1992). A feminist and psychoanalytic essay on the way Troilus' simultaneous desire for and fear of sexual union necessitates Cressida's betrayal. Once soiled for him by sexuality, she has to be a divided figure: one part idealized mother, one part betraying mistress.

Apfelbaum, Roger. *Bifold Authority: A Performance History of Textual Cruxes in Shakespeare's* Troilus and Cressida

(2002). A study of editorial debates about the text of the play, with extensive reference to how these moments were performed in modern productions.

Bayley, John. "Time and the Trojans," *Essays in Criticism* 25 (1975). Groundbreaking study of the imagery of transience in the play and the way it dissolves conventional "assurances of selfhood."

Berger, Harry, Jr. "Troilus and Cressida: The Observer as Basilisk," *Comparative Drama* 2 (1968).

Bowen, Barbara E. *Gender in the Theater of War: Shakespeare's "Troilus and Cressida"* (1993). An innovative mix of feminist, performance, and cultural criticism which traces the play's critical and performance history.

Bradbrook, Muriel C. "What Shakespeare Did to Chaucer's Troilus and Criseyde," *Shakespeare Quarterly* 9 (1958).

Campbell, Oscar J. *Comicall Satyre and Shakespeare's Troilus and Cressida* (1938). The first to argue that the problem of the play's genre can be solved by classifying it as a satire, a form Campbell shows was in vogue at the time of its composition.

Coleridge, Samuel Taylor. *Coleridge's Writings on Shakespeare*, ed. Terence Hawkes, introd. Alfred B. Harbage (1959).

Colie, Rosalie L. *Shakespeare's Living Art* (1974). In a chapter entitled "Monumental Mock'ry," this learned study shows how the play systematically degrades the literary conventions it invokes until language itself is called into question.

Donaldson, E. Talbot. *The Swan at the Well: Shakespeare Reading Chaucer* (1985). The first modern book-length study of this subject, by a major Chaucerian scholar.

Empson, William. *Some Versions of Pastoral* (1974). Among the most important modern discussions of *Troilus*, this rich essay is part of a study of the ideological meaning of pastoral. Concentrates on the double plot, claiming that "the relation between the two plots is that of a symbol and thing symbolized."

Girard, René. *A Theatre of Envy* (1991). A study of what Girard calls "mimetic desire"—desire that arises not of itself but in imitation of someone else's desire—as the issue at the center of both love and war plots.

Greene, Gayle. "Shakespeare's Cressida: 'A kind of self,' " in *The Woman's Part: Feminist Criticism of Shakespeare* (1980). Sees *Troilus* as a protofeminist play, asserting that Shakespeare "exonerates" Cressida from the charge of betrayal by placing her in a context that alternately idealizes and objectifies her, leaving her no choice but to divide herself.

Hodgdon, Barbara. "He Do Cressida in Different Voices," *English Literary Renaissance* 20 (1990). An insightful theater history, from a feminist point of view, of several moments, especially the Trojans' return from battle (1.2) and the "betrayal" scene (5.2).

Martin, Priscilla. *"Troilus and Cressida": A Casebook* (1976). A collection of recent essays on the play, notable especially for Jan Kott's "Amazing and Modern)" and Joyce Carol Oates' "Essence and Existence."

Miller, J. Hillis. "Ariachne's Broken Woof," *Georgia Review* 3 (1977). A deconstructionist account of Troilus' speech about betrayal that centers on the subversive possibilities of language. The discovery of the double, or dialogical, nature of language leads to a questioning of the whole of Western metaphysics.

Muir, Kenneth, and Stanley Wells, eds. *Aspects of Shakespeare's "Problem Plays." Articles Reprinted from Shakespeare Survey* (1982). Includes Muir's own essay, "Troilus and Cressida," R. A. Yoder's " 'Sons and Daughters of the Game': An Essay on Shakespeare's *Troilus and Cressida*," and reviews of productions from 1956 to 1976.

Rutter, Carol Chillington. *Enter the Body: Women and Representation on Shakespeare's Stage* (2001). Includes valuable essays on Helen and on the costume and image of Cressida, with reference to productions of the past fifty years.

Southall, Raymond. "Troilus and Cressida and the Spirit of Capitalism," in *Shakespeare in the Changing World* (1964). Explores the connection between the play's interest in mercantilism and exchange and the rise of capitalism in Shakespeare's England. These ideas are developed further in his *Literature and the Rise of Capitalism* (1978).

Stein, Arnold. "Troilus and Cressida: The Disjunctive Imagination," *ELH* 36 (1969).

Suzuki, Mihoko. *Metamorphoses of Helen: Authority, Difference, and the Epic* (1989). Sees Shakespeare writing in a literary tradition, from the *Iliad* to Chaucer and beyond, that is "overcrowded and overdetermined." Explores the way Shakespeare resolves the problem of belatedness by demystifying and radically revising the myth of Troilus and Cressida.

Signet Classic   (0451)

The Signet Classic
Shakespeare Series:
The Tragedies

*extensively revised and updated expert commentary provides more
enjoyment through a greater understanding of the texts*

To order call: 1-800-788-6262

READ THE TOP 25 SIGNET CLASSICS

TO ORDER CALL: 1-800-788-6262